THE WISDOM OF
RESILIENCE BUILDERS

THE WISDOM OF RESILIENCE BUILDERS

How our best leaders create the world's most enduring enterprises

Rick Tirrell, Ph.D.

authorHOUSE®

AuthorHouse™
1663 Liberty Drive
Bloomington, IN 47403
www.authorhouse.com
Phone: 1-800-839-8640

First published by AuthorHouse   12/22/2009

ISBN: 978-1-4490-5324-6 (e)
ISBN: 978-1-4490-5323-9 (sc)
ISBN: 978-1-4490-5322-2 (hc)

Library of Congress Control Number: 2009912380

Printed in the United States of America
Bloomington, Indiana

This book is printed on acid-free paper.

To the great men and women who have created lasting prosperity.
And to the many who have had the courage to try.

Contents

In Gratitude

The list of people I feel a great sense of gratitude towards goes well beyond those named here. The process of creating this book began with those kind leaders who were willing to openly talk about their life's work with me, reveal the secrets of their enterprise and allow me to share in all that succeeded and failed. Their candor and their openness are treasured. It is incorrect to think of this book as having had only one author. They authored it as well.

I am grateful to my editor, Michael C. Shaner, Ph.D., Professor of Management at the John Cook School of Business at Saint Louis University. His ability to carefully study the manuscript as well as the abstract concepts in this book is remarkable. His understanding of the real work of every business leader kept this book focused on its true intent. His skill at rendering valuable corrective feedback in a pleasant and considerate way is sincerely appreciated.

I thank the leaders of several of companies who gave me the gift of their time even though time is their greatest scarcity. To Chester Cadieux, Alvin Howerton, and Jim Denny at QuikTrip Corporation; Brian Matt at Altitude, Inc.; Bill Geiger and Steve McDonald at Geiger Ready Mix Co., Inc.; Todd Sanders and Regina Davidoff at Steinway & Sons; and Tom Nightingale at Con-way, Inc. I send my sincere thanks.

Anthony Alaimo and Apryl Mathes worked for me as researchers when they were students at Kansas University and Kansas State University several years ago. Their ability to gather large amounts of information, sift through it quickly and present it succinctly is remembered and appreciated.

I offer thanks to Nick Harn, Ph.D., for his thoughtful discussions about how the inputs and outputs that create balance for a resilient enterprise are so similar to the inputs and outputs that create balance in chemical equations. His insights influenced this work.

I thank my colleagues at Navigator Group, PA, for being so good at what they do that it allowed me many mornings and afternoons off to write. I benefited greatly from their eagerness and insight as they considered and discussed the concepts in this book. Above all, they were willing to adopt the strong Navigator Group culture and values and use them every day to deepen our relationships with those we serve. For all of this I am grateful to Shannon M. Huebert, Ph.D., Gena D. Staggs, Ph.D., Casey Talent and Linda Turner.

My deepest gratitude goes to my wife and daughters, Barbara, Kate, Sara, and Lisa. To my wife, Barbara, I say thank you for allowing this book to be one of many projects that so absorbed me. Thanks for letting my stacks of papers and reprints overflow my home office into the rest of the house. And thanks for marrying a guy whose life's work is such a large part of his life. Your love and support are cherished. To Lisa I offer thanks for your remarkable expertise on finance and the world of business, as well as for editing several parts of this book along the way. Thanks also for gathering all of those dissertations from the library, so long ago. To Kate I give thanks for your constant interest in this book, and its progress. I have gratitude for you actually reading, understanding, and dissecting so many parts of this theory and seeing the endless places in the world where it applies. I thank Sara for being a person with so many diverse interests, and for enriching our lives by sharing those interests so freely. You used your background in anthropology to teach me about how artifacts, rituals, ceremonies and heroes all join together to form a culture. To all in my family, I thank you for making my work important and always being willing to talk about it and listen. I have been blessed.

Chapter 1

Building Resilience

Our most remarkable leaders seem to have some special wisdom about how to move their enterprises beyond just being successful, or even astonishingly successful. They know how to create organizations that have the ability to prosper, become injured, and then return to prosperity. They have the ability to build firms that thrive in good times and survive the bad times. I call these leaders Resilience Builders.

We might believe it is impossible to guide an enterprise to long term prosperity in hard times. Haven't we learned that all boats are beached in low tide? Wasn't success taken away from all firms in the Great Depression, the stagflation of the 1970's, and the global economic crisis of 2008? The simple answer is no. The most resilient enterprises of the Great Depression, for example, created ongoing prosperity. In Illinois, brothers Paul and Joseph Galvin started a radio manufacturing company in 1928. When markets collapsed they looked for ways to adapt. The new firm made small radios that had good reception while moving, so they sold them to automobile makers and in 1930 they changed the name from Galvin Manufacturing Corporation to Motorola. Remember that although the Great Depression's unemployment rate was 24%, that means 76% of workers had jobs and bought cars, along with many other things.

Likewise, it might seem that all firms prosper during times of economic expansion, like the post-World War II boom, the technology growth cycle of the 1990's, and the recent development of a truly global economy. Can't we assume that growth, survival and affluence are guaranteed to any competent enterprise in the best of times? Again, no. Each of these boom-times was littered with false starts, bankruptcies, and failures. In the United States from 1950 to 1959 there were 111,000 failures of commercial and industrial firms (excluding railroads, banks and insurance). Sixteen car manufacturers went out of business during those years. Some were new ventures that are now only footnotes in the industry, like the Powell, Glasspar, and Cunningham automobiles. Others were venerable names that had been in existence for more than 40 years, like Packard, Hudson, and Nash.

RESILIENT ENTERPRISE

At first glance it seems impossible to understand which firms will and will not last. We have seen too many companies achieve meteoric success, only to quickly fade away in good times as well as bad. We have witnessed so many famous and respected firms generate prosperity for all, only to disappear with the next product cycle or economic downturn. And those of us who look inside businesses have seen how internal conflict can cause an organization to lose its ability to adapt.

But there is another story to tell. There are companies that produce long histories of strength and adaptation. They recover from the predictable and unpredictable crises that come their way. Their story is about resilience and the people who build it. We see it all around us.

Johnson & Johnson was started by Robert Wood Johnson and his two brothers in 1866 as an attempt to supply their newly invented pre-packaged sterile antiseptic dressings to treat wounds and prevent infection. In its first year it had 14 employees and established a caring culture. Today Johnson & Johnson has 119,000 employees, owns over 200 operating companies, and it still maintains that "J & J" culture. The strength of its culture has given it the powerful virtue of stability. As a result it has produced 76 consecutive years of sales growth and 46 consecutive years of dividend growth. It has built more than a great culture. It has built resilience.

Heinrich Steinweg founded the famous piano maker, Steinway & Sons three years after he emigrated from Germany to New York at 53 years old in 1850. He had the single goal of building the absolute best pianos in the world. From the beginning Steinway invented one design improvement after another, eventually receiving 126 patents. In fact, most of the important characteristics of all modern pianos were originally developed by Steinway & Sons. Today Steinway pianos are still perfect. The wood that makes the soundboard comes from a managed forest in Alaska where only ½ of 1% of a chosen sitka spruce tree has acceptable quality. 1 The loggers get to these trees by foot and the trees are removed by helicopter. This wood is dried for over 1 year before it is worked, and then it takes 400 Steinway employees another year to make the piano. Steinways have been the chosen instrument of hundreds of famous performers including Duke Ellington, Sergei Rachmaninoff, and Vladimir Horowitz. John Lennon composed *Imagine* on a Steinway. This remarkable company has survived the Civil War, two World Wars, and the Great Depression. Steinway & Sons has built more than great pianos. It has built resilience.

Nestle SA was started in 1866 by Henri Nestlé, a Swiss pharmacist, to help babies who would not drink either breast milk or any of the available substitutes. His formula, Farine Lactée Henri Nestlé, quickly sold throughout Europe. For a small Swiss firm to sell its product in other European countries was not unusual in those days. Today we realize that Nestle has had international trade in its genes from the very beginning. However, its journey has not been easy due to numerous European wars and devastating economic downturns, several of which nearly crushed the company. For example, during 1938 and 1939 its sales fell 70%. Now, with annual revenues of 100 billion Swiss francs, including 26 blockbuster products generating 1 billion Swiss francs each, it is the world's largest food and beverage company. Its products are sold in every country on the planet. It has built more than just a great geographic strategy. It has built resilience.

A New Competitive Environment

We live in the most fascinating and dangerous times. Some leaders see the current era as simply the worst of times. Clearly, the new agenda of increased taxation and regulation is here to stay. Financing is scarce, competition is lethal, and customer loyalty seems ever-more difficult to achieve. Even formerly safe sectors are at risk. Now, long-comfortable incumbents are easy prey for new challengers from anywhere in the world. Product and industry lifecycles have been reduced from decades to months. While our entrepreneurs once wanted to startle the world with explosive radiance, now this pattern brings fear of a short run. Uncertainty is everywhere. For these pessimistic leaders, confidence, daring, and hope all seem to quietly erode as they watch passively, unsure what to do.

Other leaders see these as the best of times. The developed nations still offer solid opportunities for those who understand their massive capital, skills, and talents. New technologies continue to emerge, and old players continue to become ever more nimble and competent. Emerging nations represent the greatest growth potential ever seen, as six billion people seek the means to buy homes, cars, computers, utilities, and more. Here, markets are being formed and fortunes made. These leaders are eager to generate prosperity.

Finding themselves in this mix of extreme threat and extreme opportunity, now business leaders ask different questions, feel a different hunger, and seek something more substantial. They seek resilience. This might be the resilience of the unspectacular but steady growth of Honda Motors. It could be the resilience of Emerson Electric, which creates one impressive technical advance after another, but is rarely seen in the public spotlight. Or it could be the resilience rendered to Nike by its masterful marketing skills. Sometimes these companies are favored by Wall Street while at other times they are not. All have shown a remarkable ability to grow, adapt, persist, and return to growth. And every business leader I know wishes his or her organization could have these same skills of growth, adaptation, persistence, and returning to growth. We all seek resilience.

WE UNDERSTAND RESILIENCE

We know what resilience is. We have observed the scenes after terrible storms that strike Florida or the Carolinas in America. As the local news helicopter flies over the shoreline we see one grand house after another reduced to rubble. Debris litters the beaches. Mixed in with those damaged structures are homes that still stand, seemingly untouched by the storm. Somehow their grandeur is enhanced by their ability to withstand the attacks of Mother Nature. These structures survive so nicely because they were built better in the first place. They were built with the confident knowledge that storms would come, so they are storm-proofed, wind resistant, and durable. They have strong foundations rather than wood pilings or stilts. They have Weather Shield® windows and doors. Their walls are made of aerated concrete. They are built with ventilation systems that allow the houses to breathe as the external air pressure becomes greatly different from the air inside. For all these reasons they demonstrate resilience; the ability to survive the shocks of the storms that come their way.

People can be resilient too. Recall the story of Terry A. Anderson who was kidnapped in Lebanon in 1985 and held hostage for nearly seven years. During this time he was treated kindly by some captors and abused by others. So, why do we remember him when there have been so many tragedies in that region of the world? Upon his release, Terry Anderson surprised us all by saying that he was a Catholic and he had forgiven his captors. As a result of his ability to forgive, he was able to go on with his life, both physically and emotionally. In his book, *Den of Lions*, he recounts how he had become a lapsed Catholic prior to being taken hostage and during his captivity he asked for a Bible. 2 Early in his captivity he met another captive, Father Lawrence Jenco, a priest who heard Anderson's first confession in 25 years. This was not just a moment of powerful conversion for him; it was a reaffirmation of his own deep and long standing spiritual beliefs and core values. After his release Anderson established charities for children in Vietnam and the Father Lawrence Jenco Foundation for those who provide aid to Appalachia. He lectured widely, giving the message that we all should have hope for the human race. This is a resilient man and much of his resilience has come from his ability to know who he is and to live his life in accord with his own core values.

Like the storm-resistant house, a resilient enterprise is built with the knowledge that storms will come, so it has a solid foundation and is made of durable materials. It adapts well to changing internal and external pressures. Like Terry Anderson, a resilient organization has strong values that drive its culture and guide its conduct through turmoil. Whether it is a resilient house, person, or company, there is triumph and a sense of achievement each time a crisis is survived.

This book is about the wisdom some extraordinary leaders use to build durable companies. It is about how they build resilience.

RESILIENCE REQUIRES MORE THAN THE BASICS

In order for a firm to build resilience, it must first master the basics. The leader must know how to build a team, find markets that offer opportunities for growth, fill a space in a market, differentiate the firm's products and services, and change strategies as times change.

The firm must be able to build strengths that help it to manage its way through a crisis. So, building strong cash reserves has helped Pfizer survive despite the expiration of its patents on one blockbuster drug after another. Masterful use of bonds and other financial instruments has helped 3M weather its industry's history of feast and famine. Coca Cola's massive distribution network gave it the ability to come out of a multiyear growth slump in 2006. Finding under-served niches allowed Dow Chemical to grow year after year, even after its biggest products had become commodities. Serial acquisitions followed by consistently improving people and processes have guided GE through every economic crisis since it was formed in 1892. Establishing a powerful incumbency kept Bridgestone/Firestone alive, even after its tires exploded on the highways. 3 And expansion into world markets has solidified Caterpillar's impressive growth.

Each of these firms is resilient, but their resilience was formed by more than the basic strengths I have described here. All successful firms today are able to master these basics. Mastery of this list of skills might render success for a while, but it is not sufficient to build resilience. Too many firms master these skills and then suffer or disappear. Resilience Builders have the wisdom to go beyond the basics.

The Wisdom of Resilience Builders

If you could interview or know many Resilience Builders, including those who are long into their journey, wouldn't it be wonderful to have the chance to ask them what wisdom they could offer you about how to build a resilient enterprise? This book does just that, and now we know what they would say. They would say that most of the conflicts and trials coming your way in the future are avoidable, if only you could see them coming. They would share with you the places where they stumbled because they didn't anticipate avoidable crises. They would wish that you would not suffer like they did. You can gain wisdom by observing their struggles. They would tell you that in order to survive you must do 100 things right, but to build a resilient enterprise you must master four important variables. They are:

1. The competitive platform on which the organization is built. This platform determines whether the firm will prosper by being the best in its field at efficient operations, or building deep relationships,

or marketing, or creativity. The resilient firm picks one of these platforms and develops it to extreme heights.

2. The company's location on its developmental frame. The requirements of survival are different for a start-up vs. an incumbent; a declining firm vs. a recovering firm. Resilience is strengthened by understanding and operating appropriately within one's stage of development.

3. The firm's culture. Life inside a Creative Platform firm is different from life inside an Efficient Platform firm. Marketing Platform firms are different from Relationship Platform Firms. A resilience-supporting culture is produced by the firm's competitive platform and the firm's location on its developmental frame.

4. The strategy the firm chooses. Like culture, strategy is formed by the competitive platform and developmental frame; and it supports them. If it does so it becomes a resilience-supporting strategy. Because strategy is charged with repeatedly adapting to the environment, it is the least stable of the four essential elements of resilience.

When all four of these essential elements match the competitive platform and match each other, this book calls them congruent. The firm is in a state of resilience when it makes the right choices on each of these four essential elements. This book examines these four elements and how they interact with each other to build resilience. It will show how Resilience Builders have used these elements to create successful, durable, lasting organizations.

Resilience is defined as persistently maintaining healthy growth or returning to healthy growth over time. To do this, a company must either adjust to the adversity caused by internal and external shocks that occur as things change, or it must anticipate and adaptively avoid those shocks. If a company has undergone its own degeneration or if its larger industry has declined, it can still be considered resilient if it can return to growth. Neither stunning profits nor a huge market cap are needed in order to be resilient. Fame is not needed. A celebrity CEO is not needed. To achieve resilience all that is needed is healthy growth and the ability to return to growth, despite adversities.

Using these concepts, we can observe the wisdom of those Resilience Builders who are able to go beyond success and create durable organizations. I propose that their unique set of skills is quite understandable and able to be imitated by all who have enough curiosity to read this book, and the patience to guide their firms carefully. As you read this book, you will see that you can do what Resilience Builders do. This book removes the mystique surrounding these leaders.

Young and Old Firms Can Be Resilient

Many of the examples in this book are of old companies. I chose them because it is easy to see that a successful old company is resilient. However, one unique notion of this book is that a firm does not have to be old in order to be resilient. Chapter 7 profiles Altitude Inc., a 17 year old design firm in Boston that invents, creates, and improves lots of cool products. It wins design awards year after year. It is resilient despite its young age. I propose that a young company can be resilient because resilience is not a characteristic of age. Your firm can be resilient now. In this book I will refer to a company being in a state of resilience, or having achieved resilience, or even having lost resilience. Because building and maintaining resilience is such an active process, any strategic missteps, subversion of culture, responses inappropriate to the firm's developmental stage, or loss of competitive skills can damage or destroy resilience. In a few years we will be able to ask, "Who is resilient now?", and we will see that some firms that previously had been resilient will have lost resilience or perhaps will have vanished. The good news is that if we understand how to build resilience, we can avoid such hardships for our own firms, or rebuild resilience once it has eroded.

Accidental Resilience

Some firms create massive success, or even the most sought-after products in the world, and appear to be resilient, but they are not. They might perform well on all four of the essential elements of resilience, but fail to achieve resilience. This is because although the leader might be executing all of these things correctly, he or she lacks the wisdom to understand exactly what the firm is doing right. This is pseudo-resilience, or accidental resilience. We will see in Chapter 10 that young Steve Jobs raised Apple up to a $1 billion company, but had only built accidental resilience. Accidental resilience is usually followed by a hard fall.

Previous Work

Two previous works piqued my interest in this topic. Both were written by respected authors, and both provided valuable guidance to entrepreneurs all over the world. In their 1994 book, *Built to Last*, Jim Collins and Jerry Porras compared pairs of similar companies and labeled some "visionary companies" and their counterparts as "comparison companies". 4 The visionary companies' multiyear stock values had greatly outperformed those of the comparison companies. So, for example, they deemed that Hewlett Packard was a visionary company and was superior to Texas Instruments, a comparison company. In 2007 Christian Stadler wrote *The Four Principles of Enduring Success*. 5 His approach was quite similar to that of Collins and Porras. He compared the stock market values of "gold medal" companies, like Shell, with those of "silver medal" companies, like BP. Both of these works basically asked the same question, "What makes a company a superstar?"

As I carefully examined the lesser companies (the comparison companies and the silver medal companies) I observed that all were hugely successful, all have had long-standing prosperity, and all are resilient. All have survived or adaptively avoided the predictable and unpredictable crises that came their way. So, it occurred to me that today's business leaders would be thrilled if their own companies could achieve the prosperity and resilience of Texas Instruments, Colgate, BP, Prudential, or any of these implied second-tier companies.

Rather than asking how a company can become a superstar, the more valuable questions to most leaders are: How can I build a company that is both prosperous and resilient? What are the essential elements of resilience? And what do Resilience Builders know that I can learn?

Add to this the fact that we are now aware that a single bit of advice will not be enough to create or sustain success. We have been fooled by this in the past. Innovate your way to success! Downsize! Reengineer your corporation! Create a revolution! Search for excellence! And, none of it brought us much more than a random chance at long-term sustenance. So what is the guidance that we seek? We seek to build firms that last.

THIS BOOK

It would be best to think of this book as a conversation between you and the great Resilience Builders. What would they say to you at the end of their journey? What advice would they give you about how you can build stability into your enterprise? I hope this book alters, in some small manner, how you view your life's work, your company.

This is a handbook for anyone on whose shoulders the weight of an enterprise rests. It is intended to be easy to read despite the fact that it offers a serious examination of how resilience is built by those in the forward trenches of the business world. It examines four variables and shows how these variables build resilience, so it is not intended to offer just one piece of simple advice. As a handbook, it covers a broad range of the material that relates to resilience, rather than the narrow range found in trade books. I believe you will see your own enterprise in these four variables, so you may wish to have pen and paper ready as you read it. Chapter 2 gives a sketch of the entire book, and therefore the theory of this book. It is intended to guide you into the rest of the book and also to serve as a summary you can refer to in the future. Chapter 4 examines the competitive platforms resilient companies use. Chapter 6 shows how firms must adapt as they move along their own developmental frame. Chapter 8 looks at culture and resilience. And in Chapter 10 the concept of resilient strategy is built upon a very broad professional literature. In each chapter, I freely draw from concepts that already exist and then attempt to take the field one small step further. I believe you will see that as Resilience Builders build their sturdy organizations, they use these concepts more masterfully than those leaders whom resilience seems to elude.

Between the above-listed chapters of this book you will find chapters that profile resilient companies. These have great value because, after all, stories about businesses are stories about human lives. They tell about the struggles and successes of Resilience Builders. These stories are told in personal terms in hope that you, the reader, can see how you are a lot like each one of these fine leaders. Chapter 3 tells the story of Chester Cadieux and the nice folks who built QuikTrip into one of the most successful privately owned firms in America. It is at tale of a $9 billion convenience store chain that is a multiyear resident of Fortune's 100 Best Companies to Work For in America. Chapter 5 is the story of a resilient 117 year old family-owned small business that came close to extinction twenty years ago and has since become a market leader; Geiger Ready Mix, Inc. Chapter 7 takes a grand tour of design firm, Altitude Inc., and shows how its Creative Platform and Relationship Platform skills have built a positive culture and show-stopping products. Chapter 9 provides unique insights into Apple's Steve Jobs, and his creative journey in, out, and back inside the four essential elements of resilience. My intent here is to tell universal stories, and to provide a range of examples that a cross-section of today's business leaders will value.

The four essential elements of resilience that are presented in this book are the product of my experiences on the front lines of the world of business. Starting in the late 1980's I began to interact with many leaders, some of whom built resilience and some of whom did not. The more my journey of curious observation progressed, the more I began to categorize my observations regarding exactly what builds resilience and what doesn't. This process of discovery in the field allowed me to create a logic, and then some hunches, or hypotheses. These hypotheses have become predictive. Each time I have proposed these hunches to leaders, their responses have been the same, "Ah! Ha!" They know that this book makes sense and fits their own experiences. It allows us to understand, predict, and explain.

What Resilience Builders do is wonderful. They create meaningful work, prosperity, and lasting sustenance for those around them, and they continue to do this despite the expected and unexpected shocks that come their way. These Resilience Builders are members of a unique breed of leader. Their life's work is to build an exceptional company, and this work brings them enormous joy. They know that a great enterprise brings prosperity to employees, shareholders, suppliers and the entire community the enterprise builds around itself. They pursue success more than money, and they build their firms on values that really matter to them. Their journeys are emotionally filled with the sorrow of small tragedies as well as the delight of big miracles. These are special leaders. Their stories should be told.

I hope you enjoy reading this book as much as I have enjoyed writing it, and I hope it helps you build both success and resilience.

CHAPTER 2

THE ESSENTIAL ELEMENTS OF RESILIENCE

Resilient companies are crafted by Resilience Builders. We know their names because they are the legends of prosperity; Thomas Watson at IBM, Kiichiro Toyoda at Toyota, Sam Walton at Wal-Mart, Steven Jobs at Apple, and more.

What is it about Resilience Builders that enables them to create firms that prosper and endure? Did Microsoft become the dominant software company in the world because of Bill Gates' talent as a programmer? Not likely, because Digital Equipment, Altair, Commodore, Wang, and Compaq all had intelligent programmers and those firms are gone.

Was it Meg Whitman's brilliant intellect and Harvard MBA that allowed her to grow the first virtual community and ensure e-Bay's survival after the dot com crash? No. Although some Harvard MBA alums have generated great prosperity, others have generated great failures. Some have even gone to jail. Having a great education does not guarantee that the leader will become a Resilience Builder.

Proctor and Gamble CEO, A.G. Lafley is credited with restoring worldwide growth during his tenure from 2000 to 2009. Could it have been the facts that he rose through the ranks at P&G, and once headed its Asian operations? No. His predecessor, Durk Jaeger rose through the ranks and headed the Asian operations too, but disrupted the company and resigned after only 18 months as CEO. A leader's career path does not make him a Resilience Builder.

Was it the smart strategy of building a discount airline in the face of the stodgy legacy airlines that made Southwest Airline's CEO Herb Kelleher a Resilience Builder? After all, he had the ability to lower his competitors' prices when he pulled into an airport for the first time and to repeat this over and over again for many years. Again, no. There have been many discount airline start-ups, and nearly all are gone. Simply choosing and executing the right strategy does not make a leader a Resilience Builder.

So, what do these people know, and what do they do that makes them Resilience Builders?

Our heroes can be demystified and their methods understood. Building resilience is not the product of magic, chance, or mystery. The events in our world are organized in a logical, understandable manner which gives order to our observations of resilience and explains how some achieve it and others do not. They achieve resilience not because of who they are, nor of some God-given talent, but because of what they do, and how well they do it. They all have achieved resilience by having the wisdom to understand, manage, or maneuver four variables and to know how these variables interplay with each other. These variables are what this book calls the essential elements of resilience. They are: competitive platform, developmental frame, culture, and strategy.

AN ACTIVE PROCESS

Resilient companies seem to make it all look so easy. They appear to do well in the beginning, middle and end. It seems that they glide effortlessly through the dark chapters of hyper-competition, industry crowding, declining markets, product substitutions, and difficult product life cycles. If I may use a metaphor that compares them with nature, the resilient evergreen comes to mind. It seems to never lose its needles. It is in the arctic, deserts, swamps, and the seashore. It is the last citizen of the tree line. It seems to be completely unaffected by adversity. We might believe it never stops growing and it is immune to life's challenges. Its adaptation is effortless. It is resilient. Just like a resilient company. Or, so it would seem.

A closer look reveals a more complex picture. Yes, the evergreen is everywhere, and it stays green in all four seasons. But its resilience is not effortless. For the evergreen, achieving resilience is an aggressive process, and this organism is constantly working to adapt. It holds its needles, but not forever. It sheds its needles, just not all at once. There is a seasonal needle drop in the early fall in which it sloughs off nonproductive needles and replaces them with needles that will nourish the tree and make energy and food. Each needle has stomata, openings that allow air and water exchange. These stomata close tightly during periods of stress and drought to prevent loss of moisture. There is a slowing of the growth processes during times of stress, in response to temperature and moisture levels as well as day length. All of these events are the result of complex triggers and signaling processes. Attacks from insects or disease are repelled by using food reserves gathered during the good times. The root systems are deep, fibrous and widespread. But when young, it survives on one primary taproot, just like a young business.

Like the evergreen, building a resilient enterprise is an active and complex process. This book suggests that building a resilient company is not the result of doing just one thing well, producing a great product, or being the best at something. Resilience is built by first establishing a clear competitive platform, second, appropriately operating from one's location on the developmental frame, and third, using these two variables (platform and frame) to manipulate two other adaptive variables, culture and strategy. Thus, resilience is achieved by the interplay between the four essential elements of resilience. To achieve resilience, the Resilience Builder designs each one of these elements so it matches the others, and this is called congruence. Then, as conditions change, Resilience Builders know how to alter these essential elements to adapt, return to growth, and to re-establish congruence.

GROWING IN WISDOM

Wisdom is not an inborn trait. Infants and toddlers do not have wisdom. Five year old children can have understanding and compassion, sometimes remarkably so, but they are not capable of having wisdom. Wisdom is gained from insight and experience. Our greatest wisdom comes from our times of failure, and from other times when we have avoided failure.

We can be encouraged by the fact that we do not have to start from scratch. We are able to learn from the successes and failures of others. We do this in science, medicine, and the arts. We can do this in business. We can grow in wisdom by carefully observing the journeys of others.

INESCAPABLE DECISIONS

As I studied resilient and non-resilient companies I began to feel compassion for both Resilience Builders and those leaders whose firms never quite achieve resilience. At first I could not understand my own sense of respectful concern, until it became clear that once the mission began, these leaders were in the hands of some powerful forces that would guide and challenge their journey. So as they moved forward in the optimistic days of a start-up they may have felt that this was fruitful ground and all would go well. But then the journey took them to a choice point; a fork in the road. Each one had to choose; turn right and limit the firm to one competitive platform, or turn left and take on all work. Turning left would result in a busy but poorly defined company. This book will show that turning right and establishing one clear competitive platform would enhance resilience. But this is hard to do, and perhaps not agreed upon by all members of the firm. All at once the easy journey received the impact of these external as well as internal forces. My compassion came from the fact that the leader was never spared the requirement to decide. Once a choice was made, it then required the leader to again make decisions about how to move along the developmental frame, how to build a culture, how to select and modify strategy, and how to make them all support each other. No leader could stop the journey or neutralize the forces in play. None of these decisions could be avoided. These decisions were required by the journey itself and all of the subsequent forks in the road it would present. This is a journey of gaining wisdom. There is ample opportunity to fail here. There is also the opportunity to build ongoing prosperity if one can understand and correctly arrange the essential elements of resilience. The good news is that many leaders have become Resilience Builders, and resilience is achievable.

As I have observed these Resilience Builders, I have discovered that each one uses his or her own terms or labels for these four essential elements of resilience, they have a competent mastery of them, and they manage through them. So, what are these essential elements?

COMPETITIVE PLATFORMS

Chapter 4 describes your choices of competitive platforms and brings to life some Resilience Builders who have built their companies on well chosen platforms. A brief introduction to the chapter follows:

The first essential element of resilience is the firm's competitive platform. There are four platforms: Efficient Platform, Relationship Platform, Creative Platform, and Marketing Platform. Resilient enterprises have a clear internal and external identity as one of these four competitive platforms, or as a hybrid of multiple competitive platforms, in combination. But please notice, they always have an identity. Everyone who works at one of these resilient companies knows the company's competitive platform and strives to push it to world-class levels. They know they work in an efficient company, trying to function as quickly and cheaply as possible. Or they know their intimate relationship with the customer is the single most important thing. Or they create things and focus solely on invention after invention. Or they understand clearly that their survival depends on out-marketing the competition. The important fact here is that the most successful and resilient companies have clear identities and this identity is based on the firm's choice among the four competitive platforms.

Most resilient firms are built on one platform. However, in recent years, our complex economic environment has forced more and more firms to achieve resilience by establishing a complex identity constructed on more than one platform. My work here is based on the work of Michael Treacy and Fred Wiersema and their groundbreaking book, *The Discipline of Market Leaders.* 1

THE EFFICIENT PLATFORM

Wal-Mart Stores, Inc. is a resilient Efficient Platform company. Sam Walton knew it, and now everybody who works there knows it. The pay is fair, the stores are spartan, and everyone tries to drive down costs every single day. Suppliers are expected to make large price concessions in order to participate, and no supplier has a guaranteed place on the shelf in the future. Each store is its own profit or loss center and is responsible for its own expenses.

Wal-Mart has been the victim of some negative press and public opinion recently. The popular notion seems to be that Wal-Mart is successful because it pays substandard wages. This simply is not so. Its pay scale is quite comparable to Target and all of the big-box discounters. The primary contributor to Wal-Mart's success is its mastery and strict adherence to its Efficient Platform. This involves a complex constellation of tasks that it has perfected while many others have failed. Wal-Mart has a clear identity of cost containment and operational efficiency. There is strong agreement internally and externally about its nature. A statement from former CEO Lee Scott reveals how Wal-Mart leaders think and what it measures. He said that Wal-Mart's excellent performance was the result of driving sales, reducing costs, and improving inventory management. This is pure Efficient Platform. 2

THE RELATIONSHIP PLATFORM

McKinsey & Company is arguably the most prestigious management consulting firm in practice today. It is also a resilient Relationship Platform firm. It was formed by a University of Chicago accounting professor in 1926, and soon employed consultants from other renowned universities, including Harvard. McKinsey is special. It helps solve the most unique strategic and management problems in a careful manner. Its alums include lots of famous talent like former IBM CEO Lou Gerstner. It figures out how to create success for Johnson & Johnson, Hewlett-Packard, and a long list of others.

McKinsey consultants get to know their clients well before offering guidance. These brilliant advisers offer unique solutions to unique problems, and they are empowered to offer inventive recommendations. They avoid rendering cookbook responses to complex circumstances. They intimately know their client's long-term and recent business history, industry, struggles, competitors, position in its competitive field, and all of the enterprise's challenges. Internally, McKinsey maintains a sophisticated knowledge management system which includes an advanced general business library as well as an IT reservoir of information about current and previous clients. We shall see later that Relationship Platform companies have two defining characteristics. First, they gain a lot of knowledge about their customers, and second, they use this knowledge to render something pleasing and exceptional. As a result, their customers and clients view them as partners. McKinsey excels at the Relationship Platform.

THE CREATIVE PLATFORM

We all remember Cisco Systems Inc. as perhaps the greatest of the Internet bubble celebrities. As money flowed into technology stocks, Cisco was king, at one point being the most valuable stock in the world with a market capitalization of about a half billion dollars. We also remember Cisco's dramatic crash. With the destruction of the tech bubble Cisco's telecom routers were unnecessary and excess. What is noteworthy, however, is that unlike so many of its technology brethren, Cisco is alive and resilient all these years later. How has it survived and continued to excel?

When Cisco degenerated, CEO John Chambers asked his employees what to do to fix the company. Their answer? Innovate better. Cisco's resilience is based on the fact that it never deviated from its Creative Platform. The imaginative scientists at Cisco were the first to develop multiprotocol routers, which allowed communication between incompatible computers. Even in hard times, Cisco never stopped funding R&D, and as a result it is now positioned to be the principal beneficiary of the new video and voice Internet capacities. It has invented new ways for businesses to transfer data and to use data networking, and has invented breathtaking advances in teleconferencing. In the darkest days of the 2008 global recession it launched a new network switch that will move 15 trillion bits per second. So, as the Internet becomes more burdened by all of its new uses, Cisco is the "go to" firm to keep information moving. This resilient company's complete focus is on creating and engineering new abilities that extend all of this technology.

Resilient Creative Platform companies are keenly aware of their own nature. They imagine, invent, formulate, and experiment. They give birth. They know it, and so do their employees and customers.

THE MARKETING PLATFORM

Coca-Cola produces a commodity product and has persuaded millions of people it is their favorite. Marketing, advertising, and sales dominate every element of the enterprise.

When Robert Woodruff took over the small company in 1923 he said he didn't know any more about the soft drink business than a pig knows about Sunday. But he did know about marketing, advertising, and selling. Soon, he focused his attention on his sales force. His marketing method was to have Norman Rockwell-like pictures of a boy fishing, Santa smiling, or a happy girl with a tennis racket, each holding a Coke. He was not selling caffeine and sugar water. He was selling a moment of happiness for five cents. Or quite simply a refreshing life-style.

Only two decades later when World War II ended, Coca-Cola was earning $100 million per year in profits. Then began the push to go worldwide, all under the hand of Robert Woodruff. His influence was so immense that he ushered in an era of marketing and advertising fervor that convinced us all that we could sell anything at any price if only we would market right.

People who work at resilient Marketing Platform companies know where their priorities are. They study market groups and segments very carefully. They constantly look at campaigns, sales and the numbers. Careers, promotions, and the allocation of resources all depend on the results of who to sell to and how to reach them better.

Hybrid Platforms

Every company has some amount of strength on each of the four competitive platforms and every leader must decide how far to dial-up or dial-down each of these platforms. As the requirements of twenty first century success have become progressively more complex, there has been an increase in companies who build resilience by becoming world-class at two or more competitive platforms. To do this, for example, a Marketing Platform company might press hard to increase its internal and external efficiencies. Or a Creative Platform company would enhance resilience by developing a strong Relationship Platform with its customers.

The endorsement of hybrid platforms is unique to this book. Authors Treacy and Wiersema advised against trying to steer an enterprise in more than one direction at a time. They believed the organization could become confused and unable to execute its strengths. In a way they were correct. It is exponentially harder to develop two or more major strengths that must coexist and interact with each other. The corporation's leaders of business units or heads of functions are at risk of independently leading in opposite directions. But if done successfully, a Hybrid Platform can give the firm a sustainable competitive advantage which is remarkably difficult for others to imitate.

As more industries become progressively more complex we will see more resilient firms adopting hybrid platforms.

Four Different Personalities

It is clear that there are four different personalities to these four different Platforms. Working at Wal-Mart is very different from McKinsey, Cisco, or Coca-Cola. Their strategies differ and in each case the strategy matches the competitive platform. Also, these four companies are successful because they have matched their strong external strategies with their internal cultures, each of which accurately reflects its own platform. It is the congruence between platform, frame, culture and strategy that makes them so resilient. Everything about a resilient Efficient Platform company yields efficiency. That produces a very different external strategy and internal culture than a Creative Platform company where everything is about how to create, invent, and innovate. Efficient Platform companies don't tolerate mistakes, but Creative Platform companies do. Marketing Platform companies know about their customers through focus groups, and Relationship Platform companies know them personally. Four competitive platforms, four cultures, four strategies, and each with its own personality.

Resilience Builders are masters of their competitive platforms. Their organizations have clear identities internally and externally, congruent with their platforms. These companies are distinct, well defined, and there is no confusion or doubt about the nature of these firms.

Developmental Frame

How has life changed at Microsoft as it has matured? How did American Airlines fail to adapt to changes in its own development, while Nissan and McDonald's used this as a challenge and an opportunity to build resilience? Chapter 6 shows what you can expect as your own firm goes through its developmental frame. Some highlights:

Resilience Builders are keenly aware of their company's location on its own lifecycle. In order to be fully adaptive, a start-up firm, a mature incumbent firm, and a turnaround firm must all behave differently. Their decisions must be appropriate to their developmental stage and that of their industry. Resilience Builders know this, but other executives, including some who lead large corporations, seem to be surprisingly unaware of this concept.

Resilience Builders do not see corporate lifecycle in traditional terms which use a metaphor of biological lifespan; birth, growth, maturity, and death. They might not use the term "lifecycle" at all. While they each seem to have their own terms for this, their view is a corporate adaptation cycle, which is ever-moving and constantly seeking to adjust the internal and external environments. From this point forward, this book replaces the concept of the individual firm's "lifecycle" with "developmental frame", or "frame". This allows a continuous pursuit of adaptation and encourages very active efforts of restimulating growth.

The developmental frame consists of four Quads: Quad 1 Growth, Quad 2 Steady State, Quad 3 Degeneration, and Quad 4 Conversion. Each Quad has its own work to do, and an organization can succeed or fail at any of these stages. Then, Quad 4 Conversion leads to Return to Growth. While these four categories are similar to the traditional stages of corporate lifecycle, the subtle differences are significant. The ways Resilience Builders engage these concepts is remarkable.

The developmental frame guides Resilience Builders regarding their ability to select the right strategy at the right time. This is based on external factors like industry-wide platform shifts as well as an awareness of their own point in organizational development. Like the evergreen, they seem to know when to expand and contract, when to move into new markets and when to stay away. Resilience Builders are successful because they don't misapply strategies. Their selection of strategy is based on knowing the organization's changing characteristics in each of the four Quads of the Developmental Frame.

QUAD 1 GROWTH

The essential elements of resilience begin to form as soon as an organization is created. Quad 1 Growth includes startup, early growth, rapid growth, as well as established firms that have had a Return to Growth. In Quad 1 Growth we find a category with a unique personality. All aspects of the organization are focused on growth; developing products, gaining market share, building infrastructure (accounting, MIS, supply systems, operations, and HR policies), establishing distribution networks, and most of all, borrowing and consuming money. This is an exciting time with lots of hope and some surprise at the new success. Coworkers have close relationships with each other and there is strong admiration for the founder. This is the Quad in which Steven Jobs and his friends started Apple and ignited an information revolution. They stayed up all night, ate cold pizza, and became friends. Mixed in with the excitement is a culture of few frills. This is the stage in which Jeffrey Bezos used a discarded door for his desk in order to communicate the need for austerity at Amazon.

Builders of the world's most resilient enterprises love to be in Quad 1 Growth, and if their organization departs this quad, they do everything to make sure it undergoes a Return to Growth.

In each of the four quads the process may become extreme or out of control. What happens if Quad 1 Growth explodes too rapidly? What if expansion exceeds the capacity of the firm's infrastructure to support the growth? The firm moves into a state of Chaos. Policies are not formulated, everyone defines the organization differently, major parts of the company fail to tell each other about promises made, sales grow while cash flow disappears, and the organization begins to disintegrate, despite its growth. Malignant growth results in Chaos.

QUAD 2 STEADY STATE

There is something quite attractive about Quad 2 Steady State. During the crazy times of rapid growth mixed with failure-threatening droughts of Quad 1, every leader has wished for his or her enterprise to enter Quad 2 Steady State. So has every leader whose company is in decline. They fantasize about the reward of a steady stream of orders, ample capacity, and ease of response. Some firms actually achieve this, but in the 21st century business environment, their respite here is always short.

Employees and managers can become complacent and cause an erosion of resilience. The organization's strategy might become complacent as well. Here strategies tend to focus on protecting assets and defending market share. Some companies have openly talked about not growing too quickly, or have developed wonderful new advancements, only to ignore them in favor of the long-standing cash cow. Xerox was guilty of strategic complacency. It was the first company to invent what we know as the personal computer. It created networks of these little computers. It even had a modern-day graphic user interface with icons on the desktop, but it failed to pursue this in favor of simply churning out more profitable copy machines. This was strategic complacency. This book will show that Resilience Builders are complacency killers.

What happens if complacency prevails and Quad 2 spins out of control or becomes malignant? The senior manager is seen as not caring about the employees, despite his or her remarkable efforts to be generous. Employees continually expect more. The adaptation process of continuous adjustment to the environment is compromised and opportunities are missed. The happiness of employees comes to be seen as being more important than the happiness of the customer. Internal rules and policies are fortified, resulting in layers of decision makers. Employees can leave customers on hold for a long time, fail to fill orders, or just act rudely. Malignant complacency results in a state of Arrogance.

Quad 3 Degeneration

Eventually, every business will experience Degeneration. Resilience Builders understand this and aim to have a very brief encounter with Quad 3 Degeneration. Less adaptive or less fortunate managers get stuck here and fail to recover. This is the dark chapter. Everyone in the firm sought Steady State. All employees were comfortable in their complacency. The very enterprise that was expected to support everyone for the next 100 years, pay off mortgages, educate children, and carry us through retirement begins to falter. These are the Polaroid, Pan Am, and Woolworth's of the world. These are the family owned trucking companies and small private colleges. All struggle, some recover, and some fail. All of their employees are surprised and shocked that their fates have changed. The quality of their product is excellent, they have improved their processes, they have great reputations, and still they decline. For some, it becomes clear they can't manage their way out of this. For others, an adaptive strategy, persistence, and further development of the culture will pay off. Internally everyone is unhappy in Quad 3 Degeneration.

In this Quad there is almost always a moment of not knowing what to do, a hesitation. The external market has changed and an adaptive response is needed. Instead there is a delay, a time of indecision. These leaders find themselves cast into yet another choice point and they don't know what strategy to select, so they hesitate, and that is not the best choice.

What happens if Quad 3 Degeneration spins out of control? Some of these leaders' most trusted people undermine his or her new initiatives and then leave. The "wonderful" days of complacency are longed for, and the employees believe they could go back there if it weren't for him or her, the leader. Or worse, none of this would be happening if the founder were still alive. Eventually, there is a call for the leader's resignation. What happens if Degeneration moves to an extreme? Malignant Quad 3 Degeneration results in a state of Mutiny.

QUAD 4 CONVERSION

Resilience Builders might do one of two things to rebuild resilience. First, if the organization has simply lost its platform in the absence of major changes in the larger industry, they might convert the organization by restoring the old platform. Or second, they might convert the company from one competitive platform to another, in order to adapt to a changed industry or environment.

Recent history is full of examples of the wrong remedies being applied to this Quad. Threatening e-mails, unachievable targets, motivational speakers, terminations, and team building exercises abound. Inappropriate lay-offs, sudden leaps into new businesses, and incompatible mergers are common here. It is often quite surprising to note, however, that these dramatics yield neither a motivated workforce, nor a return to a state of resilience. What's needed now is a Hope Bearing Plan.

A Hope Bearing Plan is a proposed remedy to the ills of the organization. It addresses external strategy and internal culture. It does not need to be pleasant or painless. It needs to be believable.

What happens when Quad 4 Conversion fails? When the ordeal has lasted too long without observable evidence that the Hope Bearing Plan is working, the Conversion begins to fail. Eventually the group begins to believe nothing will work. Malignant Quad 3 Conversion results in Exhaustion.

RETURN TO GROWTH

If the Hope Bearing Plan produces a successful Quad 4 Conversion, the company experiences a Return to Growth. This adaptive step is the single element that separates resilient companies from the rest. Of course. But it isn't a step all by itself; it is the product of all of the above processes. Those enterprises which are able to reinvent themselves through Quad 4 Conversion are the ones that have developed a new platform and have worked within their location on the developmental frame. They have rebuilt clear strategies and re-established well-defined cultures. They and everyone around them have come to know their new and unique identity. They have Returned to Growth.

An Optimistic Concept

The developmental frame is an optimistic concept because we all can build an awareness of these issues and begin to manage through them. This moves the concept away from a biological lifespan metaphor to a sequence of adaptive steps.

Resilience Builders seek to detect Quad 3 Degeneration early and to have only a brush with it. They create crises in order to offset complacency, or select tasks that require people to develop new competencies. They are quite willing to put their own people through the pain of redefining the entire workplace so they don't need to go through the collective heartbreak of failure. They understand that the death of a company is due to a failure to adapt. Sometimes it cannot be helped or prevented. Often it can. They know their job is to manage the interactions between platform, frame, culture and strategy in order to return to growth and build resilience.

Corporate Culture and Resilience

How is culture built similarly at the U. S. Army Special Forces, Southwest Airlines, Tyson Foods, and Charles Schwab? Chapter 8 examines this issue:

If a firm is in a state of resilience, there are two variables that should have the most powerful influence on its culture. These are, first, the firm's competitive platform and, second, the firm's location on its own developmental frame. Corporate culture is divided into three levels:

First Level:
The Constitutional Component of Culture

The theoretical contribution to culture proposed by this book is that resilience-building corporate cultures are structured in three levels, each of which functions as a separate component. The Constitutional Component of culture is the basic DNA of the organization and it provides the foundation on which culture is built. This is the primary determinant of the nature of the organization. So, in order to understand this component of culture, ask two questions. "How does this firm compete?" And, "In what Quad of development does this firm reside?" The answers to these two questions speak strongly about the culture of the firm.

The firm's choice of competitive platform is a remarkably strong influence on culture in resilient firms. Is it different to work for a resilient Efficient Platform company than a resilient Relationship Platform company? Yes. Do resilient Marketing Platform companies have different cultures than resilient Creative Platform companies? They do. To achieve resilience, the firm's culture should match its competitive platform. Many leaders have failed here. Wouldn't it be sad to watch an earnest leader try to infuse the cultural elements of an Efficient Platform into a Creative Platform company? He or she might start a program of tight cost controls, begin an aggressive six sigma quality program, and become intolerant of mistakes and waste. This leader would be doing a great job of culture creation, but it would be a culture that lacks congruence. It wouldn't match the firm's Creative Platform. Sound far-fetched? A recent BusinessWeek cover article accused famous CEO James McNerney of having done just this during his brief stay at 3M. 3

The Developmental Frame also has a strong influence on the Constitutional Component of culture. Life in a start-up Quad 1 firm is different from life in any of the other quads. In fact, each quad is unique and involves a morph from the previous stage. Culture in Quad 1 Growth is influenced by its energy, ambitions, and wonderful expectations. Quad 2 Steady State companies defend market share. Look for a culture that is based on defensiveness. Quad 3 Degeneration involves a decline and a culture filled with a resentful desire to return to the good-old days. Quad 4 Conversion brings renewed hope, signs of growth, and a culture of survival. And, in Return to Growth the culture is likely to be excited and optimistic, but no longer naively so, because the group's wisdom is the product of its previous struggles.

David Packard told a story about this at Hewlett Packard. He had worked at GE in the 1930's and while there he observed that the tools were locked up every night. He and Bill Hewlett had been very smart scientific tinkerers ever since childhood. When they started HP they wanted to promote curiosity and tinkering as part of their creative culture, so the tools were left unlocked at all times. Anyone could use or borrow any tool. Employees were even encouraged to take them home for further use, with the belief that this increased their creative skills on the job. Years later when HP had become a large organization, Bill Hewlett was visiting a plant and wanted to borrow a microscope at night. He found the tool cage locked, so he broke the lock and left a note. In this one simple act, he showed that he was not willing to forfeit this important piece of HP's culture. Wisely, he was keeping culture congruent with the Creative Platform. In addition, he was not allowing the firm to lose its culture as it moved along the developmental frame from a small start-up to an established incumbent. 4

SECOND LEVEL:
THE VALUE COMPONENT OF CULTURE

The second level of a resilience-supporting culture is the Value Component. Unlike the quietly pervasive Constitutional Component, this level is proclaimed loudly. It is based on the company's mission and its core values. It is the product of the group members' shared history and the collective experience of problem solving and survival. It is a strong statement from the Resilience Builder that, "This is who we are, and this is what we value." This builds the outwardly observable character traits of the firm.

Mission statements and core values are too often misapplied or they are odd collections of random feel-good statements that do not instruct insiders or outsiders what the basic constructs of the organization are. To build resilience these statements must stand on top of the first level Constitutional Component of culture. They must be built on the firm's competitive platform and fit well with its location on the developmental frame.

So, "We seek efficiencies in all we do, and we pass those efficiencies along to our customers" is an excellent core value of an Efficient Platform company. It guides all who encounter the firm, and it instructs. But this would not be a good core value for a Creative Platform company. Perhaps, "We are open-minded to new ideas when we seek cures to diseases," would be.

Third Level:
The Interpersonal Component of Culture

The third culture level is the Interpersonal Component. This is the "corporate culture" that most articles and executives refer to. This is the obvious personality of the organization and could be described as "the way we treat each other". Here we find the artifacts, heroes, rituals, customs and ceremonies of the organization. This determines whether we all go out on Fridays for a beer, how we celebrate birthdays, and how leaders recognize our achievements.

Resilience-Supporting Cultures

Every company has a culture. Previous authors have said it is best described as, "The way we do things around here." 5 Building a strong culture that is pointed in the right direction builds resilience. What is the right direction? Build the Constitutional Component of culture on your competitive platform, and keep it consistent with the firm's location on the developmental frame. Then select the organization's mission and values based on the same platform and frame. Use all of this to guide the interpersonal interactions within the firm, and the result is a resilience-supporting culture.

Strategies that Build Resilience

Chapter 10 tells how Disney, Thomson Reuters, Con-way Trucking and others have used resilience-building strategies in the face of dire industry dynamics.

Strategy is the fourth, and last, of the essential elements of resilience. I intentionally present it last in this book because too many leaders believe they can build a resilient organization if only they can find the right strategy and execute it well. But a great strategy in the absence of powerful strengths on the other three essential elements of resilience will yield transient success at best. It will not build resilience.

How does a Resilience Builder find a sustainable competitive advantage and move this advantage forward to a level where it builds resilience? First, decisions here must leave the firm's strategy congruent with the other three essential elements of resilience: platform, frame and culture. Beyond this there are three questions that Resilience Builders examine more effectively than others. These three questions are: Is this business planted in fertile ground? Is our collection of strengths hard for others to imitate? Has there been a platform shift in our industry? These three questions are not new to this book, but showing how Resilience Builders use them is.

Is This Business Planted in Fertile Ground?

To determine whether an industry offers fertile ground for your company, ask whether the overall industry is built on any one competitive platform or on an agreed-upon combination of platforms that create a Hybrid Platform.

As I write this, there are almost 1,500 daily newspapers in America. All are in a state of anxiety as the information they once owned is now readily available on electronic venues. Will print journalism become extinct? Not soon, and some newspapers may even thrive. Small-town papers endure because of their parochial content. Some huge papers are both respected and persistent, and some industry niche papers seem safe. But, the grand picture for the industry casts doubt on its strategic viability, and therefore on the resilience of the industry. In print journalism there is no platform a participant can select to give it a competitive advantage.

Resilient strategy is planted in fertile ground. The Resilience Builder has an uncanny ability to render an objective assessment of industry health, and he or she knows whether there has been a shift in the structure of the industry. The chapter on resilient strategy examines this issue of strategic viability.

Is Our Collection of Strengths
Hard for Others to Imitate?

As we see some remarkable firms rise in their industries and thrive in even the most difficult times, we ask the question, "How do they do it?" Competitors develop theories about how the resilient firm endures so well, and they try to imitate, but rarely are they able to do so. Rarer still are they able to copy the unique combination of skills internal to the resilient firm.

No two companies are the same, not even two successful companies built on the same platform in the same industry. There are just too many decisions that influence the nature of each firm. So, when a Resilience Builder engages his or her firm's competitive platform as an integral part of strategy, the complex combination of so many variables begins to create a competitive advantage that is not likely to be imitated. The more difficult-to-imitate the competitive advantage is, the more sustainable it is. This is because engaging a well-defined platform as the basis of the firm's competitive behavior strengthens ambiguity. In addition, each platform brings with it a collection of core competencies and skill sets which can be applied in any combination with each other. This unique combination makes the firm's success even more ambiguous and difficult to imitate.

This is even more powerful in the case of Hybrid Platforms. Multiply all of the skill-set choices the firm makes to create the first platform by all of the decisions involved in creating the second platform and the ability of a competitor to imitate begins to vanish.

Has There Been a Platform Shift in Our Industry?

All firms exist within an industry, and industries have a lifecycle of their own. We know a lot about how industry dynamics change as time passes and events unfold. In the beginning most industries are fragmented cottage industries. There are many entrants trying many different strategies. Initially, no one has a competitive advantage, and no firm seems to be able to create profits better than the others. Then something changes.

One firm develops a strategy that is superior to all the others, and this becomes the dominant strategy in the industry. There were many discounters around before Sam Walton, but none persistently drew down costs and passed the difference along to the customer. Before him, discounters tried to offer low prices, but if the discounter could get one shipment even cheaper, this was just good luck and did not result in any lower prices for the consumer. Walton called his model the discounter's paradox; the more he cut prices, the more money he made. Business school professors call it the value loop; any reduction in costs is passed on to the customer, and not allowed to reside with the supplier or the retailer. The loop is completed when the customer begins seeking these discounts and buys more from the store. Thanks to Sam Walton, this became the dominant strategy in the industry. Notice also that the establishment of a dominant strategy creates an industry-wide competitive platform; in this case the Efficient Platform. The industry-wide competitive platform comes with a collection of behaviors that will ensure either success or failure. This industry-wide platform also becomes a vehicle for the brightest leaders to become Resilience Builders, because they can begin to manage the essential elements of resilience in a manner that is congruent with this platform. The rules of the game have been established.

As an industry develops we might observe that its industry-wide platform changes. I call this a platform shift. If this happens in your industry, you must ask whether your collection of skills fits the industry's new requirements. It is difficult to give up your old competitive platform, but your firm's survival might depend on it. Chapter 10 looks at how some leaders have navigated this nicely and how some others haven't.

Platform and Frame Create and Steer Culture and Strategy

A resilient firm's competitive platform and developmental frame both create and act on its culture and strategy, as seen in Figures 1 and 2.

Here we see that the wisdom of the Resilience Builder is to build a powerful competitive platform that allows everyone to understand and agree upon the firm's spoken and unspoken rules and norms; its culture. The Resilience Builder also watches the firm move along its own developmental frame and is aware that each shift affects culture. Likewise, if the firm is in a state of resilience, strategy is heavily influenced by the competitive platform the developmental frame.

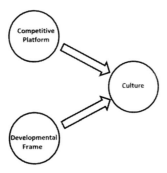

Figure 1: Resilience Builders use a clearly defined competitive platform and the influence of the developmental frame to build culture.

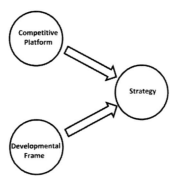

Figure 2: The distinctive nature of the competitive platform creates a unique strategy. The developmental frame impacts strategy multiple times as the frame shifts during the firm's lifetime.

THE METHODS OF RESILIENCE BUILDERS

Let's look closer at the essential elements of resilience and some of the men and women I call Resilience Builders. Their wisdom offers encouragement to all enterprises, large and small. This book will continue to demystify these remarkable leaders by showing how they understand the four essential elements of resilience, and how they use these elements to build durable enterprises.

Chapter 3

QuikTrip: Efficient Platform and a Culture of Kindness

My first fifteen minutes at the QuikTrip headquarters in Tulsa, OK, told me almost everything I could want to know about this resilient firm. Tulsa had experienced a terrible December ice storm just days prior and electricity was out for about half of the city. I was impressed that the headquarters campus was warm, inviting, and resembled a Southwest resort. As I entered the lobby I was surprised to see several hundred toys, all carefully wrapped. Some oversized toys, like bicycles and skateboards, were lined up all in rows and each one had a bow or giant ribbon on it. The friendly receptionist knew my name and that I was expected. She offered me a soft drink or coffee and said I should have a seat if I could find one that didn't have toys on it. As I watched I noticed she knew the name of each person that passed by and had a pleasant comment to make. I asked her if the ice storm had affected her and she said yes, but it wasn't so bad; putting on makeup in a dark bathroom made her look ten years younger, at least momentarily. She said the gifts were Toys for Tots, and the Marines were about to land at QuikTrip any minute. I commented that there were so many, and asked if QuikTrip was a community drop site for the program. She replied with her Oklahoma accent, "Oh, no sir, we have contests here all year where departments compete with fund raisers like bake sales, chili cook-offs, and the throw-a-ball-and-dunk-your-boss game. That's my favorite one. Anyway, we gather up all this money and then people from each department have fun going shopping. When they come back we all wrap the presents and get them ready for the Marines." Then she smiled.

Just then Jim Denny, Vice President for Marketing came around the corner. He was a solidly built man with a firm handshake and a bigger-than-life smile. He greeted me by name as if we were old friends. As we headed toward his office he told me I might hear the voices of children. Since the power was out all over town and the schools were closed, everyone was encouraged to bring their children to work. If they wanted to they could bring sleeping bags and stay overnight. Entire families were doing just that.

What is so amazing about all of this kindness? It is a popular opinion that Efficient Platform companies are unkind, penny-pinching folks who walk around with stopwatches and treat employees as if they don't care about them. QuikTrip demonstrates that this is not necessarily so. In fact, as I began my meeting with Jim I immediately asked him about QuikTrip's competitive platform and strategy, but before addressing that he said the thing he is proudest of is its culture. He said, "We are good to our customers and we are good to our employees."

This brief chapter will tell the story of QuikTrip and the extraordinary man who brought it to a state of resilience. Here we will see a slow start-up, then rapid growth and continuous adaptation in a changing strategic terrain. In the beginning this firm did not sell gasoline, and once it did it was challenged by retaliation from the major oil companies as well as geopolitical events, like the Arab oil embargo and several fuel crises. Along the way it expanded too rapidly and saw its culture slip and resilience erode. This chapter will show that the essential elements of resilience are things Resilience Builders do; not things they are necessarily able to articulate. As QuikTrip moved along its own developmental framework, there were decision points at which resilience could have been strengthened or lost. The Resilience Builders at QuikTrip knew when these choices needed to be made and they knew how to right the firm. Let's take a closer look.

A Different Kind of Convenience Store

When we think of convenience stores, most of us think of anything but convenience. We imagine gas pumps that work only sometimes, a store filled with unhealthy food, long lines, poor lighting, and dirty floors. QuikTrip stores are different. They are beautiful, clean, efficient, well-lit, friendly, and have fresh food every day. If the checkout line has more than two customers in it, the employee mopping the floor gets behind a cash register. The gas pumps are state of the art and there is paper in the receipt printer. The washer bucket always has fluid in it. Friendly clerks remember the regular customers' names and thank everyone for coming in. QuikTrip has 500 stores from Phoenix to Atlanta and the smart folks in charge there have a special formula for success that has kept this firm resilient for 50 years.

Like all convenience stores, QuikTrip is built on the Efficient Platform, generating high volume and surviving on thin margins. Its defining characteristic is operational effectiveness. But don't let this give you the impression of a barely surviving enterprise. QuikTrip has been named 28th on the Forbes list of privately held companies, has $9 billion in annual sales, and 10,000 employees. It adds as many as 35 new stores per year, and achieves steadily increasing sales year after year.

None of these accomplishments are treasured by QuikTrip leadership as much as the remarkable QuikTrip culture. QuikTrip has been named one of Fortune's top 100 places to work in America seven consecutive years now. The environment is friendly, energetic, kind, and driven. The entire culture is so ingrained that employees rarely need to be told what to do; they already know the mission and how to execute all of this company's competitive advantages. Everyone at QuikTrip has a sense of ownership in the company, and about one third of QT's stock value is in the hands of its employees. Over 140 QT employees have over $1 million in QuikTrip stock and retirement. Management treats employees with fairness, courtesy, and encouragement.

QuikTrip's ability to achieve resilience has been no accident. These folks know what they are doing and they do it well. It all began with a Resilience Builder named Chester Cadieux (pronounced Cad' joe). QuikTrip's story is remarkable and so is he.

HUMBLE BEGINNINGS

In my first conversation with Chester Cadieux I observed him to have a friendly openness and a trusting manner that are rarely found in those who have shouldered his level of responsibility. I discovered in him a sincere humility that some CEO's seem to lack. He said that much too much credit is given to him personally for the success of QuikTrip, and that he was just one of many hard working people that created this wonderful company. We will hear about some of them as this chapter unfolds, but Chester was the Resilience Builder and his personal history is instructive to us all. 1

Chester was born in Tulsa Oklahoma during the years of independent oil companies and wildcatters. His father worked for Bell Oil and Gas and also had his own part time business buying railroad tank cars and putting them into service. Without realizing it, Chester learned much from his father, who understood the needs of his customer and could charm the repair yard hands into getting his cars skipped to the head of the line and back into service quickly. He also learned that to be successful, he had to own his own business. Chester was bright and outgoing. He graduated from University of Oklahoma in the top 10% of his class and then was commissioned a lieutenant in the Air Force. While in the Air Force he observed strong and weak leaders as well as strong and weak followers. This taught him that he had to select people very carefully.

When Chester got out of the Air Force in 1957 he began looking for work that would give him a sense of accomplishment. He spent a short time as a printing salesman but this work gave him no satisfaction. He wanted to start his own enterprise and he had three requirements. First, it had to require minimal investment. Second, it needed to be a simple, nontechnical business. And third, it had to be in an industry that had little competition and could grow.

During that same time, one of Chester's boyhood friends, Burt Holmes, was watching Southland Corporation successfully build hundreds of 7-11 stores around Texas and Louisiana. Burt was an entrepreneur who didn't want to quit his job in order to go into the grocery business, but he was willing to invest.

In September 1958 when Chester was 26 years old, he and Burt opened the first QuikTrip in a strip of storefronts on South Peoria Avenue in Tulsa, paying $400 per month for 3,000 square feet. Chester ran the store by himself. He offered a limited selection of foods and charged a little more for the "convenience". The cost of the startup was $16,000 which included $5,000 that Chester borrowed from his father. Chester had dual titles of President and Night Manager. But like all new ventures, he immediately encountered unanticipated life-threatening events. Eight days after the first QuikTrip opened, South Peoria Avenue was closed for several months so it could be widened. Cars could not get to his store.

Chester became discouraged and Burt stopped by often to inspire him not to give up. Little did either of these young men know that QuikTrip would become a major American corporation. In his earliest days he hoped to someday open as many as ten stores, all in the surrounding Tulsa area. He later said, "I had no idea how much we could grow. We thought that if we had ten stores it would be as big as a supermarket. A supermarket is a real business and I wanted to be in business."

Like many Resilience Builders, Chester has the belief that much of QuikTrip's success has been the result of luck. Certainly, in the late 1950's he had no way of understanding that he had entered a new field that would rise to meet Americans' surging need for convenience. Although they were lucky, we know luck alone does not build resilience. He and his teammates at QuikTrip were about to show the world how competent they were at the four essential elements of resilience. But first they had to make a few mistakes.

FINDING CORE COMPETENCIES IN A NEW INDUSTRY

In the early days, the convenience store industry was quite forgiving, since it allowed managers to make mistakes without causing their stores to fail. (The same cannot be said today.) QuikTrip eventually became a good small business as Chester tried a lot of new things, many of which were futile. In fact Chester told me, "We did everything wrong to start with." He also said, "We were dumber than dumb".

Chester thought that his store was nothing more than a small grocery store with shorter lines and longer hours. Soon he realized that some items, like vegetables, had good profit margins but were slow moving, so they contributed little to the bottom line. In fact he said that if an onion didn't sell, he would keep peeling it down until it was the size of a golf ball. He tried to sell anything the customer might want, including fishing licenses, wigs, and television tubes. 3 Eventually he eliminated those items and replaced them with fast moving snacks, cigarettes, and beer. As time passed QuikTrip mastered the unique ability to offer a quick transaction for the consumer, leave the customer satisfied, and render acceptable income per transaction for itself. The ability to do this over and over again has become one of QuikTrip's core competencies. QT's high level of current-day skill at this has made this firm very difficult for competitors to imitate.

American society and the grocery industry were different in those days. Most women did not work and were free to shop during the day. Grocery stores did not have express lanes for checkouts, so they took time, and they closed in the early evening. No convenience store sold gas, and there was little opportunity to grab an item quickly and get going on your way. Chester began to see that his only competitive advantage would be to continuously improve QT's ability to provide efficient and convenient transactions. This, however, was quite comfortable for Chester. In fact, right on the front of Store Number 1 were the words, "Fast" and "Friendly".

As early as the 1950's Chester became an expert on the daily practices that could produce efficiency. Said one early employee, "He wanted things done fast." He told employees to carry a feather duster in their back pockets so it could be grabbed instantly. He instructed employees about how to open a paper sack with one hand while reaching for items with the other. He expected the back room to be organized. And, from the beginning he expected clerks to make change so quickly that they didn't need to rely on the cash register to tell them how much change was due. They were expected to just reach in the drawer and take out the right amount. All of these traditions, except the feather duster, are carried on today. In fact, if you go to a Quiktrip and find that you should get back 73¢ change, the clerk will often hand you three quarters just to make the transaction quicker.

THE JOURNEY TOWARD RESILIENCE

The initial start-up for Burt and Chester was rough. The winter of 1958-1959 produced little revenue due to the road closure. By December 1958 it seemed failure was a certainty. Chester's share of the losses was about equal to his weekly salary of $100. He had burned through the original $16,000 and $26,000 more.

CREATING QUAD 1 GROWTH

Faced with mounting losses, Chester did something only an entrepreneur would understand. He added two more stores. Of course, along with this expansion came employees, the cost of maintaining more inventory, and higher fixed expenses. The collection of the three stores lost even more money. What was his plan to fix this? Because he believed in his efficient and friendly methods so strongly, he added a fourth store. In fact, he convinced his milk supplier to provide the financing for it. That's when a surprising thing happened. All of the stores began making money, and this fledgling enterprise became stable.

This young company had newly arrived in Quad 1 Growth on the developmental frame. It had no written policies, and hadn't codified its own rules for success. Yet, Chester instinctively knew how to grow and make money. Long hours were the norm, and there was a healthy sense of risk. Although things were going well, everyone knew something could go wrong at any time. No one was too comfortable, and complacency did not exist. From time to time Chester stayed up all night with ledger sheets spread out on the floor, trying to decide which bills to pay, which suppliers to put off, and how to meet payroll. If one location had too much product and another was running out, rather than call a supplier he put some in the family car and moved it around himself.

As this developing firm began to build its competitive platform on efficiency, it likewise began to build the skills of efficiency into the fabric of its budding culture. This, of course, was also a byproduct of the founder's personality. By offering an efficient transaction to the customer, he believed he was doing the customer a service, saving him or her time or money. So, if culture is "the way we do things around here", 2 then from the beginning, doing things quicker and better was part of the QT culture. Also, Chester Cadieux was a pleasant, friendly fellow who thanked customers for coming in, remembered their names, and was sincere about treating his employees well. Automatically built into the culture was an expectation that everyone would do the same. In fact, as early as the 1960's he taught managers to be efficient first. If they could master that, then he taught them how to care for employees. How did he define "caring" for employees? Managers were expected to do three things: Treat employees kindly, encourage them, and give them serious and honest performance reviews. He paid all of his employees higher than the competition, not just to reduce turnover, but also so he could have loyal staff that would carry on this culture.

In these early days, the QuikTrip strategy was ill-formed, because relatively little was needed to compete and succeed. This industry had room for everybody. Running these four efficient, clean and friendly stores assured QuikTrip's success. Eventually the rules of competition in the convenience store industry would become more well-defined and this insightful man would build resilience by anticipating and adapting.

ACCIDENTAL RESILIENCE

If we could have had a conversation with Chester in 1960, perhaps he would have said his small company was resilient. It certainly appeared to be. It had good cash flow, had chosen the Efficient Platform, was in Quad 1 Growth, was building a culture to support its competitive platform, and had a simple but successful strategy. But this was accidental resilience. Chester was about to have several experiences that would make him a more seasoned leader and help him to gain the wisdom of a Resilience Builder. After these experiences we will observe Chester to know what makes QT so successful, do these things intentionally, and become very skilled at requiring others to do these things as well.

ENTRY INTO QUAD 2 STEADY STATE

During the 1960's QuikTrip grew slowly and incrementally, and seemed destined to remain a local player. Despite the fact that running an individual store required long hours and lots of energy, this team was comfortable. Efforts to improve were small and incremental. For example, during this time QT leaders decided to obtain some warehouse space. They had no system of materials management or logistics. They just went around and bought up close-outs and surplus items at low prices. In fact, only after buying the warehouse did they realize that they didn't own a truck. So they used a pick-up truck and a horse trailer to haul merchandise. At the time it would have been difficult to imagine this would become a major corporation, but this is a tale of an American organization that raised itself up by its own bootstraps.

Had it been allowed to remain this comfortable, QuikTrip would not exist today. Fortunately, like all Resilience Builders, Chester could not tolerate complacency so he became restless and sought a new market for growth. In 1968 he looked north to Kansas City.

RETURNING TO QUAD 1 GROWTH

At first, visits to Kansas City included only Chester and the second employee he had ever hired, John Howerton. In downtown Kansas City there was an upscale spot called the Buttonwood Restaurant which became their Kansas City office. Well, actually the men's restroom became their office, because it had a bank of payphones on a wall far enough from the toilets that they didn't transmit the flushing sounds.

Chester has described those days as John Howerton at his very best. John understood how to grow on very limited funds, since they had little money and the cash flow from their Oklahoma stores wouldn't support organic growth in this far-away place. Said Chester, "We didn't even have the capital to buy the dirt." Despite this they agreed on one thing. QuikTrip would grow. So from those restroom payphones, these two mavericks called realtors, developers, and land owners. They discovered that everyone was willing to participate. They found "build-to-suit" lots. Burt Holmes, QuikTrip's cofounder, was still involved and knew people in Tulsa who would build the buildings in Kansas City for a signature. So, Chester and John would buy a lot, build a QuikTrip building on it, and then find someone to buy it from them so Quiktrip could lease it back. What was the advantage of this leaseback approach? QuikTrip had limited capital, and its money would all have been depleted if they tied it up in only a few properties. By selling it to someone and then leasing it back from him or her, they could get their initial cash investment back and reinvest it in another property. QuikTrip could grow. In fact these entrepreneurs claimed that they grew the business without money. If it sounds like QuikTrip was a house of cards in the early days, it was. What we now know is that the QuikTrip senior team was developing the skills that would become another one of its greatest competitive advantages, the competent and effective use of real estate.

Chester described this to me as a time of lot of hard work and a lot of fun. He said that as the firm grew, the entire leadership team was young men, either just out of the service or fresh off the farm. Almost all were in their 20's or early 30's. They all worked hard, and some played too hard, but the organization was no longer in the comfort zone. Now, the stakes were high, and risk was with them once again. This group had vitality and energy. The firm had undergone a Return to Growth. It was back in Quad 1, and this felt good.

CREATING AN ORGANIZATIONAL STRUCTURE

During its first 20 years, QuikTrip had no overarching corporate structure. There was no marketing department, no human resource staff, and not one written policy or procedure. The firm had become too spread out and the regions were running themselves. In the late 1970's and early 1980's Chester Cadieux set about what he called "building competence at a corporate level". Of course, this was a decision-point where doing it right would enhance resilience. Doing it poorly would erode resilience. Failing to do this at all would certainly have caused the firm to falter. To build resilience, QuikTrip had to add corporate functions, maintain growth, and strengthen its platform, frame, culture, and strategy. It was about to do just that.

BUILDING A RESILIENT STRATEGY

Overlapping this time was the introduction of gasoline at QuikTrip. Chester added the first gas pumps to QuikTrip in 1971, but didn't do a major roll-out of gasoline until 1980. This roll out is one of the events of which Chester says, "We made a lot of mistakes." He also gained a lot of wisdom from those mistakes. He admits now that retailing gasoline is unlike any other, but he didn't know that at the time. The fuel business was run by a closed fraternity of men who knew each other and distrusted or maneuvered anyone who tried to enter.

HARD LESSONS

QuikTrip was too small to buy from suppliers directly, so it bought from jobbers; middle men who bought from the suppliers. Of course, they kept the prices high and included a substantial mark-up for themselves, thus making QT gasoline expensive for the consumer. Unaware that there was any other way to do this, QT managers just continued to buy from these jobbers. Eventually it became clear that the gasoline effort was failing and all of QuikTrip was at risk of collapsing. This all changed when Chester hired Lloyd Poston, who had been a manager at Derby Oil and then Vice President of Hudson Oil. Chester has always said that he was lucky to have great people at QuikTrip, and Lloyd was among the greatest. Chester said, "He taught us the gasoline business". He was smart and he knew gasoline retail, pricing strategies, refining, pipeline processes, and everyone in the business. Lloyd was a few years older than these fellows, so he was confident enough to teach his lessons by questioning QuikTrip's methods. He constantly asked, "Why do you do that?", and then persistently challenged the logic of the answer. Each time this happened a new approach emerged. Lloyd used his knowledge, connections and influence to show QT how to smartly operate in the gasoline market. Not only did QT begin to make money on gas sales, but adding pumps to a store increased sales inside that store an average of 10%. 3

Lloyd Poston's place in QT history gives us insight into the closeness of the men who formed QT so many years ago. Al Howerton (John's younger brother who was hired right out of high school in 1963) became a key player who eventually took over all of the real estate development. He described to me the times he would drive to Wichita to meet with Lloyd. He would stay overnight in Lloyd and June's home, and there would be plenty to eat. After dinner, Lloyd would get out his guitar and sing country songs. As Al told me this 22 years after Lloyd's death, his eyes welled-up. Every senior manager at QuikTrip speaks fondly of this man. He died in 1986, but he is revered to this day. 4

QuikTrip's newfound competency at gasoline retailing changed everything. Because of this strategic move, QuikTrip and others like it across the country became a threat to major petroleum companies and their retail gas stations. As the oil "majors" began to add food and convenience items to their stations, the distinction between a gas station and a convenience store became blurred. Chester Cadieux and his senior team knew that if they didn't do something right away this deep-pocketed competition could devour QuikTrip. This was no longer the tolerant industry it had been in the past. If they made mistakes now it would cause the failure of the entire enterprise.

Taking On the Competition

By the late 1980's the competitive battle was in full swing and it was time to employ resilient strategy. As the field became crowded, Chester realized that customers could get "convenience" anywhere. Even traditional grocery stores offered a wide range of snack food and had quick checkout lanes. So, to bring customers in he began to create attractive stores that sold items priced comparably to grocery stores.

During this time QuikTrip's sales were around $400 million annually, about half of which came from gasoline. When an oil company convenience store (like Shell or Amoco) opened near a QuikTrip store, its gasoline sales could decline as much as 20% per week, and merchandise sales could drop by about 10% per week. Rather than simply allow the oil companies to invade its turf, QuikTrip wisely retaliated by invading theirs. It added "gas station" type items like motor oil to its mix, thus giving the customer even less reason to go across the street. But this was just the beginning of an aggressive strategic response.

In order to take on the oil majors, QuikTrip managers realized that they had a problem. The public image of convenience store gasoline was that it was second rate or cast-off gasoline. People worried that it would "gum up" their car's engine. To offset this, QT branded its own QT Guaranteed Gasoline. It promised that if its gasoline damaged your car, QuikTrip would pay for all of the repairs. This promise was all that was needed. Customers began pulling up to the QT pumps.

Then Chester Cadieux made plans to tilt the scales back to growth, again. This was not going to be easy because this was now an aging industry in which all competitors had the same information, knew what the others were doing, and could use the same strategies.

From 1986 to 1990 Chester increased QuikTrip's growth by about 50% from about 200 stores to almost 300 stores. During that time, he moved, sold, or renovated 80 stores to add more gas pumps. He expanded geographically into new regions in St. Louis and Atlanta so by 1988 he had 8 stores in St. Louis and 10 in Atlanta. In 1988 he announced plans to continue expanding including 75 new stores in Atlanta in the subsequent 5 years at a cost of $50 million. This turned out well in the end, but first there was great struggle.

QuikTrip did not understand the Atlanta market. It was accustomed to Tulsa, Kansas City, and St. Louis, all of which had blue collar workers who bought snacks, beer, and cigarettes inside the stores. QuikTrip knew how to serve those communities, but Atlanta was different. These folks bought much more gasoline, thanks to its famous traffic snarls and long commutes, but they didn't want to come into the stores where there was much more profit to be made. After building 20 stores, QuikTrip was still struggling financially. Disappointingly, after a short but intense struggle, five of these stores were closed. Eventually the QT team learned how to serve this population, changed the product mix, began to make a profit, and resumed competent growth.

One of the theoretical statements of this book is that an organization is most adaptive when it is in growth. However, I also caution that there is healthy and unhealthy growth. It might seem at first glance that Resilience

Builder Chester Cadieux conducted unhealthy growth here, but this would not be accurate. Although QuikTrip grew rapidly at this point, it stayed within its well-developed skill sets. Building more stores and bigger stores required zoning and real estate competencies which the firm already had. They were masters at using income, leases, and creative real estate processes to offset the cost of growth. Atlanta gave them the wisdom to study a new population in order to serve it and grow.

In 1993 as the oil companies became more threatening Chester turned up the heat on his competitors by competing for the first time on gasoline pricing. By this time he clearly understood the pricing dynamics in the retail gasoline industry. He also had the wisdom to use his pricing strategy to create new customer expectations, and not to wait for customers to develop these expectations and then respond to them. So Chester decided that QuikTrip's gasoline prices would always be lower than the neighboring pumps. Then he began increasing the number of pumps so stores could serve 16 cars at the same time, but he didn't stop there.

Knowing that his competitors' gas stations which had been converted to stores had limited floor space and a small list of merchandise, he knew he could compete with them inside QuikTrip's stores. QuikTrip offered store-branded QT beer, with QT standing for "Quittin' Time" (now discontinued). He was the first to install a large selection of self-serve fountain drinks and a substantial coffee bar, and he added sandwiches and breakfasts that were fresh and attractive. In fact, QuikTrip offered $1.00 sandwiches which were of good quality (but not great quality). Although the stores were smaller than today's stores, they were premier at the time and this firm's response was very powerful and very adaptive.

Mixed in with all of this was a never-ending devotion to efficiency. QuikTrip kept its sandwiches at $1.00 from 1984 to 1997 before raising prices. How could it do this when the inflation-adjusted purchasing power of a dollar fell by about one third during this time? It did this by persistently buying, making and distributing these items more and more efficiently.

True Resilience

By 1998 the typical QuikTrip store was selling $2 million in merchandise and 3 million gallons of gasoline annually. That same year QuikTrip's total sales rose to a remarkable $1.9 billion, all built on its simple formula of quality food, excellent service, and clean, friendly stores, as well as its steady drive for healthy growth.

QuikTrip was in a state of resilience, but this was no longer accidental resilience. This was true resilience. Along the way the rules of competition and survival had become solidified in this field and QuikTrip was arguably the best in its industry. During his journey Chester had learned why QT was successful and he had become able to intentionally build his team and his enterprise around those rules of success. He had gained the wisdom of a Resilience Builder.

Chester was clear minded that QT was built on the Efficient Platform and he used this platform to guide daily activities. For example, QT did not join into the trend to put bar codes on store items. Instead Chester encouraged clerks to begin ringing up customers before they got to the counter by looking at the items in their hands as they approached the register. This made the transaction happen even faster. Of course, the advantage of bar coding is that it kept track of how much inventory was needed to replenish sold items. To offset this, QT developed its own "point of sale" software in its registers that kept track of inventory. The man who had started out teaching clerks to open a sack with one hand and reach for items with the other was now infusing efficiency into QT's use of technology.

The firm was functioning appropriately to its location on the developmental frame. After entering Quad 2 Steady State and allowing QuikTrip to become complacent in the 1960's, he tilted the scales back to growth by expanding again to Kansas City, St. Louis, and Atlanta.

QuikTrip had a resilience-supporting strategy; it didn't give up ground to the oil majors, but invaded their turf and beat them on price and product scope. It had increased the size of its stores and made them attractive shopping environments.

These elements of platform, frame, and strategy were congruent with each other, but these are only three of the four essential elements of resilience. The fourth element is culture. By the late 1990's the QT culture was solid and resilience-supporting, but how it got to be so deserves close examination.

QuikTrip Culture

Culture is a collection of expected behaviors in the workplace. ..... Constitutional Component of culture at QuikTrip began with efficiency. Everything was done quickly and effectively. Stores and store layouts were constantly studied. And, everyone was expected to have the efficiency "religion".

Kindness is Required

There was more to this culture than just being efficient. The second level, Value Component, as well as the third level, Interpersonal Component, of culture expected QuikTrip to be a kindly and friendly environment. This firm was founded on kindness, but then it lost this kindness for a while. Recall from the discussion in Chapter 2 what can happen when a company grows too rapidly. Extreme growth can result in Chaos. QuikTrip entered a period of Chaos when it initially expanded into Kansas City and Iowa, and the result was painful. As these stores were put up, QuikTrip hired too many people too rapidly. Chester promoted people who didn't share his values. QT became a big organization that lacked any formal methods to indoctrinate its store managers and employees in its strategy and the ways of its culture. Word came back to Chester that some store managers were harsh and rude toward the employees. Chester responded.

Chester wrote a letter to every manager which eventually became known as the "asshole" letter. In it he bluntly asked his managers if they were an asshole; a rude and inappropriate leader. He wrote that we all know the acceptable standards of customer service at QuikTrip, including fast, friendly service in clean stores. His letter said, "Just as there are minimum standards for customer service... there are minimum acceptable standards in the management of our employees. QuikTrip employees expect and deserve intelligent, positive, considerate, factual supervision. They do not deserve to work for an asshole. I am more tolerant of poor operations than I am of poor treatment of employees." He further said, "We cannot tolerate obnoxious, oppressive, abusive, tyrannical despots... Please be sure that you always treat your employees the way you want to be treated. This is the minimum expected standard of management at QuikTrip." Knowing they were the kind of leader Chester referred to, several of these managers resigned after reading the letter. A few others were eventually fired. These

49

firings were difficult for Chester who knew these store managers had worked hard for QuikTrip. Twenty five years later he told me, "It broke my heart to fire them." This was one more painful lesson in wisdom for this Resilience Builder. From that time on however, no one at QuikTrip believed that adhering to its culture was optional or at the discretion of local managers.

By today's standards Chester's language in this written correspondence was both inappropriate and unacceptable. But to all who read this passage, please keep in mind that it was only a few years later QuikTrip employee ratings placed it on Fortune's 100 best places to work in America for the first time, and Chester Cadieux certainly took a powerfully direct approach to enforcing QuikTrip's culture. This letter is legend at QuikTrip.

Chester always gave heavy support and recognition to his employees. When asked about QuikTrip's remarkable expansion, he said that the only reason QT expands is to create promotion opportunities for its employees. He gave the credit for the successful expansions to his leadership team and store managers for their execution of QuikTrip's basics. He knew they were the ones who actually built QuikTrip on an Efficient Platform, applied its values, and created a positive interpersonal level for QuikTrip's culture. He continued to pay them well. At the time of the great expansion into Atlanta the industry average salary for convenience store managers was $25,000 and he was paying his $48,000. 5 He made sure that entry level cashiers and clerks were paid higher than the minimum wage, had a health plan, and he created a 401K as well as an employee stock ownership plan. His philosophy was that these folks were his team members and if he expected them to appreciate every customer, he had to appreciate every employee. Said Chester, "You're not in business for yourself, you're really in business with all of these other people," the employees.

LISTENING

QuikTrip's leaders have built the culture by listening to their employees from the very beginning. For most of his career, Chester and his top managers spent about one third of their time gong to each store, listening to each and every observation of customers, customer needs, suggestions about how to do things differently, and then they listened to employee needs. In some of these meetings, division management was asked to leave, so Chester could hear candid comments from employees. Now with 10,000 employees senior managers still travel around to regions and locations. In addition, QuikTrip employees get on the store computer, log in with a fingerprint ID, and answer surveys as well as open-ended questions. Every single survey is read. Those that need a response get one. Every time. Says Chester, "From the beginning we had meetings with everybody; secretaries, store managers - everybody. The learning here is tremendous."

THE NEEDS OF EMPLOYEES

Chester realized over these 52 years that as the American culture has changed, so have the needs of the employees. How? Fifty years ago, if you had a job, you just went to work. That was that. Today QuikTrip knows that employees need time off. Now they can contact the call center, get time off, and a replacement is sent to their store. Thanks to QuikTrip's Efficient Platform all stores, cash registers, and inventories are identical, so the replacement can step right in and get to work. Culture was the fourth essential element of resilience. At QuikTrip culture is powerful and congruent with the other three essential elements.

It is not easy to get placed on Fortune's list of the 100 best places to work in America year after year. Likewise, it is not easy to start a business on a shoestring and build it to a $9 billion firm with 10,000 members that offers a positive experience for employees as well as customers. All of QT's good qualities have strengthened its resilience, year after year. QuikTrip is resilient now, and Chester Cadieux is the Resilience Builder that made it so.

SUSTAINING RESILIENCE

CONTINUOUS IMPROVEMENT

Chester Cadieux and his team had placed QuikTrip nicely in a state of resilience. The QuikTrip brand was respected and well known in every one of its markets, and customers were coming in the doors. It was successful. Its very success could have caused this firm to become complacent, perhaps arrogant, and to eventually decline. To prevent this QT began several programs of continuous improvement.

QuikTrip created a new store design in the late 1990's. A lot of thought and debate went into this, and inputs were gathered from leaders, store managers, employees, and customers. As a result, a bigger store with more room for customers, a larger soda fountain, a longer coffee bar, more room for food, and a larger storeroom was designed. Lighting was improved and security cameras were placed everywhere.

A 1999 Fortune article stated "Bye-bye number 56." 6 Number 56 was a busy and profitable QuikTrip store in Tulsa that was scheduled for demolition simply because it was too ugly. Because QuikTrip had been around for a while, some of the stores had an outdated appearance. It would be foolish to think that yesterday's success could guarantee tomorrow's and they knew that re-creating a beautiful store with improved functionality would be an investment in the future. At over $1 million each, replacing most of its stores was an unthinkably large expense, but over the next few years QuikTrip did just that.

So, QuikTrip developed a practice of building two new larger stores and closing three outdated stores. As counterintuitive as this may seem, by doing this QT continued to expand. How does QuikTrip maintain its Efficient Platform and culture in light of all this growth? It "transfers the platform and culture" by transferring a trusted manager into a new market.

Resilience and Succession

In 2002 Chester was succeeded by his 35 year old son, Chet, as president and chief executive officer. The hallmark of good succession is the fact that it is impossible to know where the father's influence ends and the son's begins. Like his father, Chet is dedicated to QuikTrip's resilience-building culture. Employees are offered dental care, profit sharing, employee stock ownership plan (ESOP), vacation, Christmas bonuses, scholarships, tuition reimbursement, disability insurance, and pleasant treatment by managers. One store employee summed this up to me, "I love QuikTrip and I love my boss." Like the days when his father was in charge, QuikTrip gives 5% of its profits to charities and is a good community citizen.

Also like his father, Chet is dedicated to QuikTrip's resilience-building operational effectiveness and continuous improvement. As I write this, there is a QuikTrip store being built inside a large warehouse. It isn't a mock-up. It is a real building inside another building. It is the next generation of QuikTrip store design. And, although this new building already exists, it is changed, walls moved, and layout altered as a result of a continuous stream of input from managers, employees, architects, and customer groups, even as the project continues. Why should QuikTrip change the stores again? Well, it seems that QuikTrip's biggest problem now is that it is so successful that the pumps get crowded and the stores get full of customers. That means the next customer might decide not to pull in, because it looks too busy. Even though this is a nice problem to have, QuikTrip's insightful leaders believe that with improved design they can further improve the customer experience and their own Efficient Platform.

QuikTrip has developed a secret strategic competence, hidden from customers and protected from competitors. It is part of what makes QuikTrip impossible for its rivals to imitate. It all began with Al Howerton, the high school boy who was looking for a job in 1963. Like almost everyone at QuikTrip, he started as a clerk behind the counter. Eventually, he developed extraordinary skills at evaluating and purchasing real estate. When I asked him to explain his method to me he did. He said it is like the children's game, rock, paper, scissors. Think of real estate as having three variables and you must decide which one is rock that breaks scissors, or whether it is scissors which cuts paper, or if it is paper which covers rock. At that point he could see the quizzical look on my face, so he explained that he learned over time when to value high traffic flow on a street, when to value a property being near a large number of employers, and when to value it being in a densely populated residential area. He became remarkably skilled at balancing these variables and always choosing the right location for a new QuikTrip.

But Al Howerton was interested in succession too, so he and the IT department at QuikTrip developed a mathematical model, called QTSite, intended to quantify his own decision-making process in which many variables (traffic flow, population density, employer locations, level of competition, etc.), are fed into a formula, enabling them to rate a potential property. Great trust is placed in the formula's outcome. Great outcomes have been derived from this trust. Chester has said that this model can accurately predict future sales volume at any location in any city. 3

To further sustain resilience, QuikTrip's recent strategy has been to efficiently improve its food offerings. In fact, its food is now so good that some customers go to QuikTrip just to get a sandwich, salad, yogurt fruit cup, or breakfast burrito. Twenty years ago QuikTrip strategy blurred the boundaries between convenience stores and gas stations. Now it is taking another step that will blur the distinction between convenience stores and fast food restaurants. How does it plan to succeed here?

QuikTrip has built its own commissaries, called QT Kitchens. Each one is a production facility that has real chefs and creates upscale sandwiches, food dishes and fresh pastries for rapid daily distribution to the stores. These items are shipped around the metro in shiny refrigerated trucks bearing the QT logo (it has come a long way since the horse trailer). When a customer reaches for one of these food items, it is fresh and delicious. It has its own food brands, including HOTZI breakfasts, Freezoni ice drinks, Hydr8 sports drinks, QuikShakes (pick a few flavors of ice cream out of the freezer and blend them yourself), Wally Drinks, and an ever expanding coffee bar. Where should we go for lunch? How about QuikTrip?

In many industries, once all players seem to have mastered the basics, the next strategic path to resilience is to dial up one's marketing skill set. QuikTrip has had a strong marketing element all along. Now, it is stronger. Every employee wears a QuikTrip shirt or red Polo, the stores proudly display the QT logo everywhere, including on the gas pump keypad. But recently QuikTrip has leapt ahead on the branding of its drinks recently. Its energy drinks each have their own mascot. Its Wally drinks feature Wally who is a disgusting little boy that makes strange body sounds with his hands under his armpits. Each Wally drink, like Honkerberry, has its own story, sure to delight adolescents and be viewed as a little off-center by parents. You can get a Wally prepaid QT card and the QuikTrip website tells children to beg, cry, and throw themselves on the floor if their parents won't give them one. It is all in good fun, but it is also powerful marketing to a specific audience, and it is good strategy.

Who will QuikTrip target next? Women. Probably disgusting Wally is not going to bring adult women in, but QuikTrip's well-lit and safe environment is a good start. Food that is attractive, nourishing, low calorie, and low on carbohydrates will also succeed. The nice people at this resilient firm are already working on it.

QuikTrip Wisdom

QuikTrip is a resilient firm. It is solidly built on the Efficient Platform. Its leaders have done a good job of tilting the developmental frame back toward growth many times. It has a resilience-supporting culture and its strategy is smart, adaptive, and aggressive. Most impressively, all four of the essential elements of resilience are congruent with each other and match the Efficient Platform on which this firm was built.

A famous quote around QuikTrip is Chester Cadieux's saying, "It's better to be lucky than smart." Everyone who has had great success believes luck has had some part of it. Chester, however, released an autobiography in 2008 entitled, *From Lucky to Smart*. 3 He suggests that in today's unforgiving and competitive environment one needs both luck and intelligence.

This story reveals the human side of a great entrepreneur, showing both his strengths and weaknesses. He was blindly optimistic in his early days, and built his firm on convenience and his own good nature. He cared about his employees, but let his culture slip away from him at one point. His efforts to grow were sometimes wonderful and other times frightening. Several times he risked the entire firm by growing too fast or not understanding the next crisis headed his way. He changed markets and the nature of his business several times.

I present this profile first because this story nicely reveals Quiktrip's movement from Quad 1 Growth into and out of Quad 2 Steady State, several times. It also shows how resilience is so greatly enhanced by building a firm on a clear competitive platform, in this case the Efficient Platform.

All leaders can learn from the steps taken by Chester Cadieux. Although his firm is now a big business, its methods are all available to all who are willing to try. Chester's story is his gift to you. I hope in some way you can benefit from the wisdom gained by this Resilience Builder's journey.

Chapter 4

The Four Competitive Platforms

Resilient companies have a clear identity; a strong and well-defined personality. We encounter this when we get a long workout on our insurance company's voice menu, then hold for the next available agent. We experience it when a bridal shop spends more time interviewing a young woman than selling to her. We see it when our cell phone obsoletes almost overnight. And we know it when our soft drink is supposed to make us young again. Most successful insurance companies operate on an Efficient Platform. The best bridal shops are built on a Relationship Platform. Technology companies build their fortunes on the Creative Platform. And soft drink manufacturers are established on the Marketing Platform. Within each industry, those companies which have achieved resilience have done so by carefully choosing their own competitive platform, communicating it clearly to their employees, suppliers, and customers, and living according to the doctrine of this competitive platform. For them, this is more than just a business model. It is a religion.

There are four competitive platforms: Efficient Platform, Relationship Platform, Creative Platform, and Marketing Platform. There is also a fifth possibility, a Hybrid Platform, which is a combination of two or more competitive platforms. As various industries have progressively become more complex, successful Hybrid Platforms are now seen more often. Effective execution of a Hybrid Platform can powerfully enhance resilience.

This book proposes that there is a distinct set of skills and competencies associated with each of these platforms, and resilient companies specialize in a specific competitive platform. Once a Resilience Builder selects a platform and dials this platform up to extreme heights, the very nature of the organization becomes clear. Each platform has its own set of defining characteristics, relationship with money, motive, and method of growth. Each also has a unique relationship with its suppliers, employees, and customers. Each has a unique set of marketing skills. This means that it is quite different to lead, manage, sell to, or work for an Efficient Platform company than it is to do so for a Relationship Platform, Creative Platform, or Marketing Platform company. In resilient companies, everybody knows upon which competitive platform the company is built.

Companies that are less clearly defined are less likely to achieve resilience. They attempt to please every constituency, satisfy the needs of every customer, and fail to establish a precise identity. They attempt to be relationship-oriented, so they avoid telephone voice menus, while their efficient competitors function more cheaply. Or they offer very efficient e-business web selling of products that need a personal relationship and a training-based sales force. They install a laboratory to innovate new products when they have never invented anything before. Or they attempt a multimillion-dollar mass media marketing blitz when they are a business-to-business supplier which never sells to the public. They function poorly because they are poorly defined. Resilience eludes them.

The competitive platform is a product of the nature of the industry in which the enterprise resides and the place the firm's leaders choose to occupy in that industry. Industries tend to favor a particular competitive platform, based on the industry's life cycle and the competitive characteristics of the industry. Hence, once a platform is chosen it may remain unchanged permanently or until the industry changes.

There are different rules of strategy and competition associated with the different platforms. Think about the land-line telephone service in an office. If one phone company offered its business clients new technology that had much greater quality of sound so listeners could hear the actual pitch, amplitude, and timbre that the speaker projected with stunningly low harmonic distortion, this might seem like a good strategic model. The company would hope to charge its subscribers more money per minute, and generate greater margins. But in reality this would not work. Sprint tried this with its "You can hear a pin drop" campaign. The problem is that the hard-wire office telephone industry is pure Efficient Platform. Phone time is a commodity item, and customers switch providers simply based on miniscule price differences. The quality of the sound is already "good enough" and no one will pay a higher fee for this commodity. Success goes to those who produce phone services in a more cost efficient way than the competition, or to those who cheaply bundle phone services with add-on services, like Internet, video conferencing, and data transmission.

Sometimes an industry offers a choice of platforms. Here, Wal-Mart is a good example of having made strategic choices that supported its resilience. Wal-Mart is a discounter and is different from a high-end retailer like the clothier, Brooks Brothers. Sam Walton knew that in small towns there were many ill-defined dress, shoe, appliance and hardware stores which were neither discounters nor high-end. Those small town stores charged high prices for commodity items, marking them up as much as 50%. He responded by creating an Efficient Platform company. His ability to achieve resilience was due to his ability to clearly define his platform and get the entire organization to live by it every day.

Once a company achieves expertise in a particular competitive platform, it should remain with that platform until there is a compelling reason to change. The issue of when to change will be addressed in the Chapter 10 which examines strategy. Imagine if Wal-Mart today were to enter the field of exclusive professional attire. It could have a store on Park Avenue in New York and compete with Brooks Brothers. There are high profit margins to be had and Wal-Mart has the finances to pursue it. Here is the problem. Brooks Brothers is not built on the Efficient Platform. It is built on the Relationship Platform. It has a professional sales staff that remembers the names and preferences of its best customers. Sales employees sometimes make phone calls to these customers to tell them of a new clothing item that matches something they recently bought. Brooks Brothers' buildings aren't plain shells made of concrete and aluminum. They don't have linoleum floors. And, they do not have the desire to function as cheaply as possible. Moving to exclusive clothing would violate the Efficient Platform on which Wal-Mart is built. It would require use of supply chain skills which are foreign to Wal-Mart.

Selecting one platform automatically involves trade-offs regarding growth opportunities. A strong platform guides the company toward some growth opportunities but not others, because there are platform-based choices to be made. In its earliest stages, a resilient Creative Platform company becomes successful by excelling at those opportunities that require creative strengths. As it becomes more resilient it infuses Creative Platform practices and Creative Platform thinking so pervasively throughout the company that everyone in the enterprise develops competency in the

Creative Platform. Imagine what could happen if the leader would ask the same employees and managers to have another product or service line that would be built on the Efficient Platform, a third that would be Relationship Platform, and finally a fourth that would be Marketing Platform. There would be no prevailing set of skills and competencies to master. There would be no clear identity to the company. Decisions would be made without any coherent ideology. And, worst, the public would not know how to define the company. Making these platform trade-offs means the firm must forgo some growth opportunities in order to achieve the resilience offered by a strong platform. Failure to do this results in temporary growth, but an eroded competitive platform and an erosion of resilience. Resilient firms seek growth opportunities that require and strengthen the skill sets attached to their competitive platform.

In the absence of an industry-wide platform shift, the firm's competitive platform is quite stable. Platform is more stable than the developmental frame (of course), culture, and strategy. It has a greater influence on culture and strategy than any other component. Under most circumstances it is a good idea to stay with the firm's established expertise, within its own platform.

The Efficient Platform

Defining Characteristic

The defining characteristic of firms who achieve resilience through the Efficient Platform is that these companies use their own internal efficiencies to produce an expedient transaction for their customers and themselves. This is intended to produce the most gain with as little waste or effort as possible. There are two components of this platform: cost containment and operational efficiency. While all companies must contain costs, Efficient Platform companies make it a central part of their identity. Operational efficiencies here include avoiding handling the product or material even one unnecessary time, effective use of IT, skilled production, skilled negotiation with suppliers, and highly efficient distribution channels. The entire enterprise is geared to reduce cost and waste, while increasing the effectiveness of the organization.

RELATIONSHIP WITH MONEY

A few years ago a newly appointed CEO of a multi-billion dollar American company began to organize layoffs on his first day. He cancelled magazines, frivolous cell phone add-ons, and every unnecessary amenity he could find. That was just the beginning. He made arrangements to sell the corporate jet. He and all managers would fly coach on discount airlines. The lavish furnishings in the executive offices were sent out the door and replaced with low cost desks and chairs, including his own. Were these acts of cruelty? Was he small-minded? Or, was his approach strategically sound? While all of these efforts might seem appropriate in a rescue situation, his was a profitable company in a mature field. However, he knew his industry was changing. Many old regional names had disappeared as profits had diminished and the field had consolidated. He knew his field was becoming more and more efficient. As he and I left his office after our mid-day meeting, he did something that surprised me. He turned off the lights even though he would return a couple of hours later. Then as we passed by an unoccupied office, he reached in and turned off the lights there as well.

Efficient Platform companies have a frugal relationship with money. Unnecessary expenses are seen as the enemy, and must be eradicated. Cost containment is the all-purpose remedy for all maladies. Expenses are seen as evil, unless there is an absolutely compelling return on investment that will materialize very soon. Large items like new plants and equipment are pursued only after a great deal of worry and hand-wringing.

Regarding the customer's money, the policy is simple. Pay now. Many Efficient Platform companies initially avoided accepting credit cards because of the 2% fee. In sales meetings an individual sales manager might be grilled for a large account which is overdue on a small amount of money. Accounts that are delinquent go straight to legal or a collector. It is a transaction, not a relationship. We serve and you pay. These companies avoid loss-leader promotions in order to win in the long run. As one senior manager told me, "We never enter a transaction in order to lose money. Never."

Most often, these groups do not have fancy offices and the headquarters building is surprisingly sparse. The headquarters staff is small but highly influential, since most functions are centralized. There is automatic climate control and a scarcity of secretaries or assistants. The décor features small cubicles and an abundance of plastic.

We can know we are calling an Efficient Platform company because nobody answers the phone. There is a voice menu asking you to press one if you want a different voice menu. Then when you reach the right place you are still put on hold. The recording says your call "is important to us", but you doubt it. Other platforms don't do this. Imagine calling a wealth management firm and being treated in this way. It doesn't happen. Why? Resilient wealth management firms are strong Relationship Platform companies. There, a welcoming person answers the phone.

In a well-functioning Efficient Platform company, there is no executive dining room. When headquarters staff members go to their plants or locations in the field, they do not rent a car. Someone from the plant comes to the airport to get them. E-conferencing is king, since it is so efficient (of course e-communicating is ubiquitous, but these people think about the postage and time they're saving). No one sends customers or suppliers greeting cards during the Holidays. That would cost too much. Even senior executives stay in moderately priced hotels. One executive who manages operations generating more than one billion dollars per year told me that on a recent trip he checked out of the Holiday Inn and walked across the parking lot to the Holiday Inn Express because he could save $10 per night. His rationale was; if the company can ask hourly employees to contain costs, he can do the same himself.

Motive

The motive of an Efficient Platform company is to increase its growth rather than increase its prices. Jet Blue could more than double its profit by raising its fares from JFK Airport to Ft. Lauderdale Florida from $89.00 each way to $109.00. It won't. It is not interested. It pays low wages, operates an efficient fleet, and wants to be known as the low price leader. Its motive is to sell more seats and run more flights, not to gain more profit per seat. It knows it is functioning in an efficient field, and it intends to maintain a cost containment strategy in order to offer low fares.

Growth Method

Nestle, the remarkably resilient food and chocolate company, has a respected research and development function. Nevertheless, often when it wants to grow it doesn't invent a new food. It waits for another company to invent a new product, test it, produce it, and make a profit. Then Nestle buys the company and works to further improve the products. It grows slowly and carefully. Growth in the Efficient Platform is typically by acquisition rather than innovation or invention. Dell Computer Corp. waits to enter a field until the technology has become inexpensive and standard, thus allowing the competition to bear the costs of development. Its resilience is ensured by the fact that the new field is established before it enters. Efficient Platform companies buy small companies with new patents (Creative Platform companies do this too) as well as their own competitors, which may be twice their size. Typically they do not have the profit margins to sustain large development staffs and labs, or to invent products, medicines, or programs. Growth occurs either by organically increasing sales or by acquisition.

RELATIONSHIP WITH CUSTOMER

Keep in mind that the defining characteristic of the Efficient Platform company is to provide an expedient transaction for itself and its customers. The word "transaction" here is important. These companies usually view their relationship with their customers as a transaction. They might say, "We will provide this much product or service for this price. We're the cheapest and the easiest. We give. You pay. That's that." They expect the customer to switch products for only a slight price difference. Think of Hunts vs. Heinz catsup. A few cents can outweigh a lot of shoppers' brand loyalty.

These vendors like to sell to the government and are not afraid of competitive bids. They also don't mind expecting the customer to wait in line in person or on the phone. Most managed healthcare organizations are efficient. So are phone and cable media providers.

Simplicity of design is valued here. Web selling is a great strength. Is Amazon an Efficient Platform company? Yes, one of the best.

RELATIONSHIP WITH SUPPLIERS

Suppliers who enjoy a cozy relationship with their customers including automatic rate increases may become a little uncomfortable here. Several of the best low price retailers are known to place tremendous pricing pressures on their suppliers. They offer very little benefit of incumbency to their suppliers who may be asked to rebid their products intermittently. Again, this is just a transaction.

Interestingly, suppliers of professional services do tend to have incumbency with Efficient Platform companies. Wal-Mart has used the same architect firm on hundreds of its new stores over many years. Why? That small firm knows exactly what Wal-Mart wants, ensures uniformity of design and construction, and offers reasonable fees. Supervising these architects is more effective for Wal-Mart than managing a complex bidding scheme, breaking in new architects, and fixing their mistakes. It's simply more efficient.

Efficient Platform retail companies have most recently begun to require their vendors to do chores that could be argued are the responsibility of the store. This means that if a vendor would normally deliver and stock store shelves once every two days and the store would have its own stocker straighten up the shelves in the interim, this has all changed. Now the vendor is asked to return to the store to straighten the shelves once or twice per day. This may require someone on a sales route to drive back to that store at great inconvenience, but it clearly is to the store's advantage. It is efficient.

Relationship with Employees

There is a popular belief that Efficient Platform companies are unkind or unfair to their employees. Chapter 3 showed that QuikTrip, a master of the Efficient Platform is both kind and fair to its employees. So are many other Efficient Platform firms. Overall, when this relationship is basically healthy the employees understand that they are valued and trusted. They are appreciated for the value they bring to the workplace and they know it. Unfortunately, this platform brings a risk that the employee will misinterpret the basic frugality of the enterprise as, "Well, they just don't care about me." It seems that the Efficient Platform company must try doubly hard to show the employee, "We care".

These organizations have rank and centralized control. Consistency and compliance are required. Performance-based bonuses are commonly found among higher ranking managers, although base pay is typically only at industry standards. Often these companies are in old industries like printing, food, paper, transportation, retail, and manufacturing. Unionized workforces are common, and benefits might be just adequate.

The headquarters is lean, but powerful. Wal-Mart's headquarters in Bentonville has shocked many first time visitors with its simplicity. Long hours are the norm. Policies are centralized. General Managers are expected to make a profit or be replaced. All are expected to participate in cost containment. Above all, everyone works hard.

TECHNOLOGY

All businesses continuously invest in technology. The technology investment alone does not distinguish Efficient Platform businesses from the others. The enthusiasm, excitement, and emotional attachment surrounding the cost-benefit of this issue does.

Many businesses are now investing in either supply chain management software, or supply chain integration methods. Efficient companies are doing this with gusto. The entire organization views this as central to the enterprise. Management Information Systems (MIS) is no longer seen as a support element. It has become a core part of the strategy. Logistics and supply/distribution management have always been the cornerstone of these companies. Long before the Internet made this easy, Wal-Mart had low flying satellites which tracked every sale on every cash register. This point-of-sale information was given not just to their own company, but also to their major suppliers. This gave them added efficiencies in the 1980's and 1990's before the competition could even begin to address the issue. In fact, Forbes magazine recently listed the top innovations of modern times, including the polio vaccine, penicillin, and memory chips. On the list was Sam Walton, not for creating one of the world's most resilient companies, but for his pioneering use of point-of-sale technology. [1]

As a result of all of this, supply chain management has become a powerful force in modern business. Efficient companies buy in large quantities and seek discounts. They use just-in-time methods in order to avoid warehousing large expensive stockpiles of products. For these companies, the "just-in-case" supplies are the vendor's responsibility, and these vendors should have supplies to fulfill odd lots. The company's massive supply chain management software programs are remarkably effective, and they expect their vendors to have the same software. This way the customer as well as all vendors can track the same system using the

Internet. Thus, for example, the system could link with transportation and include schedules, routes, and current locations. It could track the needed supplies based on recent sales orders, as those supplies are transformed from raw materials through production to the distribution system. It could inform the company as well as a network of suppliers involved in the product, so each could anticipate the next need.

Marketing

Of course, the established rules of marketing and market behavior still exist and this book is not intended to dispute or supplant them. The characteristics of low cost versus differentiated products is not challenged here. Subaru sells reliable cars at a low cost. That's its marketing strategy. BMW is the "ultimate driving machine" and is special. That's its marketing strategy. The four platform framework does not dispute this. Rather, it would simply state that Efficient Platform companies market differently than Relationship, Creative or Marketing Platform companies. The platform a company chooses should determine the value and direction of its marketing. Resilient companies have marketing and advertising programs that match their platforms. An evening of watching TV or flipping through a magazine reveals that there are many companies whose advertising is a mismatch to their platforms, and these companies tend to lack resilience.

Efficient Platform companies advertise, but rarely conduct marketing as it would be done by a Marketing Platform company. Few dollars are spent on focus groups, market analysis, and niche evaluation. The products here are often mature and difficult to market. They have lean budgets and simple slogans. Sometimes when sales decline, rather than conduct a fresh campaign, they resort to old formerly successful advertising themes. Campbell's Soup recently did this with a return to "Mmm, Mmm, Good." [2]

Marketing here focuses on the product, the brand, or the ease of use. Some famous campaigns of Efficient Platform Companies are, Wal-Mart, "We sell for less", and Dell's "Direct from Dell". Costco's slogan is in its name, "Costco Wholesale". Effectively marketing an Efficient Platform company should reveal its nature. So should the marketing of each of the other Platforms.

EFFICIENT PLATFORM VS. THE INEVITABLE EFFICIENCY OF MARKETS

The reader is cautioned here not to confuse the ongoing march toward efficiency that happens in all industries with what happens when a firm makes a careful choice to build itself on the Efficient Platform. As each day passes, every business is required to attempt to accomplish every task ever more efficiently. For example, personal wealth management firms are Relationship Platform companies, yet they use the Internet to purchase equities and send e-statements to their clients. Resilient companies in each of the competitive platforms strive to create an identity for their firm that portrays either efficiency, strong relationships, creativity, or a marketed brand image. As they do this, their competitors are trying to do the same thing a little more efficiently. These are two different issues. One is the firm's attempt to master its own platform and the other is the never-e nding requirement to do so more efficiently.

THE RELATIONSHIP PLATFORM

DEFINING CHARACTERISTIC

The defining characteristic of a resilient Relationship Platform company is that it uses its deep knowledge of its customers to provide something pleasing and exceptional. As a result, its customers view the interchange as a partnership. This competitive platform requires two types of work, or components. First, a deep knowledge of the customer must be gained and constantly maintained. Second, based on this deep knowledge, an extraordinarily special product or service must be provided. Both tasks are equally important. It is not enough to simply offer a product or service of high quality or cost. The goal of these resilient companies is to make the customer dependent on them, and there is an eagerness to do something extra for the customer; to do him or her a favor. The currency is attachment. Most often, the pleasing or exceptional thing the firm does helps the customer increase profits or improve processes.

The wisdom of the Resilience Builder here is to provide more than just sales empathy. There is a real obligation to move to the same side of the table as the customer and to conduct oneself in a way that the seller will cause events to occur that are, indeed, in the buyer's best interest. To succeed at Relationship Platform one must attempt to create a partnership.

RELATIONSHIP WITH MONEY

This is a different platform from the other platforms. The firm's involvement with a customer is more than an exchange of currency. Here resilience is achieved by having the customer leave every interchange feeling good. Sending a customer to a collection agent or court is a drastic measure of last resort. Sometimes bad debt is simply written off.

Unlike Efficient Platform businesses, this model allows additional expenses if they are in the service of the customer. An expense is not the enemy. It is a tool to achieve a deeper relationship. Return on investment is not the point. Return on relationship might be a better term. Expenses are of secondary importance in the quest to constantly prove to the customer how valuable and trusted the Relationship Platform company is. Expenses are acceptable if they help to build an intimate partnership with the customer.

Cost containment is examined, but in a minor way, and is not primary. In one strategy retreat with leaders of a Relationship Platform company, I suggested they had completely ignored the issue of cost containment and perhaps it should be addressed. There was an acknowledgement the topic had been ignored, but strong objection to the term "cost containment" and before talking about it we had to find a synonym that would be less offensive to employees. This is not an environment where employees are scolded for the amount of printer ink they are using.

Phone, cell phone, and incidental expenses might get looked at occasionally, but the entire company does not turn on this issue. Nothing is done to upstage the client. If the Relationship Platform company is traveling with an Efficient Platform client, it will mirror the travel habits of the client company. If the client stays in moderately priced hotels, its folks will as well. What is clear from the start is that travel to inconvenient places is no barrier to the project. So if the client is having a two-day review of the plant in Sidney Australia or Sidney Montana that is no problem. Let's go.

Upscale offices may or may not be needed. This depends on whether the customer comes to the offices. Climate control may be in place, but if so, it is there to make the client or customer comfortable, not to limit the utility bill. There is usually a receptionist or an operator so a person answers the phone. In large firms there may be a professional assistant to cover for a rainmaker.

Christmas cards are sent, of course, and if several cards are sent to one office each person in that office might be sent a different card. This removes any hint of mass production. The more personal, the more intimate, the more resilience is enhanced.

MOTIVE

The Relationship Platform company is motivated to establish customer dependency and attachment, based on its intimate knowledge of the customer's business, leaders, and unique requirements. Resilience is established by developing a unique ability to tailor special capabilities for the customer.

GROWTH METHOD

The Relationship Platform company grows by attempting to meet new needs with the same customer. For example, an import company that supplies fabric from Asia might spend a lot of time getting to know its customer and the customer's customers in order to find exactly the right mix of fabrics. It might demonstrate its ability to buy from a large variety of sources in order to adapt to changing style trends and to teach the customer how the trends are moving. Then it might grow by offering to provide not just fabric but also customized finished garments from a vast network of providers all over the world. This way the customer meets several of its own needs through its relationship with this vendor. Growth is almost never by innovation and rarely by acquisition. Growth tends to be incremental, organic, and sporadic.

RELATIONSHIP WITH THE CUSTOMER

This is more than a transaction; it is a partnership. Every interaction is an effort to deepen the bond with the customer and to display the vendor's unique indispensability. These resilient companies render unique products or take over a complicated process so their customers won't ever want to do it for themselves. Give customers more than they expect. The mantra is, "Make them need us."

Relationship Platform companies often are unable to compete on price alone, nor do they seek this. These companies detest competitive bids, or shootouts, as they call them. Relatively few of these firms allow government contracts to be a major piece of their portfolio, because government contracts tend to go to the lowest bidder, and they are re-bid regularly.

Price increases are approached with great trepidation. They expect the customer to stay with them after a price increase. In fact, they expect the customer to never switch. The loss of a customer is seen as a big event and is to be taken personally.

One of the cornerstones of the Relationship Platform company is its response to a customer's crisis. This is a moment the company savors. For example, once a supplier of pillows and bedding products was helping a retailer open a new store. This vendor had been a good advisor to the store owner. His warehouse was full of bedding and only ten miles from the store, but because of a severe snowstorm 300 miles away, the semi's which were to move the product to the store were stranded. They would arrive approximately two days late and the customer's store would open with many empty shelves. While the customer panicked, the vendor got on the phone. The only resource in town was a rental service with four flatbed trucks. The vendor paid for the trucks himself, bought plastic wrap (to keep the pillows from blowing away on the highway), and delivered everything on time. He and his staff stayed up all night, and the customer affectionately called it the shrink-wrap rescue. The crisis earned him a loyal customer, a new friend, and one more step toward resilience. The heroic response was not the defining quality, but his intent to use it to strengthen this relationship was.

RELATIONSHIP WITH SUPPLIERS

These enterprises ask their suppliers not to supply them with the same items as their competition. If the Persian rug here is the same as the one down the street, then how can it have been hand-selected for this customer? About 50% of fine dining restaurants fail within their first two years, because they don't get this piece right. The lobster tails here are the same as they are in

15 other restaurants. These items should be special and unique, or uniquely prepared. Relationship Platform companies expect their suppliers to have the unusual items that are rarely needed, but very important. Hallmark stores carry birthday cards for 100 year old people. They don't sell many of them, but we all know where to look for one.

The dynamics of supply are expected to mimic the dynamics of the customer relationship. If they want it quickly, so do we. If they want a wide scope of items, so do we. Supply chain automation is employed and appreciated, but it is not a central piece of the company's identity. They don't savor it, it's just good business. And, usually they don't do it as well as Efficient Platform firms.

RELATIONSHIP WITH EMPLOYEES

In general, Relationship Platform companies tend to have a good relations with their employees. Managers and supervisors look for small and large ways to reinforce their relationship with their employees. In one Relationship Platform company a woman's infant child was in an intensive care unit, and she sat with the child despite having seven other children at home. Coworkers and supervisors organized carpools for all of the other children's activities and even gave the kids a spreadsheet so they would be sure to get in the right car. These coworkers sent so many casseroles to the home, the woman had to ask them to stop or she would have to "stack them on the back porch". Relationship Platform companies strive to build good relationships with employees and they encourage employees to have good relationships with each other.

These firms are unique, however, because every employee is seen as representing the firm at all times. So, all employees are encouraged to treat others with courtesy whenever possible. Acts of kindness are highly valued, regardless of the employee's rank. This could be a sales clerk who puts a small-ticket item in her car and drives it to the airport for the customer who had left it on the counter.

In one doctor's office, a billing clerk discovered that an elderly woman could not understand her bills or insurance forms. She asked the woman to bring in her forms from all of her doctors so she could straighten out all of it for her. This is more than customer service. This is building a solid relationship.

In these companies, rank is less important than it is in Efficient Platform firms. They are rarely unionized, even in big companies. Pay is average or higher. And the headquarters might be overpopulated. Most of these companies are ripe for reorganizing or some downsizing, but it happens rarely.

TECHNOLOGY

The use of technology here depends on the industry in which the company resides. Automatic billing, routing, accounting, and process improvement are all used. It would be mistaken to believe these companies don't care about technology. They do. But here technology is in the service of the mission. It is rare for technology to be seen as part of the mission the way it is in other platforms.

MARKETING

These companies enhance their resilience by having a strong relationship with their communities. These are the firms that establish charitable foundations, scholarships for the disadvantaged, cancer research centers, and 10K "races for the cure". Small companies encourage 100% participation in United Way and the March of Dimes. Large companies establish charitable endowments and free concerts in the park. This is often done with the founder or CEO's picture in the paper, shaking hands with some local dignitary.

For resilient companies, the marketing campaign reflects the nature of the platform. The focus of Relationship Platform marketing is often you, the customer, and the word, "you" is used. For Hallmark it is "When You Care Enough to Send the Very Best," and American Association of Retired People (AARP) is "More than You Expect," and Principal Financial Group is "We understand What You're Working For". In each of these resilient organizations, the marketing focuses on customers and matches their Relationship Platform models.

THE CREATIVE PLATFORM

DEFINING CHARACTERISTIC

Resilience can be achieved through the Creative Platform. The defining characteristic of this platform is the firm's remarkable ability to develop a new or cutting-edge product or process. This defining characteristic has two components. They are; first, its ability to leverage talent and knowledge, and second, its skill at inventing or developing new products or services. These firms achieve resilience by originating new ideas, producing new things, and taking them to market. While they may own buildings and equipment, their capital is really more intangible. They leverage not just their own ideas and knowledge, but those of partners, alliances, and an entire creative community which they form around themselves. The new invention can be a grand leap or it can be incremental improvements of existing products, but it must be new. Here, creativity can be scientific, artistic, or product development.

Not included in this definition of creativity or innovation is the vast business literature which calls companies innovative if they have an unusual strategy. In this book "creative" and "innovative" are not synonymous. Innovation is what one does to a business plan or model. Creative Platform companies invent something like a computer chip, cartoon, medicine dispenser, or a movie. American Express was innovative in its strategy when it began issuing traveler's checks. Steven Spielberg and his associates were using their Creative Platform when they developed each of their remarkable movies.

RELATIONSHIP WITH MONEY

Like the Relationship Platform and unlike Marketing and Efficient Platforms, the Creative Platform views money as important, but it clearly is of lesser importance than the firm's primary task. Strange as it may seem, in this environment achieving resilience can be accomplished by winning or losing vast amounts of money on a bet. Finding and securing money or venture capital is a major task, only to go through it in the name of creativity and then trying to find more.

Huge sums of money are spent on product innovations in order to achieve resilience. To the uninitiated, the amounts can be shocking. It costs an average of about $800 million and it takes 9 to 12 years to develop a substantial new medication. For every 5,000 drugs in development only 5 make it into clinical trials. Only one makes it to the shelf. In addition, the Creative Platform company is often tasked with selling something no one knows they want. Not only is this a large risk, it is a tremendous cost, because the public must first be informed or educated and then persuaded. These companies spend a lot of money on risk management and compliance with regulations, since all medication, food, consumable, housing, educational, petroleum or most other new products are regulated by some governmental body. Getting through those hurdles costs money and time. Massive amounts of money are spent on patents and the protection of intellectual property. On the other hand, when these companies encounter a new project they want to pursue, they sometimes sell their old patents, products or projects in order to raise the necessary money. This, of course, adds to the turbulence of this competitive platform.

There is little or no emphasis on cost containment here. When a group of artists in a commercial art firm meet for an afternoon, no one in the room mentally calculates how much their combined salaries are costing for the meeting. These entrepreneurs are "all numerator". This means they look at how much money they can find and how much money their idea will make. There is far less focus on costs and liabilities. Mistakes are allowed, and some companies, like 3M, claim their best inventions have been another person's mistake. Some Creative Platform companies expect their employees to spend a significant portion of their time looking at other employees' projects. Google allows employees to spend up to one day per week on someone else's project. Time is not hoarded, and no one walks around with a clipboard and a stopwatch to determine if time is being used prudently. The most typical time conflict is the constant struggle to create something soon enough.

Internally, resources shift to the most promising projects, so life and budgets are in constant motion. Ideally, project managers should not have a great ego-investment in the size or priority level of their project, but in reality, these groups seem to always struggle with this issue. Heroes are those who develop or create something, or who can solve a problem when the group is stuck. Heroes can also be those who graciously relinquish the priority level of their projects in service of other, more promising efforts for the company.

MOTIVE

The resilient Creative Platform company is motivated to invent, develop, discover, or create new products or services and to bring them to market first. They also may offer incremental improvements in existing material. They know that resilience is achieved by staying ahead of the product life cycle. They can sell to other businesses, like the scientific measurement devices of Agilent Technologies, or directly to the public like Sony.

GROWTH METHODS

Growth is tied to new creative developments and these companies have a keen awareness of the product lifecycle as well as the always-present threat of close followers. They have a pipeline of new products, and great anxiety builds when the pipeline becomes too thin. They use alliances to develop new markets. So when the digital-camera-phone market approached 100 million units in 2004, Kodak knew it could create an attractive system of online storage and retrieval for customers. Kodak also knew it would be unable to create cell phones well enough to compete, so it developed an alliance with cell phone providers to integrate its technology. 3

Some Creative Platform Companies have a short list of customers and are highly specialized. This means their growth can be tied to the growth or development of their customers and their customers' markets.

RELATIONSHIP WITH CUSTOMERS

Creative Platform companies develop resilience by being part of their customer's solutions. They develop a close working relationship in which they share tasks, technology, and employees. Here, a creative firm might join in the design phase of a project, then participate in its execution. Cross-functional teams within the customer's departments might involve cross-company teams including the Creative Platform employees as well. Both groups are on the same software and system, and the creative team brings something the customer didn't previously have.

In retail fields, Creative Platform companies know their relationship with their customers is unstable. They expect the customer to move on if their product is surpassed by new technology or ease of use. They are aware that resilience depends on their speed of innovation. Palm had dominance in its PDA niche but was upstaged by Research in Motion's BlackBerry in 1999. In retaliation Palm added features which failed to ignite sales. Just as Wall Street was about to declare it dead in 2006, Palm released the Treo 7000w, the first PDA to offer Microsoft Windows Mobile technology. Sales jumped. Now Palm's sales have plunged because of the stunning pace at which Apple and RIM have produced new generations of improved smart phones. Things move fast in this platform and customers are lost or gained with every new technical development.

RELATIONSHIP WITH SUPPLIERS

Creative Platform companies achieve resilience through a unique relationship with suppliers. Sometimes they tell their suppliers everything and open their processes more than companies built on any other platform. Creative Platform companies are most likely to share their goals, plans and projects with suppliers so everyone can have a clear view of the group's needs. They often build their own intranet which includes all suppliers. This all leads to an effective ability to develop the timely use of software, engineered parts, materials and skills for the new project.

These firms need their suppliers, because no company can have enough expertise to be truly creative and to stand alone. Suppliers are often extremely specialized, and the purpose here is to import knowledge and skills through suppliers, consultants, learning, corporate alliances and partnerships. This allows the Creative Platform company to move about, to approach new projects and topics and to have the flexibility it needs. Enterprises built on other platforms use these alliances, but resilient Creative Platform companies thrive on them.

RELATIONSHIP WITH EMPLOYEES

All companies depend on their employees. All good managers appreciate their employees. However, none of the other platforms even come close to this one in these regards. These employees are special, talented and bright people who need cool projects to work on. They are not satisfied to be simple technicians. They want to use all of their own creative juices, solve puzzles, invent, compete and collaborate.

Just as the employee needs every challenge the employer can provide, so the employer needs every one of these creative people. As a result managers are extremely tolerant of their employees and any quirks, idiosyncrasies, or needs they may have. These employees are given wide leeway to be different. For example, once I conducted a consultation with an IT group and as I was making my presentation, a man near me at the front of the conference table began to turn his nearly empty water glass sideways while keeping the ice in the glass with his fingers. Soon, water was dribbling onto the carpet, and then there was only ice in the glass. To my amazement, the discussion continued while the group pretended not to notice his behavior. Later I asked the vice president about this, whose only reply was, "He's very bright".

These companies offer their employees extensive support, including having both employee relations departments to help them with personal problems, and generous training opportunities. There is truly a care-taking feel to these environments which seems similar to that of the Relationship Platform companies.

Stability is obtained by retaining employees. If one of these bright artists or technologists walks out the door, so does his or her expertise and all of that knowledge about the current projects.

Terminations are rare, but there can be poor job security at times. Engineers can testify to this, since many will work for several employers during a career. Projects end, concepts fail, business units are spun off, and rivals fly by. These things create job turbulence, but some industry insiders seem to adjust well to this rapid change.

TECHNOLOGY

Among Creative Platform firms we find the real joy of technology. A sampling of these clever companies reveals a treasure chest of technological toys guaranteed to enchant any inquisitive mind. They use traditional programs in unintended ways: off-the-shelf software with homemade applications, hand written code, CAD, digital art software like vector graphics and photo manipulation programs, Simply Sim's 3D underwater simulation systems for deep sea robots, Computer Generated Imagery (CGI) to develop special effects for movies, Level D Flight Simulators from companies like Canada's CAE, and more. The imaginative use of technology here is only limited by the number of new questions asked.

Resilient Creative Platform companies are unique, partly because of their unique relationship with creative technology.

MARKETING

Many Creative Platform companies are in cottage industries, and so their marketing efforts are as fragmented as their field. Some small firms attach to a small number of large customers and never seem to conduct a formal sales process. Others are quite promotional. Often it is the founder or partners who seek new contracts. The big creative companies have sales and marketing departments. If anything, the marketing element defines the Creative Platform firm by the fact that it is so uneven, inconsistent and variable across the field.

THE MARKETING PLATFORM

DEFINING CHARACTERISTIC

All firms market, just as all firms try to be efficient, have a relationship with their customers, and are creative when possible. So what makes the resilient Marketing Platform company different from other companies who market? The defining characteristic is the zeal with which they market and how extraordinarily central marketing is to the core of the firm. These groups are all about marketing. The two types of work of resilient Marketing Platform companies are first, their ability to study and then target-sell to groups of customers or potential customers, and second their skill at pairing a mythical secondary image along with the product.

These companies are driven. This is more than advertising. Marketing dominates this entire platform. These Marketing Platform companies think about markets, market segments, and their own competitive position as they go through the entire process of design, production, sales, distribution, and service. Everyone is focused on who the company serves and how to further promote the product. Resilient Marketing Platform companies are unique and have a clear marketing personality. Sometimes theirs is a special product like Starbucks coffee, but most often it is in a field of similar and equally worthy products, like Tide and Clorox, or Pepsi and Coca-Cola. Almost always, Marketing Platform companies are engaged in a crowded and fiercely competitive field.

By segmenting according to traditional demographics as well as "psychographics", marketers attempt to send specific messages to sell products. This is how they perfect the skill of pairing a mythical secondary image with a product. Often it is about which "tribe" a person wishes to belong to. It enables them to establish what is called an "aspirational identity". So, if one wants to have the identity of being a choosey mother, she should buy Jiff peanut butter. Perhaps she should buy Wonder Bread, because it builds strong bodies 12 ways. If a young man wants to appear strong, he should smoke what the Marlboro cowboy smokes. And anyone who wants to be young should drink Pepsi and be part of the Pepsi generation.

RELATIONSHIP WITH MONEY

Just as Creative Platform companies might risk great amounts of capital on an invention, so too Marketing Platform companies take risks by pouring money into the expansion of new markets. This risk is intended to gain access to new groups of people (markets) or subgroups (segments). They might invest in geographic expansion or product extensions, but they persistently risk money to add one layer of buyers on top of another. Relationship and Efficient Platform companies tend not to make these kinds of bets.

If we want to know what a company values or emphasizes, we can simply look at where it puts its money. These firms spend money on differentiated marketing, undifferentiated marketing, concentrated marketing, demographic segmentation, socioeconomic segmentation, psychographic segmentation, buyer testing trials, focus groups, surveys, traditional analysis, nonlinear analysis, and complex research models. They spend money to study groups of customers. They advertise heavily. And they have a well-developed distribution system, either their own like Starbucks coffee shops, or someone else's like L'Oreal's use of retailers.

In its earliest days, McDonald's corporation was so financially strapped that it got free advertizing by news stories. Various articles said that its hamburgers would stack up to the moon, its catsup could fill Lake Michigan, and its buns could fill the Grand Canyon. Then it launched its first Ronald McDonald ad in 1963 and changed its focus to children. One might say it was not a fast food company that marketed; it was a marketing company that sold fast food. It studied its customers, and in time it learned who they were (parents of young children), what their need was (they were busy), and what image these parents wanted (to be seen as good parents who did nice things for their children). Then McDonald's tailored its own behavior to meet these needs. This led to McDonald's birthday parties, Happy Meals, and the always-caring Ronald McDonald House for families of sick children. McDonald's sold an image and it was out to meet an entire cluster of needs. The hamburgers were excellent, the marketing was even better, and McDonald's remains resilient to this day. 4

Money here is a medium of growth and a symbol of the company's power to influence the marketplace. How it is spent depends on whether the product is new and innovative or old and incumbent. New product marketing requires large sums of money to create market share or simply to create a market. These groups tend to be completely sales driven, focused on growth, chanting, "go, go, go!" They trade in brand equity and they gain market share by taking it away from someone else. They know who their competitors are, and they understand the behavior of those competitors.

These firms spend money on market research, far more than firms built on any of the other platforms. Focus groups, telephone and mail surveys, and face-to-face shopper surveys are conducted. In addition, large sums are paid for market analyses, which examine which segments are underserved, growing, or changing their preferences. Groups of consumers are studied.

Money is also paid for large advertising campaigns. Why is it that we all grew up on Tide, Crest, and Charmin? Proctor and Gamble historically has been the world's greatest advertiser. At the time of the publication of this book, its stunning advertising budget is around $6.8 billion per year. Proctor and Gamble started the notion of "soap operas" before television existed. P&G knew which housewives were listening to which radio dramas and it knew what each subgroup needed to buy.

Motive

Resilient Marketing Platform companies are motivated to gain a new market or gain share in an existing market. They use brand image and market-share to create profits.

RELATIONSHIP WITH THE CUSTOMER

Customers are not viewed in ones or as individuals. Resilience is accomplished by examining customers by the thousands, hundred thousands, and millions. Marketing Platform companies relate to large groups and subgroups of potential buyers. They look at their own competitive "positioning", which is how their brand functions in the marketplace in comparison to other brands. Consumers are talked about in populations and examined regarding their purchasing capacity. There is constant concern about how the brand is perceived and the relative strength of the brand. This is why consumer surveys and focus groups are important. Notice how different this is from Relationship Platform companies. Their relationships are with individual consumers, and they make great efforts to communicate that to each customer. Relationship Platform firms are about intimacy. Marketing Platform companies are about mass markets.

When A.G. Lafley began quietly visiting homes of individual customers early in his tenure as CEO of Proctor & Gamble, it appeared he was violating the nature of the Marketing Platform. He showed great interest in the person, where he or she worked, what the family budget might be, and previous buying habits. He carefully interviewed a woman about various products like hair dye, noting that the dye dries hair so she might focus more on conditioner. 5 It may have appeared that the famous and resilient P&G now was interested in establishing relationships with individuals, but this was not so. Mr. Lafley was wise enough to know that each individual buyer is a representative of a large group of similar people. His impressive turnaround of his big company in 2002 and 2003 was the result of his message that P&G needed to get back to basics and this was one of them; clearly understanding the needs of market segments and linking the characteristics of the product with the characteristics of segments of consumers.

RELATIONSHIP WITH SUPPLIERS

These are usually big companies. They buy in big quantities, and they buy the same things repeatedly. They have purchasing departments and budgets. Unlike Efficient Platform companies who always need the lowest price, these groups engage a complex decision-making process when buying. A large supplier who can be more reliable and offer a national scope might be preferred to an upstart. Suppliers can develop a sense of incumbency with Marketing Platform companies.

Relationship with Employees

There is a risk built into Marketing Platform companies. Some tend to strongly favor the marketing and sales functions more heavily than they should. Increased market share is valued, so those who increase it might be viewed with the greatest favor. More value might be placed on outbound or marketing logistic employees and less given to inbound or supply logistic people. Promotions and elevation to the senior levels tend to go to marketing and sales managers. Rank matters, things are done in an orderly manner, and budgets are taken seriously.

Technology

These companies are remarkably high tech. Their analyses of market data are sophisticated. The QuickBase® program by Intuit is a data tracking and analyzing spreadsheet which is shared with all interested parties simultaneously. Pearson Data Management Group's software program is called Consilio®. This is an Online Analytic Processing (OLAP) program which allows multiple users to share a Web portal to build a scorecard for sales leads, actual sales, customer satisfaction, and location. Profix software offers data tracking for budgeting, forecasting, and "what if" analysis. Many large Marketing Platform companies have their own legacy systems for achieving these analyses. These programs identify the key drivers of revenue for understanding overall corporate functioning and the analysis of markets as well as market segments.

We are most likely to find that forecasting technology software is highly valued here. These are interactive programs which use data to predict demand and profits based on multiple variables. They might show, for example, how much market share will be lost with each small increase in price. In addition, since these companies know how much it costs to establish a new customer, it can be determined whether the price increase is worthwhile.

MARKETING

Who could ever forget the Marlboro cowboy, Pepsi Generation, McDonald's Billions and Billions Served, Listerine Kills Germs, Like a Rock, the Aflac Duck, Plop Plop Fizz Fizz, Taste's Great – Less Filling, Wash That Gray Right Outa My Hair, Double Your Pleasure Double Your Fun? And, when you are buying all of this stuff, don't forget your Visa Card, it's everywhere you want to be. These resilient firms are masters at advertising. Occasionally they advertise unique products, but more often they are commodity or near commodity items, so their goal is to sell on a grand scale.

Beyond advertising, these firms are also masters at the four P's of marketing, Product, Place, Promotion, and Price. They are adept at using their product to meet the direct needs of the customers (soap yields a clean face) as well as their secondary image needs (our soap prevents aging and will enhance your social life). These firms are called market-oriented or market-driven.

THE HYBRID PLATFORM

THE PLATFORM

Procter and Gamble sets the standard for Marketing Platform companies. It sells hundreds of different products to millions of people every day. It spends billions on marketing and advertising every year, and most of its products are household names. IBM is historically the most revered high-end computer company, it employs 3,000 scientists and is solidly built on the Creative Platform. Recently, it built the world's fastest silicon transistor using optical networks, which turns on and off 210 billion times per second. And, Hallmark Cards is famous for its proficiency at the Relationship Platform. It has solid and trusting relationships with its Hallmark Gold Crown Store licensees in malls across America as well as its suppliers. It has built an honored and cherished relationship with the consumer.

These are more than perceptions or brand images. Each of these companies has achieved resilience because of its stunning mastery of the skill-sets associated with its own platform. They are well-defined and competent at resilience building by platform building. They are champions at matching platform to frame, culture and strategy. Each was founded by, and managed by, one or more Resilience Builders.

However, there is a second shared quality of these resilient firms. They are Hybrid Platform companies. Science defines a hybrid as that which is made of two distinct breeds, species or genera. It is often seen as being of two incompatible elements. In business the apparent incompatibility seems obvious, at first glance. How can any of the four platforms coexist with another dominant platform in the same company? Isn't this what a physicist would call trying to put two objects in the same place? Wouldn't this lead to a house divided? Won't the entire enterprise become confused, ill-defined, and muddled? The answer is yes, to all of these questions for most enterprises, but, not for all. Most companies never achieve mastery of one platform and it is rare to find companies that master more than one. There are, however, a few remarkable companies skilled enough to develop multiple platforms.

In nature we usually think of a hybrid as consisting of only two elements. In theory a business could build itself on a Hybrid Platform made of more than two. However, I have never worked with a firm that was built on more than two, and I suspect that a three part Hybrid Platform is either impossible to achieve or very rare.

Proctor and Gamble is both a Marketing Platform and a Creative Platform company. We know of the billions it has spent on marketing and advertising. But it also invents products. New and improved Tide really is new and improved. It washes really dirty clothes clean in cold water. It does keep colors from fading. P&G invented Dryel so we can dry-clean our clothes at home. It has 1800 scientists and technicians in its own labs developing, inventing, and creating new things. CEO A. G. Lafley recently started a new program called "connect and develop", rather than "research and develop". It connects P&G with hundreds of small labs and creatives around the world to gain new ideas and products. P&G is a hybrid Marketing Platform and Creative Platform company.

We might think of IBM as king of high end computers, but it is a hybrid of Creative and Relationship Platforms. When the tech bubble burst, the other computer makers wanted to imitate the IBM model. They wanted to merge technology with consulting, as IBM had done for decades. IBM expanded its consulting by purchasing PricewaterhouseCoopers LLP and increasing its global consulting and "E Business Solutions" staff of 150,000 by 30,000 more employees. More importantly, it generated enough work to keep all of these tech-consultants busy, over and over again, achieving what Hewlett-Packard and Dell couldn't. How did IBM achieve this? IBM knows technology and it knows relationships.

Hallmark Cards, the icon of Relationship Platform companies is good to all who encounter it. It carefully studies the content and characteristics of which cards sell well and which don't. It studies its customers. Internally, sometimes work stops to celebrate employees' birthdays and anniversaries. This truly is a Relationship Platform company, but it takes a lot of artists to create all of those greeting cards, gifts and Hallmark Hall of Fame movies. Hallmark is known for employing the second largest group of artists in America, behind only Disney. In the headquarters, artists wearing casual and sometimes creative attire comfortably walk the halls alongside those wearing business suits. This is a Hybrid Platform company, both Relationship Platform and Creative Platform.

A Risky Platform

There is a reason why so few Hybrid Platform companies have achieved resilience. Wal-Mart, McDonald's, Coca-Cola, State Farm Insurance, Visa, all are resilient companies, and none of these are Hybrids. Exxon is resilient, but not a hybrid. Neither is Anheuser-Busch Inbev. In fact, Fortune Magazine's list of the 500 largest US companies is vastly overpopulated by single platform companies. Why?

Building a successful Hybrid Platform is difficult. In the past, most successful companies have been built on one strong platform. Few leaders are clear-minded and skilled enough to lead an entire enterprise down more than one path. There is great risk of internal conflict over which values to emphasize and which strategy to apply. There is risk that the public and consumers will view the enterprise as offering nothing special if it tries to offer too many strengths. And yet, for those companies that can competently develop a strong Hybrid Platform, the contribution to resilience is substantial. 6

The Increasing Requirement to Go Hybrid

As the competitive terrain has become progressively more complex in the twenty first century, more hybrids have begun to achieve resilience.

The field of grocery suppliers has become a Hybrid Platform industry. Until recently we bought our groceries primarily because of the marketing campaigns mounted by suppliers. So, we bought Wonder Bread to make sandwiches, Lean Cuisine to lose weight, and we went to Whole Foods to buy organic foods. All of these firms could charge more for their products, but times are changing. All participants are being required to master the Efficient Platform in addition to their comfortable skills with the Marketing Platform. Now grocer, Kroger, has its own bakeries to bake bread efficiently, put it under its own label, and sell it 20% cheaper. Safeway sells its own Eating Right brands to compete with Lean Cuisine, offering frozen dinners, cereals, and soups. And, Kroger has begun to sell its Private Selection Organic products to steer shoppers away from Whole Foods. Both the Eating Right and the Private Selection Organic lines have attractive and upscale packaging, giving customers the impression that they are buying something special and high end, even though they are produced inexpensively. In order to compete, any grocery supplier must know that this has become a Hybrid Marketing Platform and Efficient Platform industry.

Hybrids are found in some surprising places. Retailer, Target is a hybrid. It is an Efficient Platform retail discounter like Wal-Mart. It is also a Marketing Platform firm, much better skilled at tailoring its stores and product offerings to specific populations, and neighborhoods including upscale shoppers, than Wal-Mart. As we move through the 21st century we will see more whole industries become increasingly complex and then become Hybrid Platform industries.

Is it necessary for a leader in a Hybrid Platform industry to make his or her own firm a hybrid in order to retain resilience? Not necessarily. Resilience can often be retained by overpowering competitors by using only one of the elements of the hybrid. Wal-Mart has done this by remaining the predominant cost cutter. A wise Resilience Builder must know that his or her firm is in a Hybrid Platform industry and have a good rationale for the decision to go hybrid or not.

HYBRID DEVELOPMENT

How is a Hybrid Platform developed? Remember that most Hybrid Platform firms are built on only two platforms. While it is clear that these Hybrid companies have two remarkable strengths, what is perhaps not so obvious is the fact that the two hybrid factors are not equal. While the firm may have two remarkable strengths, and both are superior to its peers and difficult to achieve, one is the more dominant of the Hybrid twins. This is the factor to develop first.

Large and small companies are eager to develop a Hybrid Platform. My advice is that they should first decide whether this is worth the risks and extra efforts involved. If so, they should develop a remarkable strength first, then subsequently begin to add another, and never stop trying to develop both.

These companies should always keep the dominant strength dominant. Procter and Gamble is first a Marketing Platform and then a Creative Platform company, in that order. In 1999, CEO Durk Jager attempted to reverse this by seeking a long list of innovative creations. He sought to invent the next billion dollar product like Tide or Pringles. He poured great resources into new innovations like olestra, a fat substitute, and Fit, a detergent to wash vegetables. When the billion dollar product failed to materialize, he began shopping for other companies to buy. These were big companies, like drug companies Warner-Lambert and American Home Products Corporation. Fortune magazine called the era "rudderless". He tried to make Creative Platform the more dominant of his two platforms by rapidly inventing too many new products. When this failed, he tried to buy creativity. He demoted the importance of his Marketing Platform. He had it backwards. [7]

That's when A. G. Lafley became CEO and returned to basics. Early on, employees found this quiet man sitting on the floor of his office with old advertisements of P&G's big products spread out all around him. He claimed they had ignored Tide, and as Tide goes, so goes P&G. He converted the firm by re-establishing the primacy of the Marketing Platform and making the Creative Platform a close second. By 2003 the company's revival was a well-documented success.

Platform Stability and Platform Shifts

Platform Stability

Platform is the most stable of the four essential elements of resilience. Typically the most likely path to resilience is to choose a platform that creates a good fit between the firm and the nature of the industry in which it resides.

There is a second option. One can violate the industry characteristics in a contrarian way. Based in Rochester NY, Wegman's Grocery Stores has run a contrarian path to the overall grocery industry when it dialed down the Efficient Platform. Its stores are lavish, generous, well stocked with unusual items, and offer fresh baked or prepared gourmet items in beautifully decorated huge stores. These stores charge high prices, pay employees well and they know the wide scope of products causes an extremely high rate of discarded or outdated food. Wegman's is an industry contrarian and it is extremely resilient, but it has taken a chance and succeeded where many others have failed.

So, violate your industry's platform at your own peril. You might succeed if you are very lucky and very skilled. The easier choice is to understand the industry's nature and excel at it.

Platform Shifts

It makes sense to change platforms when there has been a platform shift in the larger industry. The reasons for this will be examined in the Chapter 10 regarding strategy. Consider the hospital industry in America. In 1980 hospitals existed in a complacent, fragmented, cottage industry. Hospital and physician revenues were breathtaking, and doctors were free to practice as they wished. Health plans were heavily influenced by doctors who sat on their boards, and those same health plans unquestioningly paid the doctors' fees for as long as they ordered the patient to remain hospitalized, even for simple procedures. Health plans almost always paid 100% of the hospital bill. The primary complaint among hospital administrators was that they had too few beds and too many patients. It was not unheard of for hospitals to put beds in hallways. Every hospital added facilities, wings, and high tech equipment.

As a result, states established restrictive "certificate of need" procedures to slow the rapid growth and limit duplication of new facilities in the field. In 1982 the federal government implemented Diagnostic Related Groups (DRG's) which was the first program to pay flat fees based on the ailment or procedure. Thus began today's managed care. Hospitals began to lose money and health plans told doctors which patients could and could not have medical procedures. A great restructuring was imposed on this field, with the greatest pain occurring between 1982 and 1997. During those years, more than 27% of all U.S. hospitals closed. This meant that over half of all for profit hospitals closed, while those receiving community or state support were slightly less impacted. About 66,000 hospital beds were lost. This became a distressed industry, and no one was happy. Major news articles reported patient groups suing their health plans, doctors threatening to refuse to provide care, and every politician campaigning for healthcare reform.

By 1998 over 140 million Americans were in some form of managed care. Under this model, both the doctor and hospital must render a discounted fee in order to be on the health plan's provider list. This remains the model of health care delivery today.

What caused all of this? This was a powerful industry-wide platform shift from a loosely organized Relationship Platform to a well-orchestrated Efficient Platform model. The hospital's relationships with the doctor and the patient were supplanted by its need to please the health plan, and the health plan was in control.

Hospitals outsourced non-core internal functions, such as housekeeping and maintenance. Many core tasks which were expensive to keep current were outsourced too, like laboratories. It became a lean industry. Vendors were asked to keep the supply room filled with just 24 hours of most products and bill the hospital only when it used these supplies. Hospital pharmacies began to send unit-dose measures to the floor, so the nurse would get only the prescribed amount of medication for this application, rather than a large bottle from which to draw. Billing the health plans became electronic and paperless, thus shortening the collection cycle from months to days.

Despite all of these changes, many hospitals are in poor financial shape today. After the platform shift, some hospitals became super-efficient while others made only modest improvements in efficiency. Those who achieved resilience had become competent Efficient Platform organizations in order to match their macro-environment. Resilience was achieved by surviving this platform shift.

So who is resilient under this system? Intermountain Healthcare in Salt Lake City is perhaps the most famous firm to embrace and surpass the requirements of this new Efficient Platform. Intermountain is a regional collection of 21 hospitals, 142 doctors offices and clinics, 14 homecare facilities, 4 Life-Flight helicopters, and 3 airplanes. In addition it generously supports 13 low-fee community medical clinics. They do all of this so efficiently that Intermountain data suggests that if this model of healthcare delivery were available nationwide, our collective healthcare bill would be reduced by one third. This organization is lean, productive, and effective. It is also a healthcare facility that is so kindly, its patient satisfaction processes are benchmarked by clinics all over the country.

Intermountain Healthcare is as resilient as any healthcare organization can be. It has embraced every nuance of the platform shift in medicine, and it has done it well. Its use of technology to support quality care and the Efficient Platform is an example. Its "CarePages" program offers personalized websites for hospitalized patients to share their progress, struggles and experiences with far away family and friends. Patients can use the "My Personal Info" program to electronically access their own medical information, including the results of x rays, tests and other data. The "Workstation" program allows the primary physician to share the entire chart with specialists who might be in-house or far away in order to get a real-time consultation. "IDX" provides the patient's physician's office with medical as well as billing information. This also aids the post-hospital continuity of care. There are bedside computers which help reduce the likelihood of adverse drug reactions. And, its robotic pharmacy system "REBOT-Rx" reduces medication errors.

What about the fact that the profits and much of the control of medicine has shifted to the health plans? Well, first, the health plans like all of this efficiency. Second, Intermountain Healthcare has its own health plan, called Select Health. It has 500,000 members and offers three levels of HMO care, large panel, group model, and a special plan for Medicaid patients.

The result is that this firm has contended with the platform shift in its industry arguably better than any other. It is a $4.6 billion organization that annually provides 500,000 inpatient days, 5.8 million outpatient visits, and 38,000 surgeries. It is a good example of developmental adaptation, altering its own platform, and the building of resilience after an industry wide platform shift.

TO BUILD RESILIENCE, BEGIN WITH PLATFORM

The first question the Resilience Builder must ask is, "On what platform or combination of platforms shall I build my enterprise?" There are four platforms from which to choose. Each platform brings with it a unique set of skills the firm must master, defining characteristics, and unique ways of dealing with money, motive, employees, suppliers, growth, technology and marketing. So, mastery of any platform will give the firm a unique personality that will be clear to customers, the public, and employees. The firm will be well defined.

Then the wise Resilience builder sets about the task of creating an organization that is so deeply entrenched in the doctrine of this platform that it reaches passionate religious levels, and everyone begins to share common beliefs.

This book will show how the resilient firm's choice of platform is affected as the company moves through its own stages of development, and how the choice of platform will determine the firm's culture and strategy. The firm's mastery of its competitive platform is the basis of its resilience.

Chapter 5

117 Years of Building Strength at Geiger Ready Mix

Every American city seems to have one or two small businesses that were started by local families and now are over 100 years old. Some are world famous and some are only known locally. These firms are enduring survivors that defy the odds and dig a deeper foothold into their markets year after year. They are respected for their honesty and integrity, and they all give appropriate reverence to those forebears who built the strong foundation on which their enterprises now stand. They are good citizens in the communities that have supported them, and they have a sense of obligation to carry on the core beliefs that have gotten them through hardship many times over.

The business press tends to ignore these companies as it looks to the new and daring, but these enterprises can be a great source of wisdom for us because they are shepherded by one Resilience Builder after another, generation after generation. Some change strategy as time passes. Some change markets as demand shifts over time. But these sturdy old firms don't change their ability to provide prosperity again and again. They are masters of resilience.

This is a story of one such firm, Geiger Ready Mix, Co., Inc. It began as a building materials supplier in Leavenworth, Kansas, 117 years ago and is still there, but today it has grown beyond the small shop that began so long ago. It has 4 large and sophisticated plants in each corner of the Kansas City metropolitan area and one in the center. Every day it sends a battalion of clean red and white trucks onto the roads proudly displaying the name "Geiger". It has grown to as many as 220 employees and it is the largest independent ready mix company in the Kansas City area.

About Geiger Ready Mix

Geiger Ready Mix is a group of courteous, bright and motivated professionals who care about the environment, their customers and each other. Its used tires get recycled into expansion joints in concrete flatwork, it turns used motor oil into heating oil, and it breaks down excess concrete to be recycled and used again. It is a Hybrid Platform company built on Efficient Platform (able to send a full truck to a big job on time every 4 minutes, 24 hours straight) and Relationship Platform (it behaves like a partner to its customers). Its operations are surprisingly high tech, and it has the best trucks on the road.

In contrast to the scandals we read about in the construction industry from time to time, the folks at Geiger Ready Mix are not just honest; they're inflexibly honest. CEO Bill Geiger once said, "This honesty is baked into our genes." If Geiger Ready Mix makes a mistake on a job, it will notify the appropriate people without being asked, have the concrete removed, and replace it correctly, all at its own expense. It doesn't make these mistakes often, but it is prepared to act if ever they do happen.

Monty Newport manages sales for Command Alkon's Western Hemisphere, New Zealand, and Australian markets. He sells sophisticated batching, dispatch, and enterprise management technology to the industry. He said, "Geiger Ready Mix is one of the best run companies I have seen." In fact, he has referred owners of other ready mix companies from all over the United States and a few from outside the U.S. to Kansas City to witness the Geiger magic and perhaps imitate what they can.

Bill Geiger is the modern day Resilience Builder who gets credit for this firm's good reputation, stay-power, and its steady 10% growth rate year after year, but don't expect him to accept this praise. He says, "If you want to know who gets the credit, start with our delivery professionals (drivers), then look at our sales staff, central dispatch and all of our good people who support these operations every day. They deserve the credit."

THIS CHAPTER

This chapter will unveil the history of Geiger Ready Mix, show how the firm first grew, and how it was later nearly crushed by a strike and the destructive impact of union decertification. It will reveal how Bill Geiger revived this firm by conducting a Quad 4 Conversion to establish a clear competitive platform and rebuild his company on strong core values. It will show how he put in place many of the processes normally associated with larger and more advanced corporations. Then it will describe the steps he and everyone in this company took to build resilience after its near-death experience.

If you lead a small or midsized firm, this chapter will encourage you to take similar steps to develop your organization, pursue constant growth, and build resilience.

DEEP ROOTS

To understand this firm it is important to know a few things about the town of Leavenworth, Kansas. Leavenworth is not a small town, but in so many ways it is. It has 38,000 residents, and even though it is only a half hour drive from Kansas City, it seems somehow remote. Leavenworth doesn't have just one or two 100 year old family-started enterprises. It has 12. 1 The families that grow roots in Leavenworth take pride in their community and volunteer their time and efforts to make it a good place to live. This is a town where it seems that everybody knows everybody, and therefore this is a town where a good reputation is always earned and never given.

This is the town that Bill Geiger's ancestors discovered when they arrived from Germany in 1860, just one year before the civil war. They were 30 year old Gottlieb Geiger and his 27 year old wife Elizabeth. Gottlieb was a stone mason who served briefly in the Union Army and then participated in the American dream by becoming a contractor and road builder.

More is known about their son, Adam Martin Geiger, who eventually started A.M. Geiger Cement Company, a building materials store, in Leavenworth in 1892. Today, in the halls of Geiger Ready Mix's Kansas City Kansas plant there are pictures of him and his store, a receipt from the store dated 1898, and there is a detailed biography by a family member written in 1932. This was an outgoing and friendly man who was devoted to family and served on many civic boards in Leavenworth. More than any of this, the one trait that is repeated about him is his integrity. In his business he was known for "honest weights and measurements". This store sold sack cement, coal, lime, pipe and plaster. This cement store eventually became what is now Geiger Ready Mix Co., Inc.

One generation later, Adam's son, E.W. Geiger, Sr. started his own construction company and took over the A.M Geiger Cement Company building materials store. Some wonderful old photos still exist from the 1920's through the 1940's showing crews building roads out of brick and concrete in locations all over the state of Kansas. It is believed that some of these crews were as large as 100 men.

THE BEGINNING OF GEIGER READY MIX

This brings the family history to modern times; almost. 1949 was one of the most important years in the history of this family. In that year, E.W. Sr.'s son, E.W. Geiger Jr. started Geiger Ready Mix Company in Leavenworth with his wife, Lura. E.W. Jr. and Lura also took over the building materials store. E.W. Jr. had hoped his father's road construction company would be his first ready mix customer and provide at least one small stream of income as well as fatherly advice, but that same year 64 year old E.W. Sr. was killed when another car crossed the center line just a few miles from home. The road construction company was sold off quickly, but E.W. Jr. was still determined to make a success of the building materials store and the new ready mix company.

The company is now run by CEO Bill Geiger, son of E.W. Jr. and Lura. Steve McDonald serves as president. 2

In my efforts to reconstruct the history of this company, I spoke with many current and former employees. I was delighted to observe that this firm tends to collect a lot of "long timers". I interviewed drivers, Terry Hiatt with 38 years tenure, Rick Snider with 31 years, Jim Anderson with 25 years, and Bob Phillips with 23 years. All still work for Geiger, all are rightly proud of their service, and almost all of these men can brag that they have never had a traffic violation while on the job. I interviewed 36 year veteran, Carlie DeCarsky. The most dedicated person I interviewed was Nellie Doyle, who started as a part time bookkeeper as a junior in high school in 1954 and stayed for 51 years.

These people described E.W. Jr. as a quiet man who was formal and polite. He was called "enormously honest" and sincere in his efforts to give good customer service. One person said that he wanted things done the right way, but was not the kind of directive leader to get up in front of the group and say, "This is how we are going to do things." If he saw something that wasn't right, he would fix it and then the group would know to do it differently next time. In this way he established the beginnings of the values and norms that are present in this firm today.

In the earliest years of Geiger Ready Mix, Lura Geiger worked side by side with her husband and the other men. Officially she managed the books and accounts, but unofficially she did whatever needed to be done, as is so typical of companies in Quad 1 Growth. One person recalled Lura working on the "ramp", which was a big wooden platform that the ready mix trucks went under to get loaded with rock, cement, sand, and aggregates. These components were stored in bins and she would pull large levers to release the material into the truck. We must keep in mind that this was 60 years ago and the American culture was not ready for a woman to be doing this work, so she would put on a ball cap and tuck her hair under the collar of her coat while working on the ramp.

Lura was much more than just an owner, coworker and teammate. Lura was different. Her family owned American Dairy in Kansas City and she had been raised in wealthy circumstance. She was described as poised, social, and compelling. She was engaging in conversation and she gave deep understanding and empathy to everyone she encountered. She offset E.W. Jr.'s quiet demeanor and shy manner. One person described her as a bright light in that ready mix plant. She had a ferocious appetite for learning, and later in life she got a doctorate in psychology and started her own publishing company.

Among the great gifts Lura gave to the history of Geiger Ready Mix is a collection of charcoal sketches that she made of drivers in the 1950's. These portraits captured the men's weather-worn faces and the good character beneath their skin. In this way, she brought her love into this work environment. Most of those sketches were given to the drivers, but the Geiger family still has a few of these cherished treasures.

When the business was started, the first four drivers E.W. Jr. and Lura hired were African Americans who had worked at the building materials store. E.W. Jr. and Lura lacked many of the prejudices of that era. Simply, they had found these men to be good workers and so they welcomed them as trusted members of their company.

In those early days the building materials store had a steady trade with a collection of small local contractors and merchants. The ready mix side of the enterprise, however, could best be described as "humble". There were two small buildings on the ready mix property, but only one had indoor plumbing. The phone was a Western Union party line, and the phone number was simply 20. A party line meant that if you wanted to use the phone, you would pick up the receiver, hear other people's conversation, wait for them to finish, and then you could make your call. There was a shack near the railroad tracks where raw materials were delivered to the plant, and E.W. Geiger Jr. hired Red Woods, the man who lived there, to help unload the rail cars and to act as night watchman. The irony of this arrangement was that Red Woods always whistled, so as he wandered around at night any crook would know when he was coming. That, however, was OK because no crook ever came anyway.

Geiger Ready Mix still has the first truck the company bought. It was a 3 cubic yard mixer with a 92 horsepower engine that carried almost 12,000 pounds of concrete, which is very small by today's standards. In fact, "Geiger 1" looks like a miniature truck on display surrounded by the current fleet. Today's trucks are massive, have five axels, and carry up to 10 cubic yards, which is about 40,000 pounds of concrete.

The firm was in the right place at the right time in the 1950's. Northeast Kansas was growing, including Ft. Leavenworth, the Leavenworth community, and several bridge and highway projects. By 1953 Geiger Ready Mix had grown to seven trucks.

This is My Son, Bill

In 1968 twenty five year old Bill came to work for his father, E.W. Jr., after completing a tour of duty in the Army. During the first staff meeting Bill attended, his father stood up and announced, "This is my son, Bill. He is the president of this company." Bill was as surprised as everyone else in that room. At the time there were 13 drivers and five support staff in the Leavenworth operation. Bill recalls feeling the weight of this sudden responsibility. From that point on, his father allowed Bill to make his own decisions, and remained his behind-the-scenes advisor.

Bill Geiger had every reason to feel confident about the future. He knew the company and the industry because he had worked in the yard or the plant from time to time since he was 10 years old. He understood the unspoken culture that his ancestors had built at this company. He knew it was his time to lead.

LESSONS LEARNED IN LIBERTY MISSOURI

Like all new leaders, Bill was about to obtain a great deal of wisdom. Unfortunately, he was also about to have some painful experiences in the process of gaining this wisdom.

The first source of this wisdom actually had begun five years earlier when E.W. Jr. had entered into a 50% partnership with Gib Denny to buy a ready mix plant in Liberty, Missouri. Gib had been a salesman of ready mix equipment, knew all of the participants in the Kansas City area, and correctly had guessed that the northeast corner of the metro was about to experience rapid population growth. He wanted to get out of sales and become an owner. E.W. Jr.'s role in the partnership was to provide the financing, and Gib ran the Liberty operations.

When Bill's father appointed him president, Bill believed the company was in what this book calls Quad 2 Steady State. However, the Liberty plant had been closed recently. Gib had lost large amounts of money over the previous years, claimed that his suppliers were unfairly selling ready mix ingredients to his competitors at lower prices and that this prevented him from conducting business. During the same time there was a long and costly strike. He closed the plant and sued the suppliers. Everyone lost their jobs. Gib sold the Liberty plant's equipment and all of the trucks just to pay basic expenses like debts, utilities, and taxes.

In 1969 Bill joined forces with Gib to revive the plant and started by batching concrete for other ready mix companies that had big jobs in the area. So, the Liberty plant at that moment resumed operations as a subcontractor. Having this cash flow, Bill began to seek contracts of his own for the plant. Within one year he had 10 trucks operating there.

During this entire time there was constant struggle between Gib and Bill. Bill was a perfectionist about getting the right mix to the job, making accommodations for each customer, and doing things efficiently. Gib was more focused on just getting the job done. Things came to a real battle when Bill insisted that they put up a portable batch plant at a big job so they could provide the right quality and get fresh concrete to the job quickly. Gib refused and decried the expense. Bill set up the portable plant anyway. Gib parked a pickup truck across the road and forbade the employees from working on that job.

Predictably, it became clear to these men that they could not work together. Lawyers entered the fray, and the result was that Bill Geiger's involvement at the Liberty plant ended in 1976. Bill related this as one of the low points in his career. Later, he said it turned out to be a good lesson that led to some wisdom about what he values and how far he is willing to go to protect those values. However, he had not actually verbalized those values in an organized way yet.

Gib ran the Liberty operation by himself for four years and by 1980 the Liberty operation was once again in a state of financial disarray. It had lost its accounts, and had laid off most of its employees. It was closed. Bill returned and bought out Gib Denny that year.

Today Geiger Ready Mix's Liberty plant is a point of pride for the company, has a positive employee climate, strong customer loyalty, and is one of the most efficient plants in the industry. But in 1980 it was clear there would be more struggles at this plant before it would right itself. Bill's journey of gaining the wisdom of a Resilience Builder was about to give him one more valuable lesson regarding what it takes to develop a resilient organization.

When Bill returned to Liberty he found a workforce that was demoralized, mistrusted management, and leaned heavily on their International Brotherhood of Teamsters representatives to deal with supervisors. Perhaps it was because the plant had been closed twice and so many people had lost their jobs. Perhaps it was simply the way they had been treated on a day to day basis previously. In fact, despite my sincerest efforts to find out why it was this way, I have been unable to discover one overriding reason for the negative emotional climate that existed in the Liberty environment during that time.

Bill put in a plant manager, Carlie DeCarsky, who was a lifetime employee of Geiger Ready Mix. Carlie was good to his employees but he had a strong personality. His philosophy was that if you work for a company, you should do all you can to help that company succeed. The shop steward for the Teamsters was Jay Robinson whose personality and personal philosophies were just as strong as Carlie's, but exactly the opposite. These were two powerful men that one worker described as, "Two bulls in the same pen, and they locked horns."

I interviewed Jay Robinson for this chapter and he described his philosophy as simply "professional". He said that once a company has a labor contract with its employees, that contract must be honored. He said that if the employees and union begin to do favors for the employer by violating the contract, then "contract creep" begins to happen in which the contract erodes over time.

So how did this play out in the day to day operations of the Liberty plant? One long-time employee said that when he was the junior driver at the plant a customer called in for an extra order. The more senior drivers had gone home, so Carlie sent him out on the delivery. In fact, the union contract specified that the runs should be offered to the most senior drivers first, even if this would have made the customer wait for the driver to come in from home. In addition, it would have caused Geiger Ready Mix to pay an extra half day's wages even though it was a run that took only a small amount of time. When it was discovered that Carlie had sent a junior driver on the run, the union filed a grievance and Geiger Ready Mix was ordered to pay the driver they should have called.

There are many stories like this one about the old days at the Liberty plant. One manager described the time as "miserable". He said everything he did was watched by the union and they filed many grievances.

Meanwhile, the Leavenworth plant was also represented by the Teamsters, but it had no such problems. Employees took their concerns directly to their supervisors and everyone conducted business the way E.W. Jr. and Bill had encouraged all along. The culture and climate were positive. Also, during this time Geiger opened a third plant in Kansas City, Kansas.

A Crippling Strike Brings on Quad 3 Degeneration

In April 1989 the Teamsters struck all of the ready mix companies in the Kansas City area after wage negotiations came to an impasse. However, the strikers focused most intensely on Geiger Ready Mix. It was the only company to have pickets in front of its property. In a daring response, Geiger immediately installed replacement drivers and continued its operations.

Bill had believed that most of his drivers would cross the picket line and continue working, but only 10 did. He later described this as great personal disappointment for him. However, none of his management team resigned, and there was no effort by them to discredit or blame him. In fact, the crisis pulled the management team more closely together.

After eight weeks, the Teamsters withdrew their demands and cancelled the strike. Both sides believed they had suffered great losses in this battle.

GOING DOUBLE BREASTED

The response of the entire Geiger leadership team was that they had "had enough", and they were not willing to go through this ever again. Meanwhile, a new trend was emerging in the competitive field: nonunion ready mix companies. In Kansas City there were two of these firms and they were strong and growing. So, Geiger decided to change its union position. It would manage a union and nonunion operation at the same time. It went "double breasted". This eventually led to an all non-union company.

This was not an easy task. Geiger set up each of its plants as separate corporations. Some retained the Geiger Ready Mix name and others were renamed Quality Concrete. All were non-union except the employees of the Kansas City Kansas plant. Setting up these separate corporations was a great administrative task, and Geiger's clear intent was to defend the enterprise against further union conflict and to keep potential problems from spreading from one location to another.

This firm remained double breasted for almost two years. In January 1992 the Kansas City Kansas plant was closed while the nonunion plants continued to operate. This firm had become 100% nonunion.

If Bill had intended to reopen the Kansas City plant he would have been wise to have waited six months or perhaps even one year. He didn't. He reopened the Kansas City plant as a nonunion company only 60 days later. At that point the name Geiger Ready Mix Co., Inc. was reinstated at all locations. The teamsters filed an unfair labor practices law suit and won. The court decided that if Bill was only going to keep the union shop closed for such a short time he should have laid off the employees and rehired them as union employees when he reopened the shop. As a result, Geiger Ready Mix had to pay substantial lost wages and pension obligations after going through a National Labor Relations Board arbitration and a Federal District Court case.

A Dark Chapter

This was a dark chapter at Geiger Ready Mix because the company had to fight for its survival every day. Having undergone a strike in an industry with tight profit margins caused an immediate loss of financial stability. The personal impact to Bill and everyone on his leadership team was profound. All of these people had made an emotional commitment to the company, customers, and employees; even those employees who had walked out. Worse, this began an era in which the company was severely distracted by legal procedures, law suits, and administrative struggles. None of this was productive.

When Geiger made these efforts to end its union certification, all of its customers who were big unionized general contractors dropped the company. Before this time Geiger had been delivering concrete to all of the big office building, municipal, and commercial construction projects. After this time, these contractors simply stopped calling. This was not a surprise to Geiger, but the rapidity and massive impact of this response were startling. The company still had business with small contractors who built foundations, curb and gutter, flatwork and some road work. Some of these small firms were union shops and some weren't. It cut its price per cubic yard by 10% from 1988 to 1992. Also, the drivers who stayed with the nonunion side of the enterprise had a cut in pay. One driver told me his pay went from $18.00 to $12.50 per hour. The pain was felt by everyone.

The total volume of sales dropped from a peak of 340,000 cubic yards in 1987 to a low of 225,000 in 1993. It seemed that Mother Nature was working against this company, too. In 1993 the Midwest had its worst floods in a century. Farm fields, roads, highways and entire towns were flooded. As a result, construction came to a halt. At one point in 1993 a sand shortage occurred as a result of the floods.

The character of Geiger Ready Mix, however, was not lost in this dark chapter. During these floods, the town of Leavenworth sought sand to build levees to hold back the Missouri River. Despite suffering its own shortage and financial strain, Geiger donated many tons of sand to the community to help with this effort.

The two years this company endured its double breasted status were more than difficult. It was a house divided, with both union and nonunion drivers, different processes for each, different quotes for different customers, and internal communications that sometimes got lost. As Geiger attempted to build a new company out of its nonunion shop, it was constrained by its own history and the precedents that had been set during its union days. Bill Geiger was trying to change some of that history.

Says Bill, "Most companies would have been gone. We shouldn't have made it through that. We had five years of steadily declining income." In fact, sales dropped from $18 million in 1987 to $11 million in 1993. He further said that neither he nor anyone on his leadership team thought about allowing the company to fail, "The worst thing that could have happened is that we could have gone out of business. But, 'quit' is not in our vocabulary."

This leadership team believed in its own future so firmly that in the midst of the darkest days of 1993 it did something that would have made no sense to anyone outside the company. It bought a property in the southwest corner of the Kansas City metropolitan area (in Olathe Kansas) and built a new plant. This part of the city was growing at a stunning pace, and Bill believed the company had to establish a presence there, especially since home builders were the largest part of its new customer base. In light of the company's recent financial state, most other leaders would have been afraid to take on new debt that could sink the company.

Like Turning on a Light Switch

This company's Return to Growth happened so quickly in 1994 that Bill described it as, "like turning on a light switch." The management team watched with some delight as new orders increased and customer relations further solidified. Sales jumped from $11 million to $15 million in just one year. Steady growth followed. In 2003 it built its fifth plant, located in the southeast corner of the area, in Lee's Summit, Missouri.

Quad 4: Building an Effective Organization

Geiger Ready Mix had been through what this book calls a Quad 3 Degeneration. In this case, the degeneration happened because of several powerful forces, like a strike that focused on this company, some cruel timing of Mother Nature, and Bill Geiger's desire to grab the wheel of his company - unencumbered by inflexible work-rule contracts. The company entered a state of decline that threatened its existence. What steps did this

Resilience Builder take to restore his company? How did he perform a Quad 4 Conversion, and then a Return to Growth?

Bill never called his recovery plan a "Hope Bearing Plan" like this book would suggest. He didn't give his recovery plan a name. He conducted his Quad 4 Conversion by increasing the Efficient Platform and the Relationship Platform, and by instilling these competitive platforms into every element of this company. He now looks back and says, "We rebuilt our company on some simple but powerful principles." Here is what Geiger's Quad 4 Conversion looked like:

DELIVERY PROFESSIONALS

The first step he took was to change the role of the drivers. They were no longer to be seen as just truck drivers, nor as just "dropping off some mud". Eventually they became called delivery professionals, and they were asked to see themselves as the face of the company to the customer. Geiger hired a consultant who rode with these delivery professionals and analyzed the interactions between them and their customers. He developed the "Thirteen Customer Contact Guidelines". These guidelines instruct the delivery professional about how to greet each customer by name, volunteer to wash off the customer's tools, be positive and friendly, thank the customer, and more.

Geiger also invested in baseball caps for delivery professionals to hand out to customers' crews, especially on hot days. Of course, each hat had the Geiger name and logo on it and they became immensely popular. Most of these hats were not expensive, but at one point they gave out very impressive black baseball caps made with a felt texture and the bright red Geiger name. A few weeks later, one of the Geiger employees stopped at a work site and asked the customer's crew why no one was wearing that hat. The entire crew got quiet and then one fellow said, "That's my Sunday hat."

The delivery professionals also became responsible for the first and last quality checks of the ready mix product. They were expected to check the order on their slip with the order the batch man provided. They measured the "slump" of the concrete, to determine how thick or diluted the mix was. They were responsible to know the customer's desired delivery time and make sure the customer was happy with the order and how it was delivered.

Get to Know the Customer

Everyone who had contact with the customer was expected to get to know everything possible about him, his foremen, and the crews. At one point, Geiger put together a collection of notebooks with information about each customer, like how many trucks he wants at a foundation job at one time, how wet he likes his concrete, and even personal notes like a statement that a foreman likes to yell, but that doesn't mean he is angry.

Today this company has a wealth of information about its customers, gathered in digital files and available to all appropriate people inside the company. This includes the names of the people in the customer's firm, its most frequently ordered mixes, its geographic range, the size of its orders, and how long Geiger trucks wait at an average job. But more than these files, the folks at Geiger know each customer. It is rare that they ever need to refer to the files, because they care about the customer and they remember.

Operationally, Geiger delivery professionals get to know some customers so well that when they arrive at a job they know how to position the truck just where the customer needs it and how to move the truck along in a smooth manner in order to support, rather than disrupt, his efforts. The delivery professionals build partnerships.

Built to Last

In 1994 Bill read the book, *Built to Last*, 3 which described the characteristics of some of the world's best companies. This book said that every great firm had a clear purpose, mission, and core values. Bill was so impressed by this book that he bought copies for each of his managers. In 1996 he hired an outside consultant to conduct a seminar in which the management team was asked the *Built to Last* questions: What is important to this company, how does it compete, and what is its purpose? Bill and his team have met every year to ask the same questions and to ask what the company's goals are for the next year. In 2009, Bill said that this first meeting was the most important meeting ever held at Geiger Ready Mix. Here is the product of that meeting:

Mission Statement

We will become the premier customer satisfaction oriented ready mix company in the greater Kansas City market, while maintaining our high level of quality and remaining price competitive.

The Geiger Way:

Purpose

In every endeavor we will add value to the lives of our customers, employees, and suppliers in a positive and professional manner.

Core Values

1. We will be "On Time and Hustle".
2. Honesty and integrity will guide us in all we do.
3. We will seek continuous improvement.
4. We will compete for the profits that are necessary to reach our goals.
5. We will show respect for our community and environment.

The leaders in the 1996 meeting did not pick any new directions for the company. They did not invent new core values or a new purpose for this company. All of these things had been there since A.M Geiger had started the A.M Geiger Cement Company in 1892. Most of the people in that room knew Bill's father, and they all knew the values that he and Bill had tried to instill in this workplace all along. What was different here was that these men were trying to put these things into words and to create company doctrine. Bill's father was a reserved man and had never dictated to the group that these are the principles they will live by. Bill had tried to instill these values all along but was thwarted by a partner in Liberty who had values of his own, and by a life-threatening strike and long fight for survival. Now it was time to announce a set of core beliefs that would guide the conduct of the firm.

On Time and Hustle

The first core value is more than a simple encouragement to delivery professionals to avoid wasting time. It is the basis of the Efficient Platform that Geiger had already built and would further develop from that point forward. This doctrine requires effective execution by the entire organization. This is important because ready mix deliveries are notoriously late, industry-wide.

Every day each plant expects its first five trucks to be "the first five on time". This means those five orders must be delivered exactly on time and not one minute late. Geiger succeeds at accomplishing this every day. Geiger then measures the remaining orders and expects them to be delivered 97% on time. This goal is almost always met, but in extremely busy times it has dipped down to 94%. In a slow economy or recession the average on-time rating rises to 99%. This is more than just mastery of Efficient Platform. It is also a strong boost to Geiger's Relationship Platform. It allows Geiger to partner with its customers, because if a ready mix truck is several hours late, then the customer's entire crew is standing around for those hours, getting paid, and the job is delayed that much further.

Honesty and Integrity

This core value was the one that drew the most immediate support and the least debate in the 1996 meeting. One participant later talked about how he had caused a big mistake when he was a young new employee. It happened while building a road intersection and he ordered the wrong mix. He was terribly embarrassed to tell this to E.W. Jr., but to his surprise, E.W. Jr. didn't get angry. He thanked him for coming forward, said that this will teach us for next time, and then called the municipality and offered to have the concrete removed and replaced. The municipality took him up on the offer.

Many of the long time employees know that Bill is as inflexible as his father was regarding honesty. Etched into the memory of the corporate culture is the fact that many years ago a senior manager tried to sell excess concrete on the side, "off ticket". This, of course was not a mistake, it was intentional. Terminations are rare at Geiger, but this act brought one on.

Continuous Improvement

As Bill began to rebuild his company after the strike, he poured money and time into new technology. Walk into the batch room at one of Geiger's plants and you will see a row of computer screens monitoring each ingredient of the next batch of concrete. They measure the moisture of the aggregates because wet materials weigh more and moisture probes will adjust for this in order to create an exact mix every time. These batch processes are done by large underground storage bins using digitally triggered switches to load materials onto conveyors. In the winter the water used in the mix is heated to ensure the product absorbs it as expected. And, no one stands on a wooden ramp pulling levers to manually determine how much of each ingredient to drop, like in the old days. Geiger is capable of perfectly producing over 4,000 different kinds of mixes at each of its modern plants.

Everything is automated at Geiger. Geiger's truck radios are state of the art and production activities from every location are automatically sent to accounting by T1 lines. Trucks have GPS and can be monitored at each plant by "yard cam". Payroll is managed digitally. How does Geiger manage all of this hardware and software? It has a well-respected full time technology guru, Everett Watts.

COMPETING TO REACH GOALS

Before the strike, the four plants behaved very independently from each other. One long time employee said that the plants quietly competed with one another. Plant managers had full discretion regarding where to accept jobs and where to assign trucks. Another employee explained how counterproductive this was. He said that one day things were slow at his plant but busy at another plant. His plant manager asked the other plant manager if his guys could do some of the excess jobs. The answer was no, these jobs were all local to the busy plant. However, when he was driving home and was only a few miles from his own slow plant, he drove right past a Geiger truck from that busy plant headed toward a delivery.

Geiger has attacked this problem by installing a powerful central dispatch supported by Command Alkon technology. Now customers call "central" rather than their favorite plant in order to place an order. Central has the authority to shuffle trucks and drivers around to all of the plants. It also routes the trucks to jobs using its own GPS technology. Central knows where every truck is at all times. It also knows where trucks are backlogged on a job, so it can delay the next truck until the clog is fixed. Central has dispatchers as well as customer service representatives to keep things moving flawlessly and to support the customer's needs for efficiency.

This function has done more to reduce competition between plants and to build "One Geiger" than any other.

COMMUNITY AND ENVIRONMENT

Recently the Environmental Protection Agency launched an initiative to visit construction sites. It found many small violations in Kansas City, especially regarding the disposal of waste by contractors. Geiger Ready Mix received no violations, and was openly praised by the EPA auditors. It does not pour excess concrete onto a vacant lot in a new development. Geiger's delivery professionals do not conduct their rinse-down procedure into the curbs in front of a house, because that water will join a stream or river at some point. Geiger is serious about supporting the environment.

BUILDING RELATIONSHIPS

Nellie Doyle told me that in the 1950's E.W. Geiger Jr. was greatly concerned about his relationships with customers and he tried to build trust in every way. So, if trucks were promised at a particular time but they were delayed elsewhere, he would leave his office and drive to the job (or send someone else) simply to let the customer know.

Terry Hiatt started work in 1971 and he delivered materials for the cement and building supply part of the company when he was new. He said that Geiger had such a strong bond of trust with its customers that sometimes a customer would call him at home in the evening with an extra order. He would jot down the order and go in early to get it ready. Often the customer would pick up the order or Terry would deliver it before anyone else at Geiger had come to work. He often filled out the paperwork after the office opened. It all happened as a verbal request up to that point.

Geiger has a long history of trying to accommodate every customer. In the 1950's and 1960's foundation builder Otto Ruebhausen stopped in the Geiger office at 11:00 every day to place his order. E.W. Jr. would fill the order and have a truck ready and on site for him at 1:00. Every day.

The Relationship Platform piece of this company is just as strong today as it was in those old days, and it is still built on getting to know the customer and providing a unique service. In 2008 General Sales Manager

Bill Yunghans started a system in which an employee monitors whether a customer's order gets delayed. If this happens, this employee calls the customer and apologizes and says that if there is ever a tie-up again that could cause someone's job to get pushed back it will not be his.

The customer loyalty built by Geiger's combination of Efficient Platform and Relationship Platform is strong. In researching this chapter, I met with Bill and Cleda White, founders of William White & Sons Construction in Kansas City. They have been 30 year customers of Geiger and described a two-way relationship built on trust. Bill White said he can call Bill Geiger on the phone and set up a $2 million project, get a price and solidify the deal without the complicated contracts that are found so often in construction today. He also said that in the past when the price of materials has gone up as projects have moved along, Geiger has never tried to modify the agreement.

Bill White also commented on Geiger's Efficient Platform. He has had very large jobs that required trucks to arrive every few minutes. He said Geiger's dispatchers knew how much time it would take for a truck to pull up to the pour, empty the load, get reloaded and get back to the job. He said the dispatchers knew how to pace them and how many trucks to "put on that string". It worked flawlessly.

GETTING GEIGERIZED

Before the strike, new driver training consisted of making sure the driver could correctly manage the truck. Sometimes that was the complete extent of it. If the driver had a lot of experience with other large trucks but was new to the ready mix truck, then the training would be a little longer.

Today, new employee orientation is extensive. Safety is drilled into every aspect of the training, including conduct at the plant, courteous driving on the road, and how to avoid accidents at the job site. Delivery professionals are trained to start the day with a walk around the truck, using a checklist. They learn about the start-up, load checking, and evaluating a need for maintenance. Training about how to build relationships with customers includes listening skills and customer service. They are trained on quality and teamwork. Every new employee is trained on Geiger's unique culture, core values, mission, and purpose.

Training does not stop at orientation. Geiger has its own certification program for delivery professionals, called, The Geiger Ready Mix Driver Certification. Obtaining this certification gives the employee a pay raise, and he or she must recertify every two years to keep the raise. Geiger also encourages its employees to complete other certifications like the American Concrete Institute's Field Technician Certification and the American Concrete Institute's Flatwork Certification.

Building a Team

Geiger has made skillful efforts to let everyone know that he or she is part of a team. Every six months the entire company gathers for a town hall-like meeting in which awards are given for safety, productivity, and anniversaries. These awards might be an insulated lunch box to keep food in a car or truck, a leather jacket with the person's name and the Geiger emblem on it, a NASCAR adventure, or even a trip to the national World of Concrete convention. Managers and supervisors call the employee up in front of everyone and tell the group some of the great things the employee has done and why the award is being given.

Geiger's pay scale has moved up since the dark days of 1989, and employees have a full range of benefits including retirement and health plans. As one employee told me, "It's a real job." Employees are given bonuses during prosperous times. Managers are evaluated annually by a 360° Feedback Survey and they take their employees' ratings and comments seriously.

Geiger has a promote-from-within policy, whenever possible. Some jobs are technical and require an outsider, but very few. Steve McDonald explains Geiger's policy to promote from within, "We want to create a company that offers opportunities so all employees can build new skills, take on the challenge of more responsibilities, and be rewarded with promotions. At the same time we are happy to have the person who would like to be a delivery professional his entire career. When we welcome someone into our company we want him or her to find an environment that makes them want to stay for a whole career." Steve should know. He started as a part time yard boy in 1980, has had several jobs inside the company, and is now president.

GEIGER WISDOM

Geiger Ready Mix, Inc. stands as an example of how a new leader believed he understood the nature of his company and the industry in which it resided, but was surprised by the powerful forces that had him in their grips as he went on his journey of building and rebuilding a resilient enterprise. There were several points at which Bill Geiger was forced to choose a direction for his company, and he was not spared the choice. To have done nothing would have been a choice. He was called to act.

This story beautifully displays that a Quad 4 Conversion does not necessarily end with a Return to Growth. Bill continued to relentlessly push his firm's Efficient Platform and Relationship Platform even after the company regenerated prosperity. He continues to push these platforms today as a part of the Geiger culture and a way of life at Geiger Ready Mix.

Bill has said with some humility that he wishes he had the wisdom he has today when he went through his early struggles. We now see that he made many right decisions. Clearly, he was gaining the wisdom of the Resilience Builder.

Look at your own firm and ask whether you have a mission, purpose, and core values that are understood and agreed upon by everyone; as they are at Geiger Ready Mix. Ask whether everyone understands and buys into the competitive platform you have chosen. Look at your location on your developmental frame.

This is a privately held firm, so I will not present current or recent financial figures. However, from all we have seen, this firm is in a state of resilience. Or, one could take a phrase from the book Bill admires so much; Geiger Ready Mix is Built to Last.

CHAPTER 6

RESILIENCE AND THE DEVELOPMENTAL FRAME

Resilience Builders have a unique understanding of their organization's location on a developmental continuum. This is evident in the historical way they tell the stories of their enterprises. Listening to their narratives reveals that they put the organization into what this book calls the developmental frame, or "frame". This is not the frame one might expect and it is not the corporate lifecycle typically found in textbooks. These are the stages of development as we have all read and heard them described by Resilience Builders. Some of these talented leaders have used words similar to the terms proposed here and others have used their own unique language, but Resilience Builders all seem to focus on the same four stages of development. So what are these four stages?

Resilience Builders lump all of the expansion phases into one simple group, which I call Quad 1 Growth. They seek Quad 2 Steady State, but they are aware of its transient nature. They fear the Steady State will be destroyed by either adverse industry changes or the pernicious influence of internal complacency. They are aware that if these external industry changes or internal complacency go unchecked, the organization will enter Quad 3 Degeneration. If they find themselves in Degeneration, they seek Quad 4 Conversion, in which the very platform on which the enterprise was built must be either renewed or replaced. A successful Quad 4 Conversion creates the possibility of a Return to Growth, and then the enterprise will once again be in a state of resilience.

The existing literature includes several models of the developmental stages a firm can experience, but the stages I propose go one step further.

They are subtly specific and their delicate differences are extraordinarily powerful. Therefore, this book calls the developmental frame one of the essential elements of resilience and I hope that as you read about these stages of development you will see where your firm resides.

To be clear, these Quads exist. The concept of the developmental frame is real. The organization's location on the developmental frame has a tremendous impact on everything. Life in a start-up Quad 1 Growth organization is vastly different from life in an incumbent Quad 2 Steady State firm. Life in Quad 3 Degeneration is different from life in a Quad 4 Conversion firm. In fact, the influence of these four Quads is so strong that a person viewing the same enterprise at four different times in four different snapshots of the developmental frame might think it is four different firms. And, as powerful as each Quad is, being between Quads is when the most disruption, struggle, and anxiety occur.

THE DEVELOPMENTAL FRAME

Most theoretical models describe the developmental processes of a firm's lifecycle in biological or human terms. They talk about birth, growth, maturity, decline, and death. Some talk about the expected lifespan of a business, while others use labels like middle aged, or have said maturity will come after a certain number of years. This is a curvilinear view of organizational development, and it is somehow discouraging. It is shown in Figure 1:

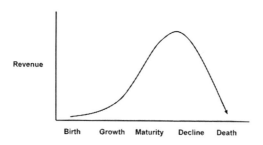

Figure 1: Curvilinear Model

But a business is not biological. Although it is able to learn, grow and adapt, it is not organic. It is not predestined to have only a limited number of years, and Resilience Builders know this. If a business "dies" it is due to a failure to adapt or a drift into complacency and then into Quad 3 Degeneration. Instead of corporate lifespan, I use "developmental frame" as a better term to describe the way Resilience Builders interact with this process. The four Quads are shown in Figure 2:

Quad 1	Growth
Quad 2	Steady State
Quad 3	Degeneration
Quad 4	Conversion

Figure 2: The Four Quads of
The Developmental Frame

Each of these Quads can be viewed as the developmental progression which will occur when an enterprise is able to exist over time. Once a business experiences healthy growth and becomes relatively stable, it can be expected to have at least a brief stay in Quad 2 Steady State. Its time in Steady State will be disrupted by more aggressive growth or by complacency leading to a fall into Quad 3 Degeneration. Once in Quad 3 Degeneration it will either fail or, if it is to establish resilience, it will undergo Quad 4 Conversion, which will bring about a Return to Growth.

The external and internal environments can be theoretically rated from –10 (very negative) to 0 (neutral) to +10 (very positive). If the internal environment is plotted horizontally and the external environment is plotted vertically, and the Quads are in place, Figure 3 results.

Here a positive external environment is due to favorable marketplace conditions, demand, access, ease of supply, availability of loans, and any of the known favorable factors. A positive internal environment is characterized by employees who demonstrate productivity, enthusiasm, a desire to succeed, interdependency, and other positive factors. When placed on the frame, these factors put each firm at only one location.

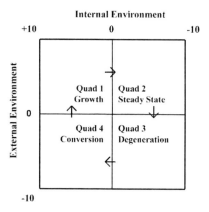

Figure 3: The Developmental Frame

The interplay between the internal and external environments is substantial. If there is a strong internal environment marked by drive and competent productivity along with a positive or receptive external environment, Quad 1 Growth will result. If there is a negative internal environment, lacking drive, but still a positive or receptive external environment, some form of Quad 2 Steady State or complacency will occur. A negative internal environment mixed with a negative external environment results in Quad 3 Degeneration. A positive internal environment marked by redirection and hard work in the presence of a negative external environment yields Quad 4 Conversion. Overall, the combination of internal and external factors can be said to set the stage or create the circumstance for each Quad to exist. Why is this important?

Many business leaders try to make their employees less complacent simply by demanding it. More commonly, boards of directors or other stakeholders blame the CEO for Quad 3 Degeneration without looking at how the market has truly changed. Trying harder to do the same things in a dying market or after a platform shift in the larger industry will not work. Of course Quad 3 Degeneration can be the result of inept leadership, but ignoring the external market is a foolish mistake. The best Resilience Builders have the wisdom to examine all of these factors simultaneously.

EXTREMES ON THE DEVELOPMENTAL FRAME

What happens if one of the Quads spins out of control? What if Growth, Steady State, Degeneration, or Conversion becomes extreme or develops a destructive quality? What if they become too much? Extreme Quad 1 Growth will bring about a company which is scattered and poorly organized, creating Chaos. In Quad 2 Steady State, if the comfort zone begins to devour the organization, unchecked complacency will result in Arrogance. Relentless Quad 3 Degeneration will become self-fueling and produce a state of Mutiny. And, Quad 4 Conversion might take too long before it produces results, thus causing Exhaustion, as shown in Figure 4:

	Stage		Extreme
Quad 1	Growth	→	Chaos
Quad 2	Steady State	→	Arrogance
Quad 3	Degeneration	→	Mutiny
Quad 4	Conversion	→	Exhaustion

Figure 4: Quads and Extremes

During the extremes on the developmental frame leaders tend to allow the competitive platform to drift or to become weak and ill defined. Instead of pouring their energies into building a competent organization, all energy is expended to just make it through another day. At times strategies might be described as desperate and poorly chosen as they reach for any new stream of revenue.

If the extremes are charted to mark the extreme or out of control processes, Figure 5 results:

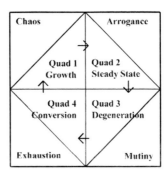

Figure 5: The Developmental Frame
With Extremes

A NATURAL PROGRESSION

Implied in this model is the notion that there is a natural progression here. Any organization in Quad 1 Growth will eventually to move into Quad 2 Steady State. Allowed to remain in Quad 2 Steady State for a prolonged period of time, the firm will move to Quad 3 Degeneration. At that point in its development, the firm will either fail or conduct a Quad 4 Conversion and a Return to Growth.

This grid is not circular. It is not intended to imply perpetual life, nor have we discovered the economic fountain of youth. Rather, the intent here is to describe and categorize the stages of development and the hard work that Resilience Builders do to adapt again and again. This is an active process and requires tremendous effort. Failure to do the needed work in any Quad results in diminished resilience. There is a powerful influence here of Quad 4, Conversion. This factor makes the model renewable rather than circular. This theory does not suggest that the enterprise must go through a prolonged Quad 3 Degeneration before entering Quad 4 Conversion. The best Resilience Builders are able to detect a slight decline or mild degeneration and react strongly to convert back to growth.

FRAME SHIFT

As a leader sees that the firm has changed Quads, an interesting thing happens. He or she personally begins to react to the new stage of development, but at this moment he or she is alone. His or her employees, partners, and senior managers tend to lag behind in the previous Quad. Imagine a leader whose enterprise has moved from Quad 2 Steady State to Quad 3 Degeneration. When the leader eventually discovers this, he or she begins to formulate a plan, then shares his or her thoughts, feelings, and newfound sense of urgency with the senior team. They all nod their heads and agree. Something has to be done. They all are in this together. But the next day one of the VP's uses a sick day to take a car in for repairs and to interview a lawn care service. Meanwhile, a meeting about how to operationalize the new plan gets bumped to next month, and everyone leaves promptly at 5:00, empty-handed. What's the problem? The leader has detected Quad 3 Degeneration and has personally already moved to Quad 4 Conversion, but these team members are still lagging behind in Quad 2, and they are complacent. Leaders need to know that when they attempt to respond to a frame shift, their group will lag behind in the previous Quad. This pattern causes tremendous internal struggle between leaders and their teams, and contributes to the angst felt when the enterprise is between Quads. Resilience Builders are wise enough to see this. Other leaders are not.

The powerful impact of a frame shift on internal dynamics occurs whether or not the team is aware the Quads have changed. So if a founder and his or her start-up group go through a sustained time of impressive but choppy Quad 1 Growth, everyone might seem happy. Perhaps none of these group members has ever severely confronted another and none has argumentatively threatened to leave the group. While there have been ongoing frustrations, they have remained mostly beneath the surface. As more contracts come in the firm grows and more employees are hired, money is plentiful and things really are stable. Departments are formed, regular workdays are the norm, and more decisions are made by fewer people. Look here for the first big blow-up in the founding team. There might be an attempt to renegotiate responsibilities and relationships, and we might see members attack one another about personal things that have always bothered them. Anger might seem to come from nowhere.

This turmoil may be because the Quads have changed from Quad 1 to Quad 2. Or it may be that the group is developmentally between Quads, and this leaves them nervous, not sure how to relate with each other, and afraid they will be injured as they begin to feel insecure about their role in the organization. The effects of this frame shift can be strong enough to disrupt teams. Many battles fought here are proxy battles. A bitter speech about why I must park in the remote lot might really mean, "You have displaced me in the decision-making process and I feel demoted." Yet, no party is aware of these hidden dynamics; it seems like a petty complaint about the parking arrangements.

Resilience Builders are surprisingly able to adapt to frame shifts because they understand that during and after a frame shift everyone feels ill-defined and unsure about how to proceed or succeed. Rather than allow their organizations to indulge in these conflicts, Resilience Builders create new tasks, make new demands, and push the organization forward. They also know that as they try to restore resilience, this is where they will lose friends, coworkers, and partners. Here Resilience Builders should begin to prepare themselves to adapt to their own personal and emotional journey.

Frame and the Predictable Crises of Resilience

Few of the resilience crises that leaders encounter are random or unpredictable. Yet so often, leaders either seem not to expect these crises or they don't know how to respond. Mixed into the remainder of this chapter will be the concept that many of the resilience crises managers face are the result of the Quad in which the organization resides or the organization's movement between Quads, which I call a frame shift. Knowing this, Resilience Builders are well equipped to understand that staff low performance, defections, accusations, or resistance are not personal betrayals, but are the result of the organization's movement from one Quad to another. So the first thing Resilience Builders do in regard to the frame is just to know it. Second, they understand that a frame shift is often caused by changes in the external environment and they prepare to deal with this by altering strategy. Third, they respond to changing internal dynamics by working to retain the desired elements of their culture as the firm moves along the developmental frame.

Here we see the Resilience Builder going on a journey. Each phase of this journey will seem to be permanent, as if the firm could remain in this Quad forever. But as the journey moves along the leader will discover that he or she must make new choices, and will not be allowed to decline from making new decisions. Turning one direction foregoes all that would have occurred if the other direction had been taken, and vice versa. No leader wants to make these decisions, but no leader is spared. All would wish to remain in Quad 1 Growth or perhaps Quad 2 Steady State forever, but this will not be allowed. There is a strong sense of human drama to all of this, because the Resilience Builder cares, and because these decisions matter.

Quad 1 Growth

The world loves a winner. Even more, we love the race that produces a winner. We love the winner's story. In this Quad there is a sense that we are all in the race and we are all going to be winners. Maybe the business is new and small and taking on the incumbents while doing things "our way". Maybe it is established and is buying the competition or the technology. Either way, there is excitement here. There is doubt and there is hope. For a new business, there is doubt about whether the business can attract enough customers and deliver the product or service well enough to become self-sustaining. Can we move past that one product or service? Can we grow beyond that big primary customer? Can we really develop a sustainable competitive advantage? At this point everyone in the organization believes the answer to all of these questions is yes. They believe this because they believe in the founder or the venerated leader.

Place in the Market

Often a new company exists by creating a new market, just as Palm did with hand-held digital devices. This includes the task of educating the public and persuading them that they want something no one has ever heard of. Or, it could be creating a market variation like Starbucks did with coffee. It was no small task to convince the world to forgo the commodity brands and buy coffee at quadruple the price. Either way, here we find new companies attempting to create, fit into, or alter a market. This is at once a formula for excitement as well as failure.

Established companies who attempt to jump-start growth by acquisitions, innovations, international expansion, new distribution channels, or by buying the market are also at high risk. In all of these methods there is a high failure rate, some anxiety, and surprisingly, a lot of enthusiasm.

For new companies as well as established firms growth is exciting. The risk and potential for reward make it so.

ORGANIZATIONAL STRUCTURE

Those large, old, incumbent firms which grow carefully and methodically tend to have well established and deeply ingrained organizational structures and operational procedures.

Start-up firms are quite the opposite. In the beginning these young companies have few rules and there is little structure. Decisions are made without deliberation. Some of these organizations resemble a group of nine year olds playing soccer. Everyone is in on every play and they all run to where the ball is. No one has a role with limits or boundaries. Here, meetings are impromptu, bonuses happen when the founder says so, and much time is spent on deciding what the future nature of the firm will be. At first there may be no meetings, or if there are, the agenda is easily ignored because of some pressing issue. There might be no written policies. Despite this, the organization can build resilience here if it can continue to produce growth.

However, a resilience crisis awaits the start-up leader here. While still in Quad 1 he or she will be challenged to take the next step, which is the development of an internal structure. The tasks of product or service development, finance, production, IT, sales, distribution, and marketing become complex and the founder realizes that he or she cannot do it all singlehandedly. If he or she can do well at creating this internal structure, resilience is enhanced. If he or she shies away from the task, things may remain temporarily more comfortable, but resilience will begin to erode. It is time to build an organizational structure.

Why does it seem so easy to avoid creating this new structure? As a middle layer of managers begins to form, so does the beginning of conflict powerful enough to destroy resilience. Suddenly, these middle managers must jockey for the founder's time and influence. They do not all share the same view or values, their departments have to compete for money, and here we look for conflict to ensue. Some who have been there since the beginning are upstaged and lose influence. Big decisions are made without them. They feel like outsiders. Here are the seeds of the first defections. Some who helped found the organization resign and move on. Others resign, take customers, and compete. Things are no longer as easy or innocent as they once were. But out of this struggle, an organization is formed. This crisis is a test of the leader's ability to build a robust organization. This is a point at which he or she can gain some of the wisdom of a Resilience Builder.

Many founders become bitter at this point, but fostering bitterness is a mistake that will wear down the founder's will as well as the firm's resilience. These changes are the pain of giving birth to the firm. There can be a wonderful outcome. In order to create an organizational structure, there will be defections. This must not be taken personally, although almost always it is.

FINANCE

In the beginning, Resilience Builders must do more than just build an organization that can render a product or service. They must develop finance skills and truly understand what the numbers say about the firm and to investors or lenders. Finance and the valuation of firms is perhaps the most overlooked and misunderstood element of the young developing enterprise. Often the founder only wants to ask simple questions like, "What are our earnings (NI)? And, he or she might try to determine the health or value of the firm based on this measure. Missing from this logic is any awareness of the developmental stage or Quad of the company. Start-up companies often have few or no assets in terms of buildings, equipment, or other capital, yet it has been asked, "What is the return on assets (ROA)?" In order to establish resilience, value must be built, but the Resilience Builder must not be misled into using the wrong metrics.

The value of a company is the product of two concepts, the value of current assets, and the expected value of its future growth opportunities. Each of these factors can be discounted according to its anticipated risk. Hence, a new start-up may have no assets in place and poor cash flow, but still have great value because it has great growth opportunity, as was the case with Google in its early years. Despite the fact that the business community knows this, there is a never-ending discussion criticizing the value of start-up companies because they lack assets and profits. The point is that this should not be expected. The greatest component of their value comes from the value of their expected future growth.

To begin building resilience in this Quad, the leader should look at cash flow and hope to see some gradual improvement over time. In addition, a second measure becomes important in the early stages of growth, cash flow from financing (CFF). That is, how able is the company to attract investors, borrow, or obtain financing? Some substantial part of its cash flow comes from its financing efforts. To the entrepreneur, the right question is, "How can we get our hands on a large amount of cash, burn through it to create healthy growth, and then get some more cash?" This can be an indication of healthy functioning in this early stage, but could be a great danger sign at a later stage.

So, the resilience of firms in Quad 1 Growth depends on a unique set of financial skills, and a unique relationship with cash flow. The Quad 1 Resilience Builder must demonstrate skills here that are not needed in the other Quads and use those skills to fuel continuous growth.

Sustained Quad 1 Growth

More than any other characteristic, Resilience Builders have the ability to create growth again and again. How this occurs is remarkable.

Picture a Resilience Builder and his or her young company standing on level ground. The group has survived the birth of the firm and now is making at least a small profit. Ahead, he or she sees a first level opportunity, but this enterprise does not have the resources to fulfill the opportunity. It lacks the financing, internal expertise, technical skills, and ability to do the new task efficiently and competently. As he or she stands on this level ground, this project seems like a giant step up. It is not clear that the group can do it, and to attempt but fall short might cause the firm to fail. Yet the opportunity makes sense. Imagine also that it fits the firm's platform, culture and strategy, and although he or she might not know it, this is the perfect project for this company in Quad 1 Growth. It is the next right thing to do. Picture also that there are other second and third level opportunities all around but they are so huge that he or she doesn't even consider them. The requirements to support them would be way too great. He or she can't even imagine ever being in that league. The metaphor is like looking up a staircase and each successive step is exponentially larger and larger. 1

The Quad 1 Resilience Builder attempts this first level opportunity by taking a giant step up to the next stair, a lot like like a small child attempting to go up one huge step. It is a hard stretch. The distance between the level ground and this new level represents the resources, expertise, and skills required to succeed. This also causes all of the firm's Quad 1 employees to stretch in order to get there. Long hours, doing two jobs, failing and succeeding at learning new skills, overloaded telecommunications systems, new software which sometimes works and sometimes doesn't, new employees with treasured expertise who see the frantic pace and quit, and once again a shortage of cash all become part of daily life. This is the stretch and a risk to resilience, but once success is achieved a new organization emerges that is more competent and has new resources and new skills.

After a time of stabilizing the group, he or she begins to look around and sees those second level opportunities that once seemed too big. These are much greater than the previous opportunity. The stretch is larger. The new organization with its new strengths is able to take a bigger stretch. So he or she does it again. The organization goes through the same process again, and it gains new capabilities in doing so.

After doing this several times, the Quad 1 Resilience Builder might be surprised to notice that the firm is in the range of opportunities and capabilities that are quite large, and they are the level of opportunities that he or she once saw but avoided long ago. The firm has climbed a staircase. With each stretch the organization has added skills, resources and expertise. Each addition has allowed the next even larger stretch and a firmer grip on resilience in Quad 1 Growth.

A note of caution should be considered here. This process of sustained growth creates its own crises. The demands here are substantial. They tax the company and put it at risk. As one Resilience Builder told me, his first step was a stretch of nearly one million dollars. His second was a five million dollar stretch and his third was a 20 million dollar stretch. He said his first was like a plunge into deep water, and the rest seemed somehow less frightening. Internally this process can exact a dear price on the group. With each stretch, good people are lost. Some will not say why they leave. Others may explain their departure honestly by saying the pace has become too difficult and the demands too high. The company has become a different creature than the one they first joined. What they are really saying is that as this company has stretched and stretched again it has built resilience, but it has become a very different organization. There are many team members who cannot accept these changes and many leaders who have allowed their own fear of this turmoil to erode resilience.

Outlook and Climate

In the beginning, the phrase "unjustifiable optimism" would best describe the outlook maintained by almost everyone in Quad 1. There are many opportunities to pop champagne corks: when the deal is sealed, when the first financing comes in, and when the first customer orders are placed. All are good reasons to celebrate, but beneath this external image, there is an awareness of the risk. We all could be out of jobs. We could go bankrupt, or spend years paying off debt we cannot service. We could be upstaged by the competition. It has happened to others. Here, fear is not a bad thing, it can help to establish a culture of hard work, camaraderie, and mutual dependence.

The Resilience Crisis of Healthy vs. Unhealthy Growth

A central tenant of this book is that to build resilience an enterprise must be established on a competitive platform and this platform must be clearly identified to employees and customers. The platform defines and guides the company. However, many companies become progressively more ill-defined as they move through Quad 1 Growth. This is because they pursue every growth opportunity that comes along including those that do not fit the company's platform. This means, for example, that a Creative Platform firm should not accept a new opportunity that requires it to operate on a severe Efficient Platform, unless the Resilience Builder is intentionally trying to create a Hybrid Platform firm.

Predictable Crises of Resilience in Quad 1 Growth

Each crisis is an opportunity to enhance or erode resilience. The leader's journey has begun and he or she is firmly in the grip of some powerful forces that have already required him or her to make choices. The work here includes selecting a competitive platform and then guiding the enterprise as it responds to the following predictable Quad 1 crises:

1. Find a market and customers. Address this market in a way that allows the firm to be built on a clear competitive platform.

2. Use this platform to give the firm a competitive advantage over competitors.

3. Learn about and secure finance and investors to support growth.

4. In the beginning, create an organization where even specialists are generalists. Everybody does everything. Everyone stays late stuffing envelopes. If the offices flood, everyone grabs a mop. Everyone gets to vote on major decisions.

5. Begin to build a culture. This culture will be heavily influenced by the values of the founder, the competitive platform on which the business is built, and the fact that the company is in Quad 1 Growth.

6. As the firm grows, decide whether new opportunities are healthy growth, and ensure that new product or service offerings support the chosen platform.

7. Begin to ask whether the firm's competitive advantages are sustainable over the long term.

8. As the firm grows, create evolutionary changes in organizational structure. Encourage the development of distinct functions, and specialists who really are specialists. No longer can everybody be expected to do everything.

9. Become structurally more formal as functions develop. Build a middle layer of managers, and allow healthy struggle internally as roles change.

10. Expect to lose people as the firm changes. The Resilience Builder must work to not become emotionally resentful, angry or discouraged.

THE EXTREME STATE OF GROWTH: CHAOS

Growth that is too rapid can destroy resilience. To understand this location on the developmental frame, think of the experience of living in one of America's fastest growing towns or communities. It all seems to be exciting, and one could conclude that he or she is in the right place since everyone else wants to live there, too. There are new houses everywhere and most have upscale cars in the driveways. New businesses have moved in, and expansion is robust. It sounds great, but the downside is significant. There aren't adequate roads so the morning commute is a crawl on a good day. The schools are overwhelmed, and the high school is going to a split session schedule. By Sunday afternoon the produce in the grocery store is picked over. The electricity is shut off regularly because of construction. And, the only hospital in town is full and has no beds for new admissions. Eventually it becomes clear this is not paradise.

There are countless examples of similar things happening in business. While most leaders would be pleased with 10% to 20% growth, imagine what it is like for a firm to grow at 50%, 100%, or 1,000%. The answer is that hypergrowth can become chaos. While there are some firms that have built resilience at these rates, like Microsoft and Dell, most cannot. How extreme can growth become?

Every year BusinessWeek, Fortune, and Inc. magazines render their lists of fastest growing firms in the United Stated. These numbers can be impressive, like Vaalco Energy's revenue growth of 81%, 2 or Heely's growth of 104%. 3 Others are just stunning, like reports of three year revenue growth as high as 19,812% for Northern Capital Insurance. 4 As attractive as these results are, the Resilience Builder must be prepared for a crisis here.

One overriding resilience issue in rapid growth is the nature of the firm's finance, or more specifically, the firm's operating cash cycle. For those who hold substantial capital inventories, or have large pre-sale costs, or who must endure slow collection of accounts resilience tends to erode. An example of this might be a manufacturing firm which must buy materials, pay people and ship the product before being paid. In contrast, those who have minimal presale costs, get paid up-front, or have rapid collection have it easier. An ideal example would be a retailer's gift card "float", in which it gets paid prior to the transaction and keeps the proceeds that are never used or redeemed.

The reason this book calls extreme growth, "Chaos", is because that is how resilience is destroyed at this point in the developmental frame. The sales group pursues a random and scattered pattern of leads and makes promises that fall outside the firm's product or service line. Even within their own scope, they offer delivery deadlines that cannot be met. They might sell to groups that are unable to pay. Production is caught off-guard. Based on a momentary surge in one type of order, production builds a big inventory of items that clogs the warehouse and never sells. Perhaps there is a huge blitz of items that are immediately outdated by new technology or styles. Rapid hiring brings in candidates who are not qualified or are untrainable. Everyone is a novice, making simple mistakes. There is no enterprise resource planning software so each cubicle does things uniquely. Pricing is random and might be offered below the firm's actual costs. Finance is caught up in basic functions and is unable to guide the firm, and no one really knows which products to promote and which to reduce. Collecting money happens in a random and intermittent fashion. The excitement of growth is replaced by a mood of frustration and anger.

The story of Gazoontite.com in California is instructional. It smartly pursued a brick-and-mortar approach along with Internet retailing of anti-allergen products such as bedding, sheets, and stuffed animals. When the initial orders came in extremely rapidly, these entrepreneurs had to borrow a minivan and then clear the shelves of local Sears, Costco, and other stores, losing money but meeting the demand. In the first year, they went from one store, four employees, and 800 feet of storage to four stores, 100 employees, and 8,000 feet of warehouse space. In rapid sequence, founder Soon-Chart Yu bought a $50,000 computer tracking system, discarded it for a $300,000 tracking system, and discarded it for a three million dollar system. Meanwhile, the warehouse decided to reduce inventory of expensive allergen resistant sheets while the firm ran ads on the local radio stations for the same sheets. Overall, Mr. Wu was known as a good manager by the business community, and soon opened 5 stores in the San Francisco and New York markets. But after a short life Gazoontite.com filed for Chapter 11 bankruptcy protection because of its rapid growth and Chaos. 5

QUAD 2 STEADY STATE

Secretly, most managers wish to be in Steady State. This is the relatively stable time when the firm is able to accomplish two seemingly incompatible conditions; first, comfortably meet the needs of employees and stakeholders, and second, sustain healthy growth. This is a state where anxiety is reduced and success is assured. It might seem to be only a hypothetical state, perhaps too good to be true. But it can be true. Look at the tobacco companies after World War II, IBM's multi-decade dominance over corporate computing, or Microsoft's subsequent near-monopoly. Look at the ability to charge high tuitions at elite universities, or the enduring stability of the major oil companies. Quad 2 Steady State can exist, and history contains many examples of companies who have enjoyed a long tenure in Steady State. Unfortunately for most firms, especially small and mid-sized companies, steady state is usually brief, at best, and there are predictable crises of resilience here.

Establishing Equilibrium

All of this relates to the scientific notion of equilibrium. This is the condition in which balance is achieved between the two sides of a chemical equation. In chemistry the Steady State is said to remain in place until somehow disrupted. This concept is known as Le Chatlier's principle. Le Chatlier said that chemicals exist in systems with reagents on one side and chemical products on the other. This system will work to achieve equilibrium, and once achieved, it will try to maintain equilibrium, or balance. The equilibrium can be disrupted by stressing either side of the equation. A stress to one side of the equilibrium will disrupt the balance of the equation and as the system attempts to establish equilibrium, the other side of the equation will react equally. So reactions can travel either forward or backward, depending on which side is first disrupted. In fact, the only way out of the state of equilibrium is to provide some form of stress or disruption.

Here, one can think of a teeter-totter. It can remain level if it is in perfect Steady State. Apply stress to one side and it moves while the other side moves an equal distance. In business, of course, this is only a metaphor, but arguably an accurate one.

Many business leaders seek Quad 2 Steady State, hoping for a chance to experience easy long-term stability. They hope for a good run, acceptable profits, and grateful employees. They hope to impress investors again and again. However, danger lurks behind these wishes. If the chemistry metaphor is extended a little further, we see that Steady State can be maintained permanently by the scientist in a laboratory, because he or she can control every extraneous variable that would disrupt or stress either side of the equation. In the business environment no leader has this power. Although some leaders might relax and enjoy their firm's Steady State, Resilience Builders know that something will soon stress the equilibrium and Steady State will be disrupted. In anticipation of this they begin to plan for the next disruption during the good times.

Even in seemingly calm industries Quad 2 Steady State is quite active. The teeter-totter is always in motion, leaning a little one way, then leaning a little the other. In comfortable organizations these swings might be so small as to be barely noticeable. Some Quad 2 Steady State organizations experience larger swings, and require great work to maintain balance. If the organization leans one direction, it experiences mild decline. The other direction yields some growth. The cycle is growth vs. decline; decline vs. growth.

Many leaders are unaware of the small movements here. Or, if they detect a decline, they offer an excuse. If there is some growth, they take the credit. Rarely do they see that this is a system trying to serve itself. Resilience Builders see it, and they are aware of the factors that can and will disrupt this equilibrium.

DISRUPTING EQUILIBRIUM

Equilibrium can be disrupted by three things: market forces, complacency, or an intentional disruption initiated by the leader.

Market Forces. Market forces can upset this balance in Quad 2 Steady State, and thereby erode resilience any time a competitive field begins to crowd, thus increasing the customer's choice of suppliers and over-extending supply. New competitors can upstage the field with superior products, and customers can increase their ability to negotiate. 6 All of these factors represent external stresses that disrupt the balance of equilibrium that is found in a Quad 2 Steady State enterprise. These disruptions are tangible. They influence the prices a firm can charge, the costs it must pay its suppliers, the amount of investment a company must endure in order to remain in the industry, and the new rules of success as determined by the changing platform. Any of these forces might impact an enterprise. Resilience is lost for those who ignore them, who believe the past methods of success will continue to work, or who refuse to change. Resilience is built by those who recognize these changes and adapt.

Complacency. The second disruptor is complacency. Alfred P. Sloan, the legendary CEO who oversaw the stunning dominance of General Motors from 1937 to 1956 said in his memoirs, "Success, however, may bring self-satisfaction. In that event, the urge for competitive survival, the strongest of all economic incentives, is dulled. The spirit of venture is lost in the inertia of the mind against change. When such influences develop, growth may be arrested or a decline may set in, caused by the failure to recognize advancing technology or altered consumer needs, or perhaps competition that is more virile or aggressive. The perpetuation of an unusual success or maintenance of an unusually high standard of leadership in any industry is sometimes more difficult than the attainment of that success or leadership in the first place." 7

Complacency comes in two forms, employee complacency (all employees including the CEO can become complacent) and strategic complacency. Usually employee complacency and strategic complacency coexist and develop in tandem.

In many ways it makes logical sense that once Steady State is achieved, both the employees and the strategy would become complacent. And, why not? Hasn't this success been hard-earned? Upon entering Quad 2 Steady State there is a feeling that the firm has concluded all of its struggles. There are no more arguments about selecting a competitive platform or choosing a strategy. Those disruptive employees who had become unhappy as the company grew left long ago. The group has survived its climb to success. It has won its struggle to find good suppliers and distribution networks. It seems the element of risk is gone. We won't fail. We are a household name, an icon.

Now everyone can sit back, relax, and enjoy the fruits of prosperity. Of course there will be hard work, but the company has stable customers, a good name, reasonable profits, and financial stability. That's what's great about this Quad. And that is also the problem with this Quad. Every employee including the leader is at risk of succumbing to a complacent approach to the workplace.

Some groups become extreme in employee as well as strategic complacency. Look at the legacy airlines in the United States from the early 1990's until the current day. As the public's lifestyle began to include more travel, planes filled up and the airlines became complacent. We can recall pilots earning more than $200,000 per year and going on strike. Airlines overbooked flights, so customers who had paid for a seat got "bumped". What of the ticket agent who announced that a flight would be delayed for two hours and told the travelers they could leave the area to shop, wander, or go to the bar? Fifteen minutes later she boarded the plane and it departed without them. Major media sources covered stories of rude interchanges between flight attendants and customers. The "me first" airline employee so outraged the public that it led to an airline traveler's bill of rights in the U.S. congress. Of course, this bill was abandoned due to the sad events of September 11, 2001. Amazingly, soon after 9-11 the mechanic's union, the International Brotherhood of Machinists, called for a strike against United Airlines, even though the airline was losing roughly $15 million per day and had cut almost 20% of its employees and flights. The mechanics didn't need to worry. If the airline failed, the government would simply give the airline bailout money or loan guarantees. Anyway this pay raise was owed to them. Self-centered employees? Yes. Self-centered union? Yes. But complacency has a way of working its way into management's ranks, too.

At American Airlines, after painfully receiving $1.8 billion in pay concessions from its employees to help avoid bankruptcy in 2003, it was discovered that AMR (American Airlines' parent company) Chief Executive Donald Carty had arranged a special executive retention plan for AMR's top six executives, equaling twice their pay if they would remain until January 2005. This self-entitled attitude of management caused resentment that lasted so long that in April 2009 the pilot's union rented billboards near the Chicago O'Hare and Dallas Fort Worth airports decrying ongoing executive bonuses. 8

The complacent attitude of entitlement can be present in a flight attendant, a mechanic, a pilot, and even a CEO.

Behind all of this was a strong dose of strategic complacency. Despite watching their peer airlines fall into failure, the legacy airlines persisted with business as usual. They clung to their hub systems, profit-draining first class cabin, and poor service, while ignoring new entrants who crowded the competitive field. They further ignored increased buyer power provided by the Internet. They lobbied to keep foreign airlines out of the U.S. local markets, and campaigned for government bailouts. When it finally occurred to them that the field had undergone a platform shift and all of the winners were operating on an Efficient Platform, their first response was to remove the pillows from the coach cabin. It took 10 years for them to understand the platform shift. In this case, employee complacency marched hand-in-hand with management complacency and strategic complacency.

In contrast, Resilience Builders do not tolerate complacency. Even in the best of times, they relentlessly push the teeter-totter away from the slightest hint of complacency and toward growth.

Intentional Disruption. The third method of disrupting equilibrium is for the leader to intentionally stress the Steady State. This is how Resilience Builders are different from all other leaders. They understand the small variations of the teeter-totter might be mild at this time, but soon they will be large. They understand that mild periods of small decline can become Quad 3 Degeneration. They also know that an organization in Quad 2 Steady State can be pushed directly back into Quad 1 Growth without going through a Quad 3 Conversion. They understand that the only way to disrupt Steady State is to provide a stress, and they would rather that stress come from them than from the malignant power of complacency or the impact of new market forces. So they impact the organization themselves.

Place in the Market

By the time a firm enters Quad 2 Steady State, it has carved out a good place in the market. Customers know the company and there is a solid sense of confidence. However, this "good place" in the market is a bad thing. It begets comfort and complacency. The internal dynamics of the firm can generate two patterns capable of destroying resilience. One involves comfortable employees and the other involves unhappy employees.

First, there are companies that have a solid place in the market and employees that are too comfortable. K-Mart is a good example. It was founded in 1962 and quickly became the dominant discount retailer in the U.S. In the 1970's its phrase "Attention K-Mart shoppers," became part of the American culture, and it enjoyed over a decade of comfortable prosperity. Its employees were happy and management became relaxed. It truly seemed like this could last forever. But by the mid-1980's the stores looked worn out, checkout lines were long, and the discounts were less attractive. K-Mart became the victim of jokes in the media, including a famous slam in the 1988 movie, Rain Man. K-Mart declared bankruptcy in 2002 and still struggles.

The second pattern here would be companies with a well established place in the market and unhappy employees. These employees are so over-confident that they indulge themselves in the luxury of openly complaining about the employer. Meanwhile the comfortable employer's strategy produces little growth. The teeter-totter tips away from growth and towards complacency, despite being unhappy. Campbell Soup Company would be a good example here. It actually invented condensed soup in 1897 when a chemist found a way to separate excess water from the other components. This was the first real convenience food. The Campbell brand became a household name. Then competition emerged, tastes changed, microwaves arrived, and fast food outlets took a toll on these products. Sales of condensed soup peaked around 1970 and then declined for over 30 years. Campbell's leaders did little in response. In the late 1990's they consistently cut operating costs and gradually raised prices. Although this brought some financial relief, it neither increased sales nor added new products. So, how is this a form of unhappy complacency? Employees were unhappy and under-motivated. Sales were weak. Up to this point, management's response was akin to the deer in the headlights, failing to react. This changed in 2001when new CEO Douglas Conant disrupted the company, improved quality, acquired competitors and then expanded aggressively in Europe, Australia, Asia, and Russia. He initiated new marketing campaigns, especially for Campbell's Select soups. The result: In 2005 he announced that Campbell had a more engaged workforce. And from 2001 to 2008 Campbell increased its sales from $5.7 billion to $7.9 billion. Despite being in a good place in the market, complacency was out, growth was in. 9

ORGANIZATIONAL STRUCTURE

Most firms that established departments and functions in Quad 1 now believe this task is done, but it needs to be done again in Quad 2. In addition, now comes a need for professional managers. It is likely that the founder who is credited with creating all of this prosperity is not capable of adequately leading the firm at this point unless he or she develops some new skills or brings in a powerful manager to help. The two tasks of redesigning the organizational structure and deciding who can continue to lead the firm represent the next resilience crisis for the Resilience Builder. This is a choice point and it must be addressed. If the leader chooses to do nothing, this is his or her response.

Entrepreneurs have some unique characteristics which serve them well in the beginning. They are builders, change-seekers, and quick responders who detest bureaucracy, and can act on an impulse. They are individualists who don't tolerate frustration and don't cohabitate long with people they don't like. Their methods of motivation and communication are one and the same, personal. These men and women know each of their key employees and usually view each of them with gratitude for their ability to satisfy the leader's high expectations. They have been through a lot together and their relationships are personal.

These traits have not been weaknesses up to this point in the developmental frame, but they might become so now because the firm needs routines which are stable and uniform. Growth is slower and steadier. The firm offers more standardized products and services. Life is more predictable, and this is good. The firm begins to build much stronger internal functions, like finance, sales, production (or its equivalent), and distribution. These functions need to have enough credibility to be able to disagree with the leader or founder. Employees inside each function should be specialized, but this means they will be unable to do the more general tasks of the organization. This is a time when some employees don't know one another, and even more important, they don't know the founder. Here Resilience Builders learn that they might need to tolerate some people they don't like. Processes become more formal, communication happens in layers, and it becomes difficult to manage this large group.

So to gain or retain resilience, a new kind of personality is needed, a professional manager. He or she is neither an entrepreneur nor a founder. If the founder wishes to stay at the helm, he or she needs to let go of some old traits and become more like a professional manager. Some can do this and some cannot. The organization needs to be guided in an orderly, routine, and methodical manner. Committees replace informal meetings. Reports are valued for the information they give. Regulators are dealt with in a competent manner. Budgets are taken seriously. It is the job of the founder to learn these management skills. This is the leadership crisis that comes in Quad 2 Steady State.

Finance

Resilience Builders know that as the company matures from a start-up to eventually reach a mature stage of stability, the components of company valuation change. In the early days, growth opportunities are the greater part of the firm's value, but in Quad 2 the firm's assets become the more significant factor. While in the early days it was acceptable to go through a lot of cash and profitability was not primary, this all changes in Quad 2. Here factors like earnings per share (EPS), return on equity (ROE), and return on assets (ROA) have meaning and serve as good report cards for the firm. Simply, in this Quad it takes assets to make money. Growth rate is typically now more moderate, and future opportunities might involve unexciting projects like replication or scale.

Nowhere is there a better example of the changing role of finance than Microsoft. When Bill Gates handed over the CEO title to Steve Ballmer, in 2000, Microsoft was a mature Quad 2 Steady State company. One of the first things Ballmer did was to divide Microsoft into seven separate business units, each with its own financial measures, to be tracked as indications of its ongoing progress. Each unit was given its own finance function and the company headquarters was given a larger and more influential finance department. Who did Ballmer imitate? General Electric. This was all new for Microsoft, because previously finance had been viewed as a support function, tagging along behind the company's immense growth and profits. Once growth leveled, the company issued its first dividend, it gathered assets like buildings and patents, and it accrued $50 billion in cash and short-term investments. At that point finance managers gained new importance in this organization.

OUTLOOK AND CLIMATE

For firms that are new to Quad 2, the inner circle of leaders may remain aware of market trends and the overall health of the organization, but even they seem much more secure than they were in Quad 1. Almost always the outlook is said to be good.

As the organization spends time in this Quad there is increased likelihood that a culture of complacence will emerge. Employees begin to ask, "What's in it for me"? No longer is the role of every single person to give a little extra in order to breathe life into the company. Now the expectation shifts to the desire for the company to nurture us.

It is encouraging to note that the Resilience Builder has options here. For example he or she could tie rewards to individual, departmental, or organizational achievements. These could be offered as rewards from their grateful coworkers and company. He or she could increase demands for performance and constantly increase the responsibility placed on people and their departments. He or she could tip the balance back toward growth.

MOVING BACK TO QUAD 1 GROWTH

Resilience Builders are strikingly different from other leaders in their ability to monitor the teeter-totter in Quad 2. They tinker with this equilibrium and steadily push their group toward healthy growth. They create cultures that require constant progress. They alter strategies in response to market forces. They reinforce the basics of their business, and most of all, they are complacency killers. From Quad 2 one can move directly back to Quad 1 Growth, and they are eager to do so by destroying complacency.

Under CEO Jack Welch General Electric became known as "The house that Jack built." That is not really accurate, it is the house that Thomas Edison built, but Mr. Welch was a great Resilience Builder. To discourage complacency, he rated subordinates as A, B, or C players. He required that leaders get the C's to be B's, and the B's to be A's. He instituted practices that measured everything and set standards of improvement. He eliminated GE's culture of complacency and entitlement and replaced it with a culture of growth and performance.

Ray Kroc, the legendary man who built McDonald's was so ardent about his business model that if a complacent franchisee was becoming lax about cleanliness, efficiency, or conformity to McDonald's standards he would personally go and visit the location to gain compliance. He once drove from Chicago to California to do just that.

Sam Walton so aggressively stamped out complacency that his managers were required to attend his famous Saturday morning meetings to answer questions about the smallest detail of what items were and were not selling in a specific location. Sam's own wife criticized the Saturday morning meetings saying these people have families and children's activities. Sam's response was that if the leaders expected their store managers and floor employees to work Saturdays, they could too. This was the world of retail.

PREDICTABLE RESILIENCE CRISES IN QUAD 2 STEADY STATE

The leader must not allow Quad 2 Steady State to lull him or her into a state of comfort. Strengthen the competitive platform internally and externally. Be careful to avoid new opportunities that will cause the enterprise to drift away from the platform. Force the organization to build strong departments and competencies. Kill complacency.

These crises will be addressed by the Resilience Builder in Quad 2:

1. Adjust strategy as you grow and as the competitive field changes. Don't become too comfortable or believe you will succeed because you have succeeded thus far.

2. Some changes in the market will demand your firm offer goods and services that come from a different competitive platform. Most often, remain within your own platform and its skill sets.

3. Shift platforms only for good reason, like after a platform shift in your larger industry.

4. Broaden leadership beyond your own direct influence. Begin to build a corporate structure rather than just being a charismatic entrepreneur.

5. Choose, develop, and indoctrinate leaders who execute your platform and live your culture. Use them to solidify your competitive platform, culture and strategy.

6. Share the wealth but avoid entitlement. Give benefits and rewards that require employee performance. At the same time, show you care.

7. Develop your skills at monitoring the balance of equilibrium in Steady State. Constantly tilt it toward growth even if this requires a leader-generated crisis.

8. Kill complacency.

THE EXTREME STEADY STATE: ARROGANCE

Arrogance occurs when the comfort zone is taken to an extreme. In these environments it is not unusual to hear an employee say that the reason the company exists is to employ, pay, and care for employees. Gone is the focus on the customer or the changing markets that challenge the organization. It is impossible to imagine this state of affairs existing under Jack Welch, Ray Kroc, or Sam Walton.

These arrogant organizations have plenty of rules, and these rules always protect the convenience or wishes of the company or the employees. So, you want your product shipped overnight? They have a rule that shows why they can't do that. Tired of standing in line? They don't care, others will soon replace you. They have voice menus that say to talk to an operator, press zero, but this only brings a dial tone. There is perfect comfort letting the client wait on the phone for a long time. You can't figure out your cell phone bill? They don't care. What time will the furniture be delivered? Sometime between 8:00 am and 3:00 pm. These are the people that answer the phone by asking your ID number without ever saying hello or asking your name. Your health insurance claim was denied? Send it to their appeals committee. Oops, you've already missed the deadline. Of course, it is a deadline they invented themselves. Want to get on an earlier flight? OK, but you will have to pay more and then return to the airport at 10:00 pm to retrieve your luggage, because it would be too much trouble for them to put it on your new flight.

Arrogance is a nosedive into the comfort zone. The core of this state is entitlement. Many of these environments are protected in some way like the laws that prevent foreign airlines from operating from city to city inside the US. In contrast, some firms have the luxury of their arrogance because of a true first mover advantage, like the biggest American car companies from the 1950's to the 1970's. For everyone else, arrogance destroys resilience.

QUAD 3 DEGENERATION

Every business that exists long enough will experience Quad 3 Degeneration eventually. This is the dark chapter. This is the Quad that one Resilience Builder, Lee Iacoca, said if he knew how it would be before he got into it, he would have blown his brains out instead.

There isn't a bright side to this Quad. The bright side comes from moving out of this Quad or making it so brief as to be barely remembered. Unlike the previous Quad, here it is not possible to move backwards. The company cannot move directly back to Quad 2 Steady State, or directly to Quad 1 Growth. The only way to Return to Growth is through Quad 4 Conversion.

Lee Iacoca, however, overstated the case. While some enterprises become mired in Quad 3 Degeneration, others have only a mild brush with it and the Resilience Builder moves quickly and adeptly to convert the organization. Some firms seem to remain in this Quad forever and others don't. Some die here and others establish a new beginning by selecting new products, services, customers, platforms, or business models.

Things change. One cause of this Quad 3 Degeneration is internal. The destructive seeds of complacency begin to bear fruit.

A second cause is external. Market forces change and produce a market shift. This can cause a change of industry platform producing a commoditization of the product, price wars, shifting supplier power, more sophisticated buyers, or the emergence of big players with better resources.

These market factor patterns vary according to platform. Creative firms seem to have the quickest rise to glory, but are quickly surpassed by a progression of more innovative or advanced competitors. One author called this pattern a succession of bottle rockets. 10 Relationship Platform companies find that as they dig deeper into the client relationship, the special qualities of their services become less special. The tasks and skills that only they had offered might be learned by the client. Efficient Platform companies begin to believe cost cutting is the only goal and then operate so cheaply that they fail to support their own internal functions or they fail to spend on the replenishment of systems so competitors become more efficient. Marketing Platform companies find themselves outdone by new firms with fresh campaigns.

As the firm begins to degenerate, some leaders' efforts to intentionally disrupt steady state appear to lack any correlation with the ongoing changing market forces. New organizational charts are drawn, the company is moved to functional management, then that is discarded and it is redesigned as site-based management. Layers of middle managers are added. Then they are removed. Management's own complacency as well as the company's strategic complacency tilt the equilibrium away from growth and survival.

HESITATION

The fact that the company is now in Quad 3 Degeneration is nearly always accompanied by a deep sense of surprise or disbelief even when the warning signs have been present for a long time. Everyone has believed this is the company that does it better, it has been around for so long, it can't be true. But it is true. Even in today's economy where few people expect lifetime employment, still there is a sentiment that this company's decline cannot be real.

Once there is an awakening to the truth of this situation, the first strategic response is to render no response at all. There is a silence; a pause. There is hesitation. It is as if the leaders need time to absorb this reality. This delay is best seen as a time of indecision. Then when the next response comes it almost always is to do the things that got us here, but with the intent of doing them better. We will try harder. But if the firm is truly in

Quad 3 Degeneration none of this works. It consists of doing more of what didn't work in the first place. It is an unrealistic attempt to go backward to Steady State.

Place in the Market

Either the market has had a platform shift or the firm's place in the market has fallen. In Quad 3 numbers can be deceptive. Delta Airlines, United Airlines and American Airlines absorb the greatest market share in their industry. They are big. But in the past decade their fall into Quad 3 Degeneration has been epoch. Size doesn't prevent Quad 3 Degeneration, nor does volume, reputation, or a vast stable of assets. TWA, Pan Am, Eastern Airlines, Northwest Airlines and many others had all of those things and degenerated out of existence. Growth prevents Degeneration, but here caution is advised. Inappropriate mergers and acquisitions create growth, but do not prevent Degeneration. Untested new products, entering inappropriate new segments, or errant diversification all create growth but destroy value. Only a return to healthy growth counteracts Degeneration. And, this healthy growth will require a trip through Quad 4 Conversion.

Organizational Structure

Organization restructuring can be a smart and adaptive thing to do. As the market changes, often the internal structure that supported the organization in the previous Quad is no longer adaptive. Reorganizations make adaptive sense when they match the new industry dynamics, a platform shift, or the structure of the market, especially if they enhance culture or support strategy.

Some groups appropriately jettison excess capacity, half-empty warehouses, and bloated staff ranks in order to match the current market demand. However, other groups plunge deeply into cost containment programs that render no adaptive value. This can be window dressing on a sinking ship. Simply laying off large numbers of employees or closing plants does cut expenses, and the benefits fall directly to the bottom line. This improves earnings per share momentarily, but is of no value if it simply buys time for the firm to continue a failing strategy.

FINANCE

The world's view of the firm changes in each Quad. In Quad 3 Degeneration the basis of determining the value of the firm is still a product of the current assets plus the expected future cash flows generated by these assets. If the firm is in a mature market which has lost most of its profits, and if products or services are viewed as commodities, then growth opportunities will be seen as diminished. So, as the progression into Quad 3 continues, the financial community tends to view the assets in place as the most dominant valuation factor. This is not a good thing, because if some form of growth potential is not developed, the markets begin to ask what the firm would be worth dead.

Unfortunately, the change in how the firm is viewed and valued brings with it an adaptive burden. As the company moves into Quad 3 Degeneration and its profits level off or decline, getting money to rejuvenate the firm becomes more difficult. Investors become hesitant and access to new financing becomes limited or more expensive. It is common to hear managers complain that they could get all the loans they wanted when they didn't need them, but now they simply are not available.

If the company is able to get financing but can't earn the cost of the capital needed to re-establish its growth, then increasing debt only erodes the value of the firm. The requirement is that the company must earn money on the capital it invests if it wants to increase its value. The two great barriers to making this happen are the effects of Quad 2 complacency and the fact that almost always the external competitive field has changed at this point.

OUTLOOK AND CLIMATE

You are in Quad 3 Degeneration. At first you will deny it. Then you will know it. It's easy to deny. The firm has been through many downturns, why should this one be different? Remember, the management group lags behind the leader in a frame shift. So the leader catches on first. The profits are down or gone. Orders have diminished. The marketplace has shifted and the outlook is somber or gloomy. There is little room for hope. In severe cases there are rumors that the company is being closed, sold, or broken up. There are also rumors of layoffs, and that this will be done in a cruel way. The entire organization begins to blame the leader, including his or her most trusted allies.

This is a place where Resilience Builders separate themselves from ordinary leaders. Resilience Builders attempt to avoid revenge or retribution, and do not waste personal energy on hatred or becoming helpless. They remind themselves that the goal now is to create a healthy company and they are not there to win a popularity contest. Resilience Builders begin to formulate a Hope Bearing Plan and consider what type of campaign must be launched to revive the organization. They begin to move onward.

THE SELF-FUELING NATURE OF QUAD 3 DEGENERATION

Unlike any other Quad, Quad 3 Degeneration has a self-fueling character that is remarkably strong. Once a company or industry begins to decline, the degeneration can develop its own downward drive which further fuels the deterioration. The stock market may label the firm a loser and move away quickly. Key staff may begin to defect, resulting in decay of talent and intelligence. Employees who stay feel trapped and helpless. New ideas either drag or are lost. Ultimately each of these negative steps is perceived as further proof that the company is incapable. This perception fuels further decline.

At this point everyone wishes to travel backward in the developmental frame, but it is too late for that. The only way to return to health is through Quad 4 Conversion.

PREDICTABLE RESILIENCE CRISES IN QUAD 3: DEGENERATION

The wisdom of Resilience Builders in Quad 3 requires you to put your own enterprise under the microscope and examine it with cold objectivity. Try to set aside all of your emotional attachment to the firm's old ways and look at them carefully. Be able to truthfully explain what happened to bring about Degeneration. Prepare to act. Here are the predictable Quad 3 crises:

1. Find the firm's location in the developmental frame. This is Degeneration; don't allow denial of this fact to continue.

2. Know, then, that the pathway back to Quad 1 Growth is through Conversion.

3. Learn why the Degeneration occurred. Look for adaptive ways to deal with the field's platform shift or new market dynamics.

4. Examine the firm's failure to adapt. Understand the two frame shifts (moving from Quad 1 into Quad 2, then Quad 2 into Quad 3) that brought the firm to this point.

5. Detect the strategic hesitation; the pause. Get ready to offer a strong response.

6. Avoid trying to go back to the firm's original methods. Make plans to convert the organization's internal culture and external strategy.

7. Begin to develop a credible Hope Bearing Plan, but don't offer it yet. This comes in Quad 4.

8. Begin to prepare a campaign. Know how to apply resources to it. It will be launched in Quad 4.

9. Understand the interpersonal dynamics of Quad 3 Degeneration. Expect some people to resign, be fired, or betray the leader. Work to avoid the deep resentments and anger that can develop here.

THE EXTREME STATE OF DEGENERATION: MUTINY

Imagine a time centuries ago. A sailing ship is lost at sea. The compass is broken, there is no wind and the sky has been overcast for weeks, so there is no way to navigate. The food and drinking water are gone, and fights have erupted among the men. Then the men decide the source of the problem is the captain. The crew kills him and throws his body overboard. There is a momentary sense of justification among them, when suddenly it becomes clear. They are no better off. They still don't know where they are. They still have no food or water. And now they have no captain.

Up to this point in Quad 3 Degeneration there have been two internal dynamics. First, there has been denial. Second, there has been a regressive desire to return to the good old days of complacency in Quad 2. Now these dynamics are replaced by a new one, fear. The discontent of the group so far has been diffuse and unfocussed. Then it begins to focus on the leader. Whereas thus far they have attempted to marginalize the leader, now the ill-defined sense of unease is placed squarely on the leader. No longer are there efforts to deride or marginalize his or her initiatives. At this point the frontal attacks begin. Perhaps someone whom he or she trusted completely offers the leader's weaknesses to the board of directors. Consensus begins to build that the firm would be better off without him or her.

Of course, all of this destroys resilience. The list of formerly great firms that have fallen apart as a result of this type of sabotage is long. Yet, there have been other firms that have been aptly guided through this dark chapter. Resilience Builders know the best course is to prevent things from becoming this bad in the first place. And Resilience Builders also know that if one finds oneself at this point, the only way out is to begin Quad 4 Conversion.

Quad 4 Conversion

Consider what it was like for George Washington in 1777, when his men were stranded and freezing at Valley Forge. The British had taken New York City and Philadelphia and were just waiting to finish him off. Two thousand of his 11,000 men had died and another 2,000 had deserted. Things were bad. Now imagine the joy when, in the end, his rag-tag army won the war. These stories are everywhere. Nelson Mandela forgave all the bitterness of his 27 year imprisonment to become a peacemaker and a great president of South Africa. Lance Armstrong overcame cancer and won the Tour de France 7 times. And who can forget all of the classic movies of love lost and love regained, like when Richard Gere and Julia Roberts had given up on each other in Pretty Woman and said goodbye? Then he rode up to her on his white chariot (well, it was a limousine) and swept her away.

Just as we all love a winner, even more we love a recovery. We love it in sports, politics, business, and human relationships. We love to see the battered underdog rise to victory. In Hollywood they know that every good story needs a dark moment; the time when the hero has tried but failed and failed again. The dark moment is most powerful if the situation seems truly hopeless. Somehow the joy of victory is even richer after a sense of despair.

For all those Resilience Builders who find themselves in this Quad, it becomes a challenge that gives them life. This is the task they have spent a lifetime preparing to meet. They seek the chance to recover, break through the dark moment, and win.

CONVERTING AN ORGANIZATION

Chemists say that a conversion occurs when the nature of the chemical outcome is different from the starting materials. Conversion causes one chemical species to change to another. It is a process. So, if we combine water, sugar, and yeast, we know that at first the substance will be an unattractive poor-tasting liquid. But if we allow the yeast to act upon the sugar in the water, and give it time, it will convert to alcohol. The key here is that alcohol is different in its nature from any of the three original parts.

This book uses the term Quad 4 Conversion because here the character of the organization must change in order for the organization to recover. Most often a Quad 4 Conversion is based on changing the competitive platform of the company. Conversion requires an examination of the firm's place in its industry, as well as its mission, values, culture and strategy. To conduct a Quad 4 Conversion, one or more of these elements will be altered. After the Conversion, employees will think and act differently. Managers will reward different behaviors. It will be a different firm.

Most competent leaders are able to perform a pure turnaround. Resilience Builders are able to do more. They can perform a Quad 4 Conversion. Resilience Builders have the remarkable ability to start with an injured or failing enterprise and act upon it in such a way that the preexisting elements are converted into a new substance. Conversions almost always involve drastically changing the competitive platform, culture, and strategy, and therefore habits and values. So, changing a small ailing Relationship Platform company to a large Efficient Platform company is Quad 4 Conversion. Changing a Creative Platform company to a Marketing Platform company is also the work of Quad 4 Conversion. In these cases the buildings, assets, and many of the people will be the same. The company will be different. Very different.

Once again, I have chosen the chemistry metaphor carefully. The notion of changing the nature of one substance into a different substance is instructive to business leaders, and this is a skill Resilience Builders are uniquely able to perform. However, I have observed that in my consultations to business leaders, they often replace the chemistry metaphor with a religion metaphor. One manager said, "We need to change religions around here, from the efficient religion to the relationship religion." One comment was, "We don't have a religion. We are platform atheists. So, we need to pick a religion and become true believers!"

CONVERSION VS. PURE TURNAROUND

Why does this book not call this a turnaround? "Turnaround" is a commonly used business term that involves restoring the financial health and profitability of a company. Conversion does this as well. But one can conduct some turnarounds simply by getting back to business basics. These turnarounds are done quite mechanically and without changing the platform, strategy, or culture of the organization, like by cutting excess capacity, dropping unprofitable products, altering the supply chain, or improving collection processes. These turnarounds might simply add new product lines or repair dysfunctional distribution systems. None of these things involve changing the nature of the firm, like changing water into alcohol. A Conversion does change the nature of the firm.

Here I use two terms for these two processes; pure turnaround (a turnaround that does not involve Quad 4 Conversion), and Conversion. A pure turnaround is conceptually straightforward, because it is only about tactical and operational improvement. Pure turnarounds usually don't qualify as a Quad 4 Conversion. If simply returning a company to the basics of good business practice resolves the problem, even in difficult cases, no Conversion has occurred.

Carlos Ghosn's famous revival of Nissan Motors from 2000 to 2006 is a good example of a Quad 4 Conversion. Before he announced his Nissan Revival Plan (NRP) in 2001, Nissan was a failed car company, having made money only one year between 1993 and 2001. It had lost market share globally 8 years in a row and in Japan for all of the preceding 26 years. It is now a healthy firm. In the five years from April 1, 2003 to March 31, 2008 Nissan's net sales increased 31.4 %. Operating income is now a healthy 7.3% of net sales. And now Ghosn is eager to upstage his competition by an early worldwide launch of all-electric vehicles. 11

How did Ghosn do it? First, he conducted a pure turnaround that involved returning to business basics. This required Nissan to break the keiretsu business alliances, lay off employees (unheard of in Japan), and break the cozy historic relationships it had with banks. Second, he conducted a Quad 4 Conversion by creating a competitive platform for this company. Nissan had become ill-defined. It was slightly Efficient Platform, slightly Marketing Platform, and slightly Creative Platform. That means it was lost and it really had no platform. Employees and consumers could not define the company and its cars would best have been described as lackluster. So, because the auto industry requires an Efficient Platform, he developed quick, low-cost transactions through the entire supply chain. Also, because auto industry dynamics are as image-based and marketing-based as the fashion industry, Ghosn chose Marketing Platform. He created beautiful and tasteful cars that sold style and enhanced the image of those who would own one. He called them "sexy". This Quad 4 Conversion was all about creating a Hybrid platform. Nissan became both Efficient Platform and Marketing Platform. In the end, every employee knew it, and customers responded to it.

What was the underlying motive of this Resilience Builder? He revealed it quite directly to a meeting of his top 500 executives, which was televised to all employees. "Success breeds complacency and sometimes arrogance." Like all Resilience Builders, Carlos Ghosn abhors the destructive influences of complacency. 12

An example of a Conversion performed by renewing the company's original platform is McDonald's. It recently returned to health after a long slow decline. Its products had become boring and the franchisees' compliance with McDonald's standards was spotty at best. In 2001 and 2002 it had changed its protocol, so each hamburger was made to order and therefore it was supposed to be fresh. In reality, it was just slow. Customers were infuriated that McDonald's had changed its formula for the sauce on the Big Mac. Marketing campaigns were changed often, and easily forgotten. In January 2003 it posted a quarterly loss of $343 million which was the first quarterly loss since McDonald's had gone public in 1965. Shares plunged to their all time low of $12.00. Since same store sales were lagging, McDonald's increased the top line by adding more poorly performing stores, thus further killing profits. The death bells began to ring when fund managers began to buy the stock, betting on its vast real estate holdings, rather than its business value.

CEO Jim Cantalupo enacted a Quad 4 Conversion in 2003 by returning McDonald's to its original hybrid of Efficient Platform and Marketing Platform. He called his revival campaign "Plan to Win". True to the Efficient Platform, he demanded uniformity, made the restaurants cleaner, made the food faster, improved the fries, and restored the Big Mac sauce. He dialed up the Marketing Platform by attending to new segments of adults and health-conscious customers with premium salads and tasty chicken meals. Further, he launched McDonald's biggest marketing campaign ever, "I'm lovin it", featuring Justin Timberlake. This campaign was kicked off in Munich Germany and instantly reached over 100 countries served by McDonald's.

McDonald's was back. It had been born and raised as a hybrid Efficient and Marketing Platform company, and then it had lost its way. Now these platforms were reestablished. This Quad 4 Conversion only took one year to produce results. By the Quarter ending July 2004 profits were up 25% compared to a year earlier and sales were at a 17 year high. Morale was up and the culture had been restored. Since then Mc Donald's has now had 5 years of impressive revenue growth, is gaining its international market share, and in the U.S. is now taking on Starbucks premium coffees. During the 2008 stock market plunge, McDonald's stock actually increased, and hovered around $60. Resilience had been lost but is now regained.

The Hope Bearing Plan (HBP)

In the beginning, life in Quad 4 Conversion is no different than it was in Quad 3. This seems to surprise most leaders. In Quad 4, Resilience Builders are all about recovery, creating Conversion, and conducting a Return to Growth. They want to drive the organization upward and rebuild prosperity. But the entire team has heard all of this before. So have the investors and creditors. How would any of them know this time it is different? The latter part of Quad 3 was miserable; all of the stakeholders blamed the leaders for everything, or came to view the firm as a lost cause. Now in Quad 4, employees recall that during previous downturns predecessors have said other kind and reassuring words. Promises were made, and none of them bore fruit. So why would they have any enthusiasm now?

The driver of Quad 4 Conversion is what this book calls the Hope Bearing Plan (HBP). This plan gives form to the recovery.

By this time, even the most ordinary managers have huddled their teams together to derive a new plan of action. It is based on their view of recent market changes, their changed place in the market, and their view of the future. They have ideas about the ways the company might pursue this plan and the resources needed to achieve all of this. They have a new business plan. Most often they communicate this to creditors, investors, Wall Street, and each other, but they do not communicate it to the employees. Resilience Builders do. Carlos Ghosn's Nissan Revival Plan (NRP) and at McDonald's, Jim Cantalupo's Plan to Win are good examples. They gave their Hope Bearing Plans a name, and they communicated these plans widely inside their firms.

Please note what the HBP is and what it isn't. A successful Hope Bearing Plan identifies the new or revived platform. It is a plan intended to inspire as well as guide. It is appropriate for this stage of the developmental frame. It is a blueprint for Quad 4 Conversion. It is intended to give the organization a sense of confidence.

PLACE IN THE MARKET

By the time a firm is in Quad 4, most markets and investors have given up on the company. So now the Resilience Builder has a great plan about how to revive the enterprise and the market seems to have no response at all. If the firm is in a declining industry, this is even more pronounced.

At this point, most Resilience Builders sense that they are alone. They have surveyed the market terrain and have decided that this company can generate prosperity. They have hope. No one else does. They communicate their hopefulness to everyone, and get nothing in return. The Resilience Builder's motive here is to revive the company by converting it to a new competitive platform.

ORGANIZATIONAL STRUCTURE

One of the greatest challenges in Quad 4 Conversion is to establish an organizational structure that matches the new market and adapts to the platform shift. For example a Relationship Platform which involves either a company sales force or independent sales representatives might be replaced by telecom, Internet, or direct sales methods if the firm is converting to Efficient Platform. Each department or function must be reviewed or modified in order to convert the organization.

FINANCE

There are two factors in play regarding finance during Quad 4 Conversion. First, in a manner remarkably similar to Quad 1, profits should become a much less important measure of success. This is a time when growing the firm is much more important than harvesting money. During Quad 4 the firm is either learning to do its work differently or learning to do different work. In either case, the potential of future profits is more important than current profits. And like Quad 1, Cash Flow from Finance (CFF) should become very important. The question is, can the company acquire funds, use them, and then acquire more in order to execute the Hope Bearing Plan?

The second finance factor in this Quad is something that is almost always thought of as part of the start-up phase of an organization. It is what authors Neil Churchill and John Mullins call SFG, or self-financeable growth rate. This is the rate at which a company's self-generated revenues can sustain expansion. In Quad 4, this requires a delicate touch. Applied too sparsely, the company will not meet its expenses and fail. Applied too generously, the firm will run out of its reserve of money. The SFG is based on three factors. First the company's operating cash cycle. (This is the amount of time revenues are tied up in inventory and other capital before the company actually receives payment.) Second, the amount of money needed to generate each dollar of sales. Third, the amount of cash each dollar of sales generates. Delicately managing SFG in Quad 4 is essential to building resilience. 13

The similarities between the finance issues of Quad 4 and Quad 1 are striking. In both Quads the firm is trying to increase its value based less on current assets and more on the promise of future growth. However, in Quad 1 the financing seems to come easier. In Quad 4, investor confidence in the company is low because of past failures. It seems as if the investment community believes in the linear model of development (inevitable growth, maturity, decline, and death) rather than the adaptive model of the developmental frame proposed by this book. They overlook the fact that Quad 4 is not a fresh start from zero. The firm has assets, resources, talent, and a market, or it wouldn't exist, so one might expect eager investors. Instead, investors and lenders become scarce in this Quad, and securing finance is one of the greatest challenges of the Resilience Builder.

Outlook and Climate

This is the time of recovery, the transformation, and the new beginning. It is based on the Hope Bearing Plan. The entire intent of this Quad is to bring optimism to the enterprise. So imagine the shock and heartbreak of a leader when he or she has lifted his or her saber, yelled "Charge", and realizes that he or she is running uphill alone. Pessimism and sarcasm are in high supply. There is dissent and opposition everywhere including among the top leaders. Worse yet, it seems everyone has a better plan in mind than the Hope Bearing Plan.

The Resilience Builder will observe in this Quad that the group first goes through a phase of Internal Resistance when all employees and managers cling to past power and their own skepticism. Then as the Hope Bearing Plan begins to produce positive results, the group enters the second phase, Internal Recovery.

Overcome Internal Resistance. This is the first of the two internal stages of Quad 4 Conversion. To overcome Internal Resistance, the Resilience Builder has two tasks. First, establish a credible plan on which to base this Quad 4 Conversion. And second, convince every individual, employee, supplier, lender, investor, and potential customer that this plan will work. It is the second task that usually receives inadequate energy in this Quad.

There is much to be done. The Resilience Builder must determine the cause of the decline or crisis; communicate this cause clearly and with resolute honesty to all stakeholders, and establish a plan to address these shortcomings, even if the shortcoming is just that the market has changed. This includes a statement of the resources needed to succeed. He or she must show how the Hope Bearing Plan meets the requirements of the new marketplace. Then the Resilience Builder should state whether the firm needs to change its competitive platform, and why. This frank and honest evaluation will gradually improve employees' trust in management and in the Hope Bearing Plan.

The Hope Bearing Plan must be communicated aggressively and tirelessly to all levels and to every single person involved. Then communicate it again and again, campaign style. Try to persuade disbelievers. Listen well. Look at their reasons for resistance and attempt to persuade. This involves energetic two-way face-to-face communication. In order to win more converts, establish small successes that show the plan has begun to work.

Having won over most of the organization, the Resilience Builder must become more aggressive with remaining resisters. Tell dissenting managers, supervisors, staff, and employees what is demanded from them and how to do it and by when. Wherever this has not worked, begin to reassign, directly manage, or remove pockets of resistance. Say it, sell it, persuade, steer, and then direct the organization.

Promote Internal Recovery. After Internal Resistance comes Internal Recovery. Most often this internal recovery begins after some financial successes occur, even if only in a few compartments of the firm. These small successes are heralded by the Resilience Builder as proof that the HBP, in fact, does bring hope. Then the internal climate improves to reflect this view. This improvement might be only a mild sense of enthusiasm or it could be at the level of a celebration, but once it arrives, it is unmistakable.

Having gone through this, the leader is a changed person. Gone is the naïve character who once innocently thought that all allies would be in this together forever and who believed that good things are guaranteed to those who try hard. Now he or she is a seasoned veteran and a capable, powerful master of the art of leadership. He or she is a Resilience Builder.

Predictable Resilience Crises in Quad 4: Conversion.

The following challenges will be addressed by the Resilience Builder in Quad 4:

1.	Operationalize the internal and external causes of the Quad 3 Degeneration. The real question is, "How did we get here?"
2.	Courageously assess the internal state of the organization including any complacency, fear-based turf battling, and resistance.
3.	Determine how drastic the Quad 4 Conversion needs to be.
4.	As in Quad 3, the Resilience Builder should be aware of his or her own emotional processes and avoid anger and resentment.
5.	Match the Hope Bearing Plan to the platform shift that has happened in the industry, if one has occurred.
6.	Do the pure turnaround steps, like improving processes, collections and distribution, while conducting the HBP.
7.	Empower employees by letting them know what their role is in the HBP.
8.	Relentlessly drive the HBP campaign, eliminate internal resistance, and win support.
9.	Highly publicize the few small early successes and continue the campaign.
10.	Allow a learning curve as the group attempts to execute the Hope Bearing Plan.

THE EXTREME STATE OF CONVERSION: EXHAUSTION

The greatest risk in implementing a competent HBP is that it will take too long to succeed. In mild cases this might be of less importance, but when an organization has been placed deeply in Quad 3 and the climate is uniformly negative, the Resilience Builder is under great pressure to provide evidence that the Hope Bearing Plan does in fact bear hope. This is why it is wise to mount a strong campaign and to publicize even small victories. Business news publications are filled with examples of excellent recovery plans that take too long and then the group loses faith or the board replaces the leader. Sometimes the journey is just too long. This leads to a depletion of emotional resources, a loss of energy, and then a belief that nothing will work.

This is fertile ground for Resilience Builders. They understand that their tasks are strategic, cultural, financial, and tactical. They engage the group, launch the campaign, and they don't take no for an answer.

They understand the power of exhaustion. This was the case with Rich Teerlink at Harley Davidson, Carlos Gutierrez at cereal maker Kellogg Co., and John Lampe at Bridgestone/Firestone. All led embattled or distressed firms. All rebuilt their brands and regained prosperity, and all steered their organizations away from the state of exhaustion.

RETURN TO GROWTH

As the Hope Bearing Plan begins to succeed, as cash flow begins to improve, and as the benefits of prosperity begin to emerge, it becomes clear to all that the work of the Resilience Builder has borne fruit. Gradually a sense of relief moves through the organization and there is some return of comfort. This is more than financial comfort. This is comfort being together, comfort telling a stranger what company we work for, and comfort that we will be OK. The evidence of this newfound health is subtle, like telling employees they no longer need to do two people's jobs, as well as dramatic, like announcing that the new production line is having trouble keeping up with so many new orders. Sales meetings are no longer hostile and even seem to be a little self-congratulatory. Antiquated and unreliable software programs are updated and machines are replaced. The organization feels the benefits of this new nourishment.

Return to Growth happens when the organization makes one more frame shift. This is a shift from Quad 4 Conversion to Quad 1 Growth. And, although there is no Quad in the developmental frame called "Return to Growth", it is the most important transition in the steps toward building resilience. This is the Resilience Builder's most unique skill. Many leaders can start or manage an enterprise. Nearly all leaders can conduct a pure turnaround. But Resilience Builders can convert an organization and then cause it to once again reside securely in Quad 1 Growth. At this point, resilience equals the Return to Growth.

Return to Growth is not a step unto itself. It is the product of all of the steps of building resilience. It is sensitive to the developmental frame because it can be done directly by moving from Quad 2 back to Quad 1, but it cannot be done by moving directly from Quad 3 to Quad 1. Once the firm is in Quad 3 a Quad 4 Conversion is needed in order to Return to Growth. The Resilience Builder selects the right platform and then establishes congruence between the essential elements of resilience; platform, frame, strategy and culture. The value of this congruence is substantial. It represents getting each of the essential elements of resilience to operate in support of the others.

Not all Return to Growth experiences are the same and the difference comes from the level of trauma produced in Quads 3. A Return to Growth following a shallow penetration of Quad 3 Degeneration might seem like normal business adaptation. But a Return to Growth after a deep penetration of Quad 3 will have a traumatic impact. These are two starkly different experiences for the Resilience Builder and for everyone involved.

Life in Quad 1 Growth this time is quite different than it was the first time through. Gone is the naive conviction that we can achieve success simply by intelligence and willpower. Gone is the myth that if we make it past the next great hurdle everything will be easy. And gone is the belief that if we can find the right mix of people, product and position, this will bring us security for the rest of our lives. Now this is a group of seasoned veterans who have tried hard, used all of their willpower, and achieved success simply to fall victim to either powerful internal forces or powerful market forces. This is a group of realists who know the value of the essential elements of resilience.

A VERY PERSONAL JOURNEY

Recall from chapter one that this is a very personal journey for Resilience Builders. Every leader I have known who has developed his or her enterprise to a level of resilience has done so with great effort and a loving hand. This means that he or she has made a huge personal investment in the business and in the people who went along on this journey. Resilience Builders can tell you the names of their teammates 20 or 30 years hence. They can recount with amazing accuracy the details of every resilience crisis they encountered and how they resolved it, for better or worse. They can describe those who rendered both loyalty and betrayal. They remember well the times the market was both kind and unkind to them. They can do all this because they invest themselves. They care.

Most leaders who read this book don't sign up to go all the way around the developmental frame. But watch out, the trip may be coming to you anyway. Some leaders are surprised by the changes that come from powerful internal and external forces. Others are not. Either way, the concept of the developmental frame is optimistic because knowing what to expect in the four Quads can help you adapt. Knowing how to respond in a way that is appropriate to your location on this frame might be just the wisdom you need to be a Resilience Builder.

CHAPTER 7

ALTITUDE INC: PERFECTION IN DESIGN

Isn't it amazing how some products seem to have great design, fit perfectly in your hand, and get complex things done in a simple way? Likewise, isn't it interesting that some products are hard to open, difficult to use, and cause extreme frustration even when you follow the "easy to read" instructions? Welcome to the world of Altitude Inc., one of America's premier design firms. 1

A design firm, or product innovation firm, usually consists of engineers, designers (with various degrees in design), and an assortment of researchers, strategists, and technical experts. Some of these firms even have psychologists and anthropologists in house. All of this is intended to enable them to design everything from a better folding chair to a blood analyzer, to your TV remote control. The people who work at these firms are smart, creative, and practical in a way that is not found in any other environment. They understand form, function, color, social context, and consumer relevancy. They know a lot about ergonomics, material science, mechanics, and manufacturing. The best design firms know a lot about people.

These firms are sought out by companies that invent, manufacture, or sell items to business, medicine, science, or the public. A good product innovation firm has the power to make or break a product, because a great product that is uncomfortable to use is not a great product. But a great product that meets the obvious and subtle needs of the consumer and is easy to use has tremendous stay-power in its marketplace.

Most of these firms are solidly built on the Creative Platform and most have exciting internal environments. All have bright employees. And, all can point to some product they helped to create or improve. But that's where the similarities end. After that, each of these firms has its own strengths, personality, and better or worse combination of the four essential elements of resilience. Each firm has its own atmosphere or "feel".

This is a fragmented field with essentially no entry barriers, so any engineer or designer can start a single-person or small firm and compete with the best in the profession. There are hundreds of these firms in the United States and Europe. It is hard for these firms to stand out or differentiate themselves from the others because they all promise to design the best item, object, feature, or capabilities. The most resilient and successful firms appear to be either small with 20 people or less, or large with 50 people or more. As with all fields that lack entry barriers, new entrants constantly chip away at the profits of incumbents, and failures are common among both new and established firms.

In this field, resilience is challenged by more than new entrants. Firms might fail because they underestimate the time and expense of a big project. They might simply lack enough capital to make it through the slow times between projects. They are enormously affected by the ups and downs of the economy. It is difficult for a design firm to offer its employees a nonstop diet of challenging opportunities and an internal culture that can entice them to stay and build a collective knowledge base. But the single greatest challenge to resilience here is to become that special firm that the customer returns to time after time. Very few design firms have mastered this. Very few have mastered it as well as Altitude, Inc.

ALTITUDE, INC.

Located between Harvard and Tufts University, Altitude has the ability to draw from a rich academic environment, and to offer its employees the benefits of the greater Boston area. This 17 year old firm has 35 employees serving clients worldwide. From the outside, the building looks like an old warehouse, but enter the lobby and you will find yourself in front of a wonderful collection of the most delightful products of Santa's workshop. There is a sophisticated Bose home theater system, a Herman Miller office divider that looks like a sail, a hand-held spectrophotometer that helps hazmat teams identify dangerous materials, a blood gas analyzer for Bayer, a T Wave System for Cambridge Heart, a new Mr. Coffee brewer, and a Margaritaville® Frozen Drink Maker. All were designed by the bright and energetic folks at Altitude. Altitude's designs have won national and international accolades, including the People's Choice Award from The Industrial Designers Society of America (IDSA), many Gold and Silver International Design Excellence Awards sponsored by BusinessWeek, several of Europe's prestigious Red Dot Awards, and lots of awards presented by specific industries like the Product of the Year Award offered by Engineering Plastics Magazine.

These wonderful products and impressive awards are important to Brian Matt, Altitude's founder, but they are only great to the extent that they bring an improvement over whatever existed in the world before, and to the extent that they help a client achieve its goals. Altitude's success rests on the success it brings to its customers.

Altitude was born out of frustration. Prior to Altitude, Brian was a young managing partner for the Boston office of a large design firm (name omitted here) and while he was employed there he had two kinds of frustrations. First, there were the ones he could describe in words. So, he knew he disliked the sense of cranking out a project just for the sake of getting it done. He knew he didn't like the emphasis on how a project was to be a moneymaker for the firm. He abhorred wasteful bureaucracy. And he wanted an environment where everyone's opinion had real value. Those frustrations were the easy ones, because he could identify them. Then there was a second set of frustrations that remained below the surface. He could not label them, nor could he even describe them very well at the time. These frustrations only became clear when he left his employer, established his own firm, and did things his own way. It was in the process of creating his firm that he discovered how those hidden frustrations became strengths. These strengths were the skills and competencies of both the Creative Platform and the Relationship Platform.

Brian's life changed in 1992. His fiancé's father died a few weeks after Brian proposed to her, he bought a new car and a house in the upscale town of Wellesley, MA, and he left his job to form Altitude, Inc. When it was founded, Altitude had no clients of its own. Because of his own personal integrity Brian made no effort to take his "book of clients" with him. However, there was one client, Davol, Inc., that petitioned his former employer to let it work with Altitude when it discovered Brian's new move. We will hear about this client in a moment, but first this young entrepreneur had some lesson to learn about building resilience.

Altitude was formed as a three way partnership with Brian and two other men. All three were intelligent, energetic, and gifted at the craft of design (names of the others are omitted here). Before the launch they spent hours every evening planning Altitude, Inc., and dreaming of how they could do things in positive and meaningful ways. These were good times and the future appeared to have endless promise. All three were filled with naive hope, but that was about to change. About four months after Altitude was officially launched, the second partner resigned for personal and family reasons and abruptly moved to California. This was a blow to Brian who liked the fellow, and has felt his absence ever since.

At first, Brian and the third partner got along well, and seemed to share the same vision of the future. In the earliest days of Quad 1 Growth they both scrambled to get new contracts and serve their clients well. But as time passed it became clear that these were two very different personalities who wanted to lead this small firm in very different ways and did not share the same core values. As Brian strengthened his views that Altitude should be built on both the Creative Platform and the Relationship Platform, the divide between these two men grew wider. As the firm added new employees, the conflict between Brian and the partner began to involve staff members, some of whom threatened to quit if the conflict didn't end.

Imagine Brian's struggle during this time. Altitude was growing and Brian rightly believed he had found a formula to create great success. He had relocated the firm to its large new office space, at considerable expense. He was putting in long hours on the road, growing Altitude, but back at the office the culture was in disarray. In 2000 he offered to buy out the partner, and once again he believed he could see a bright and promising future for Altitude. Just then the tech bubble burst, the economy tanked, and revenues declined. At the same time, he underwent a personal tragedy when his mother succumbed to a 10 year battle with cancer. Despite these things, and because of Brian's relentless optimism, he believed he should still go forward with taking on a lot of debt to buy out his partner. After some difficult negotiations, a price was determined and the partnership was ended. But, there was more bad news on the way. The economic downturn caused two of Altitudes biggest clients into bankruptcy, making hundreds of thousands of dollars in overdue invoices uncollectable.

Brian now looks back at this time as evidence of how naive and innocent he was. He was taken by surprise that a recession could injure his enterprise so deeply. He was shocked to discover that professional tragedies always seem to arrive at the same time as personal ones. He was astonished that his partner couldn't understand or embrace his formula for success. Today Brian is ready for anything and surprised by little. Altitude has a diverse portfolio of clients and it nicely survived the 2008 global recession.

To avoid repeating history by bringing in people who are incompatible with the Altitude culture, Altitude has an extensive screening process for new applicants. It evaluates whether the applicant is a good fit for Altitude's basic values and creative processes. In the beginning Brian was like many new entrepreneurs, because he had a belief that if he tired hard enough he could do anything and work with anybody. Now, like most experienced veterans, he is so much wiser and better prepared. He is a Resilience Builder.

THE ESSENTIAL ELEMENTS OF RESILIENCE

As this chapter tells the story of Altitude, Inc., it will become clear that this firm has been crafted by a Resilience Builder and that all four of the essential elements of resilience (competitive platform, developmental frame, culture, and strategy) are congruent with each other. To do this, Brian Matt has found and encouraged some of the brightest and most creative people in his industry.

When I first encountered Altitude I attempted to ask its staff and employees about the two parts that make up its Hybrid Relationship and Creative Platform. I asked about them as independent subjects. This method of interviewing has worked for me in the past, and I fully expected it to do so here, but I was mistaken. No one could separate the parts of the Relationship Platform from the Creative Platform in any way. They viewed these two collections of competencies as completely intertwined, inseparable, and enormously important. In fact, I do not recall any firm that had a more perfect hybrid of two platforms than Altitude. The discussion that follows will attempt to dissect these two platforms in order to allow us to understand how this firm has built resilience. Please keep in mind that the gifted people at Altitude would view this as an artificial dissection.

Altitude is now nicely placed on Quad 2 Steady State on the developmental frame. It had rocky start, then a rapid rise through Quad 1 Growth. Like most firms that create or invent things, the early days were feast and famine, a rush to deadlines, and great efforts to find resources and vendors that could help. Now, even in the wake of a global recession, Altitude continues to work, remains in Steady State, and remains stable as a firm.

Altitude's culture nicely reflects the values of its founder, and it matches the Hybrid Relationship and Creative Platform. It is also the product of Altitude's place on the developmental frame. This chapter will take a look inside the halls of Altitude and show how congruence is established by the Constitutional Component, Value Component, and Interpersonal Component of its culture.

Finally, Altitude's resilience is strengthened by the nice match between its strategy and its Hybrid Platform.

Building Altitude's Relationship Platform

The firm that became Altitude's first customer not only paid some bills; it also helped Brian identify one of those frustrations he had been experiencing at his former employer. Further, it helped him develop Altitude's proficiency at the Relationship Platform.

The client company was Davol, Inc., a medical devices division of C. R. Bard Inc, then headquartered in Rhode Island. Davol was best known for its orthopedic surgical devices. Because orthopedic surgery is aggressive and often leaves small bone fragments and other debris in the blood, its scientists were attempting to develop a blood scrubbing device. Its purpose would be to recycle the patient's own blood by cleaning out bone particles, crushed platelets, and other substances in order to allow the patient to re-use his or her own blood. This was in the very early days, so at the time Altitude consisted of Brian Matt, his partner, and one designer.

Early Exposure to the Relationship Platform

Brian went to Davol's offices and found that as he asked a lot of questions about Davol, its previous work, blood scrubbing, and orthopedic surgeons, he was quickly included as part of the Davol work family. Brian has a natural curiosity and the more he learned about Davol, the more the Davol staff wanted to tell him. He became ever-present with Davol scientists, listened to sales staff, and wanted to know about production possibilities. He was interested in the potential market size of this product and how

Davol had marketed other orthopedic devices. As the project progressed, Brian sensed that he had moved from vendor to partner, just by taking the time to listen and learn about Davol. This was a turning point in Brian's professional development. He had discovered how gaining a lot of knowledge about a customer could pay off for him. He began to guide his newborn firm in the ways of the Relationship Platform. (Of course, Brian didn't call this the "Relationship Platform", that's my term.)

His Relationship Platform skills increased significantly when he worked for his second client, Symbol Technology, now a division of Motorola Corporation. It was making laser bar code scanners which we now know are used to check out shoppers in retail stores, manage warehouse inventory, and even connect the right medications with patients in hospitals. This was an international firm and a big project for Altitude. So, Brian began steadily adding new staff positions, and these Symbol Technology scientists took Brian and some staff members with them to interview customers all over the world. Altitude learned a lot about Symbol Technologies, its image in the marketplace, the science involved, and what Symbol Technology's customers wanted. And once again Altitude learned that all of this knowledge was the glue that bound this small firm to its client.

Around the same time Brian met Black & Decker Housewares Design Director, Mike Laude at an industrial design conference. These two men hit it off and Mike gave Altitude its first Black & Decker project, a second generation of snake lights. Brian immediately engaged his new Relationship Platform skills with the enthusiasm of a zealot. He learned everything about Black & Decker, how its various products were doing in the marketplace and why some were strong while others were weak. He learned about Black &Decker's competition, and what each one actually did to compete. And, he learned what Black & Decker was hoping to accomplish with these new snake lights. The result was simple and powerful. Each piece of information Black & Decker gave to Brian further strengthened the relationship between these two firms and gave Brian the ability to create something special for Black & Decker. And, like the Davol project, Brian sensed that Altitude had become less a vendor and more a partner.

The snake light project was a success, and the way it fit nicely with the rest of Black & Decker's products delighted this customer. That was good news for Altitude. It was especially good news because the Black & Decker Corporation, headquartered in Towson, MD, is actually a conglomerate. It owns Porter-Cable, Kwikset, K2 Commercial Hardware, and Price Pfister, among others. Where Altitude Inc. leapt forward was with Black

& Decker's DeWalt line of high performance professional power tools. This is also where Brian Matt crystallized the collection of skills that formed Altitude's Relationship Platform.

Three Sources of Knowledge

Brian entered DeWalt with the theory that if Altitude was to design the right product for this customer, the design must be based on three sources of knowledge. These three knowledge areas are still the basis of the Relationship Platform at Altitude today. They are:

Understand the client company.
Understand the client's customers.
Understand the client's competition.

Regarding the client company (DeWalt), he wanted to know the history and size of the company, the corporate mission, how decisions were made, how wide its market scope was, what DeWalt saw as its own competitive strengths (product quality, innovation, service, add-ons, etc.), what its brand image was, how elastic its brand was, and whether the company had held tightly to this brand image in the past.

Regarding the client's customer, he wanted to know whether this was a clearly defined market segment or the general public. Who selected these products and why? How price sensitive were these customers? In what environments were these customers found? What else did they buy? How did the company's branding entice the buyer, or was its branding effort mostly ignored? What were the buyer's expectations?

Regarding the competition, he wanted to know whether this was a crowded field with lots of look-a-like products, or did each product occupy its own space? Was DeWalt up against superior competition (products, funding, R&D staffs), or was this a fair fight? How did the competition identity itself to the buyer? And most important, by using the answers to all of these questions, how could he help DeWalt surpass the competition?

This process was complicated by the fact that DeWalt could not tell Altitude what it wanted. It knew it wanted to add something to its line of products, it just didn't know what new product to add. And, so far all that Altitude knew was that DeWalt products had a brand image of being so durable that an electric drill that was dropped off a roof would still work, and professional contractors liked these products. Altitude would help DeWalt decide what to do.

Swing a Hammer, Dig Ditches, Paint

By this time Altitude had grown into a capable group of designers, engineers and strategists. So now a new client could be studied by a team. These team members knew they had a lot to learn so they went to DeWalt's retail channels including small hardware stores, big box hardware stores, general retailers, and home centers. The Altitude group went on shop-alongs with senior staff from DeWalt. They also went on shopping trips by themselves. They discovered that there were two types of construction customers. The first group did big jobs with girder and masonry materials. The second did home "stick" construction as contractors, remodelers and professional woodworkers. At the time, DeWalt's biggest market was with this second group.

After they talked with DeWalt's customers in stores they went to job sites. To gain more knowledge about this customer, the Altitude team joined some construction crews, hammered nails, dug ditches, and painted. While they were immersed in the environment they asked questions; lots of questions. How can this tool be better? What new tools would you like? What are some areas of opportunity? What would make your life easier? They also observed all of the obvious and subtle elements of the work.

They found a treasure chest of opportunities. Contractors said things like, "I need a way to lock up my tools at night when I go home. I need to plan and sequence the construction schedule. I need ways to minimize the disruption of a family when rehabilitating an occupied home. We need entertainment for our employees. We need a more efficient lunch routine, because sometimes the employees have to travel far to buy food. We need to find efficient ways to transport workers from one location to another on a job site and back again. We need better communication between foremen and workers".

The first project to emerge from all of this was the DeWalt Worksite Radio. It is a sturdy-looking, yellow and black gadget that has two roll bar handles and resembles a small generator. (A radio generates sound, so a generator design made sense.) They learned that most contractors replaced three radios per year, because they were stepped on, dropped, hit with a board, or thrown around when someone tripped on the electric cord. So this radio is durable enough to be dropped without breaking, and it has a flexible antenna that will not snap if it collides with another object. It uses the same battery platform as all of the DeWalt cordless tools so it lasts a remarkably long time and if it is allowed to run out, a battery from another tool can be plugged into the radio. The radio can also act as a charger for all size batteries in the system. This model did not include a CD player, because foremen felt that when the CD ended the worker would have to interrupt work, change the CD, and then return to work. The CD capacity would have been a time killer.

Making History

When DeWalt launched the radio in 1994 it had prepared to sell about 30,000 units per year. During consumer validation research it decided to double this estimate. But when it launched the radio at National Hardware trade shows it took in orders for almost 1,500,000 units. This was a blockbuster product whose success shocked even those who had designed it. In fact, it is still the most successful single-item product launch in DeWalt history. It remained essentially unchanged for 11 years in an industry that prides itself at modifying products annually. During those 11 years it had no price erosion, and became a standard part of job sites everywhere.

In 2000 Altitude won a Gold International Design Excellence Award from IDEA for the DeWalt Radio because of its unique design, durability, and fit with its environment. In 2004 Altitude won an IDEA Catalyst Award for the DeWalt Radio. This award honors the business success of an invention and is given to blockbuster products that remain on the market for at least 10 years.

Altitude's powerful competence at its Relationship Platform starts with gaining a great amount of information about the client and then leveraging this information to provide something special for the client. When I asked them, the good people at Altitude denied that they were trying to make the client firm dependent on them, but I wonder. Altitude builds strong and long-lasting relationships with its client firms.

As Altitude has increased the complexity of its projects and the number of its employees, it also has strengthened its Relationship Platform. Now it is automatic for the folks at Altitude to spend an unusually large amount of time learning about a new client company, the client's customers, and the client's competition. These projects are bid on a fixed-fee basis, so Altitude does not get any extra money for spending this much time learning so much about the client. But Altitude knows that this knowledge allows it to create a product that fits with the client firm's brand image and that it will nicely meet the needs of its end users. It also knows that this deep knowledge of its clients allows it to innovate their businesses, not just their products. Altitude also knows this will delight those clients and keep them coming back.

BUILDING ALTITUDE'S CREATIVE PLATFORM

In the beginning, Brian knew that everyone who worked at Altitude was creative. That is the nature of this work. And in the beginning, everyone had great leeway to pursue creativity his or her own way. This ad-hoc management method worked in the early days. Brian was a good rainmaker, so the new jobs came in and Altitude was well placed in Quad 1 Growth. From 1992 to 1995 Altitude went from two employees to eighteen. Revenues were good and opportunity seemed to be everywhere. Brian was keenly aware that one of the frustrations he had experienced at his previous employer was constrained creative processes, so he encouraged this independence. Why not? These were crazy times. There was an impromptu feel to the place and lots of decisions were made "on the fly" because Brian was often out of the office, or even out of the country.

In 1998 things began to change. The work was steady, finances were stable, and group members became comfortable with each other. Brian created a small corporate structure and established collective project groups made from the various in-house disciplines, like design, engineering, brand, and strategy. These project groups could be established in flexible ways depending on the client's problem. Departments were established. Altitude was entering Quad 2 Steady State. As the group began to benefit from its own learning curve, the creative processes at Altitude became more formalized, more operationalized. Less and less did each member do things his or her own way. Now there was an Altitude way.

Altitude's maturity enabled it to examine the creative processes used in its profession, and then to use them to establish a formal structure to its own creative processes. It divides these processes into five phases. As time passed, Altitude mastered them and morphed them to fit its Hybrid Relationship and Creative Platform model of building resilience. Please note that these phases are presented in a sequential order, but the Altitude team often goes back to revisit a previous phase or does two phases at once. The phases of Altitude's creative process are as follows:

Phase One: Discovery

The discovery phase at Altitude is the most powerful connection between its Relationship Platform and its Creative Platform. Everything the previous pages said about Altitude's Relationship Platform also describes the discovery phase of its Creative Platform. Some design firms do almost no discovery at all. They simply put in a bid to design a new product, gather the desired specs, and begin to design. Other design firms can be found providing all levels of discovery; some shallow, some moderate, and some substantial. In contrast, Altitude takes the discovery phase to extremes.

Understand why this project exists. Altitude begins discovery by asking how the project has come to them. There are three possibilities: 1. There is a tired product that has lost its market prowess and needs to be revitalized, like Altitude's work on the new Mr. Coffee brewer. 2. There is a new technology that is filled with potential, but the client needs help to productize it, like the way Ahura can use lasers to excite molecules. Altitude helped turn this into a tool Hazmat teams can use to instantly determine whether an unknown substance is safe. 3. There is a problem to solve, like the way Altitude helped Delphi Consumer Electronics build portable live video receivers that get good reception in cars as they move. The creative processes are different for these three needs. So is the client's vision of the outcome of the project. Altitude begins the Discovery Phase here.

Understand the client company. Sometimes the task of understanding the client company comes easy, and Altitude can move forward quickly. But if this part of the discovery comes hard, it is remarkable to see the extremes that Altitude can undergo in order to gain this understanding. The team might ask about the history of the company, its financial health, how the client company came to be formed, its organization structure and they might even ask for previous annual reports or other seemingly farfetched information. They always ask about the firm's brand image, place in its market, and the range of its other products. They want to know how the firm defines itself and how its new product will fit this image.

They wonder whether the client will be capable of producing the product once they design it. Everything about the firm is relevant, both to the Relationship Platform and to the Creative Platform.

Understand the client's customer. This step involves shop-alongs, market research, consumer ethnography, and basic questions about which customer buys which product, under what conditions. They look at distribution channels, what the customer wants, and how customer's needs are currently being met and unmet. This is why Brian traveled the world, interviewing scientists for Symbol Technologies and hammered nails with carpenters for DeWalt. In the end, he asks what the customer needs now.

Sometimes amazing things happen when Altitude takes the time to understand the end user. The original design for Bayer's 800 series blood gas analyzer was a machine that was slender and tall. However, Altitude discovered that it wouldn't fit under shelves in Asia, and some lab technicians couldn't reach the controls, so it proposed a product that was shorter. Also, it learned that left-handed people wanted to inject the blood samples into the right side of the machine so they could type on a keyboard on the left side of the machine. Surprisingly, right-handed people wanted the same arrangement, because they felt more comfortable injecting the sample with their right hand. One design met the needs of both groups, but no one would have known this if Altitude hadn't asked.

Brian is emphatic about this; design for the purpose of design is artwork. But design for the purpose of the end-user is about meeting needs. In Brian's words, "If you don't create an idea that is relevant to your audience, what's the point? You get fool's gold." He suggests that some design firms design cool things just because they can, not because they intend to leave the end-user well served.

Understand the client's competition. The design of the new product must give it the ability to stand out in an often crowded field. Creating differentiation and relevance in context with the client's brand image and purpose is the surest way to achieve this. This is not easy. Sometimes CEO's just want a new toaster, or a drill that is lighter. It is only by a careful examination of competing products that Altitude can persuade the CEO that a unique product is needed. That happened with Jarden Consumer Solution's Margaritaville® Frozen Drink Maker.

Jarden makes and sells branded items that we see everyday around our homes, like Rival crock-pots, Coleman camping equipment, and

Sunbeam blenders. When it bought the rights to market Jimmy Bufffett's Margaritaville brands, it hoped to create a blender with parrots and palm trees on it. The folks at Altitude studied the competition and found the market was crowded with blenders, and adding some decorative items would not compel the customer to reach for a new one. Then they went into the margarita marketplace (that's right, bars) and studied margaritas. Said one Altitude team member, "Who said market research isn't fun?"

The results of the discovery phase showed that the reasons the margaritas made in bars are so much better than the ones made at home is because they shave the ice. They also have a drain to remove the water as the ice melts. Home blenders chop, crush, and explode the ice, but they do not shave it. They allow the ice to melt and become slush. Home blenders are cheap and undifferentiated. Altitude saw the need for an expensive, up-market, well designed luxury item that would be the centerpiece of a party.

Phase Two: Conceptualization

At Altitude, the task of conceptualizing the new product is not a task at all. It is a process. Mastery of this process allows Altitude to apply its Creative Platform skills to any industry, like medicine, computer technology, or household appliances. But the process of conceptualization is not pretty. Sometimes it is just plain painful.

From the earliest steps of the discovery phase through the delivery of the final product, Altitude teams are made of members of every profession; engineers, strategy & research, design, and brand communications. As the project progresses they all come to care about it. This can create a great deal of emotional tension. As the group brainstorms about how to meet the needs of the client firm, its end-user customers, and how to outperform the competition, more than one idea emerges. Often all of the ideas that come forward are viable, so these teams give permission to the members to disagree, argue, and brainstorm aggressively.

This process is strengthened by the fact that the team will travel the entire journey together. This is one of Altitude's secret competitive advantages. Many design firms use different teams to do each step of the creative process. Typically in other firms the discovery group "throws the project over the wall" to the conceptualization group, who then throws it over the wall to the next group. In those firms, each team is responsible for only one step, but not for the whole product. Each group tries to translate the most important issues to the next group, but with each translation, something is lost. Not so at Altitude. Each team member deals with every issue from the beginning, and they all take responsibility for the entire project. This causes them to make a very personal and emotional connection to it.

At times the debates look for two creative concepts they can collide together in order to find the best product. Says Brian, "Sometimes a new idea is nothing more than two old ideas colliding." In fact, Altitude has trademarked the term, creative collision. So the DeWalt radio was the collision of workplace efficiency with workplace entertainment. It was efficient because the contractor would no longer need to replace his radio every few months, and because it didn't have a CD player. It saved money and time. It was entertaining because it reduced boredom and monotony on the job.

PHASE 3: THE DESIGN BRIEF

Finding the right product that is intended to occupy the right space in the market and leave the end-user well served is a great achievement, but it is not enough. Now Altitude's Creative Platform must be taken to the client. Just as the creative processes have been emotionally challenging for Altitude's team members thus far, so now comes an honest debate between Altitude and members of the client firm. At first glance some clients are surprised by the proposed new product. Altitude staff members offset this by returning to the three ways the project came to it in the first place. They place the discussion in the context of revitalizing an old product, productizing a new technology, or solving a problem. This almost always softens the discussion and leaves the client ready to benefit from Altitude's long hours of sifting through its creative options. In fact, only those clients that are open to this process become long term clients of Altitude.

The design brief is strengthened by what Altitude calls "modeling". This is where Altitude breaks out its coolest technology to make life-like images of its proposed product. This might involve off the shelf illustration software like Adobe Photoshop or Adobe Illustrator. Or, it could use any combination of 3D drawing packages like Pro-engineer, Solid Works, or surface based modeling and animation packages with rendering capabilities like Rhino and Maya. Altitude's folks are happiest when they can present a computer image of the new product that is so realistic, it looks like you could reach into the computer screen and touch it. They might make the image rotate in front of the client. They might put in the shading, soft and hard light, shadows, and perhaps some little beads of water on its surface.

The design brief and modeling methods are powerful here. Seeing the finished product in near-reality is so compelling that it usually aligns the client with Altitudes proposed product. This overcame DeWalt's objections that DeWalt is a tool company, not a radio company. This is how Altitude persuaded Jarden Consumer Solutions to go beyond their stable of less-than-$99.00 household items and produce the Margaritaville Frozen Drink Maker as a $300.00 family treasure. In the end, there is much to be gained by accepting Altitude's advice. Like the DeWalt radio, the Margaritaville Frozen Drink Maker became the most successful product in Jarden's history.

Phase 4: The Implementation Phase

All of Altitude's work thus far really has been a debate about how to turn the most important client issues into a real product. Now it is time to show the client company how to actually make the product.

In this phase many things happen simultaneously. At the center of all of it, Altitude's engineers work with the client's engineers to create the steps of production engineering. The Altitude team begins building real models, makes some decisions regarding branding and naming the product, and designs the product's packaging. Any disputes regarding these important issues are referred back to the initial concepts of how the project came to Altitude, why the client wants this product, and how to best serve the end user.

Phase 5: The Delivery Phase

Handing the final project over to the client company is a moment of pride as well as mutual accomplishment for everyone involved. Members of the Altitude team experience a deep sense of ownership. In fact, they are so attached to most of these projects that in future years they will refer to the things they did and learned on this assignment. Members of the client company not only feel the joy of receiving this gift, they also have a clear sense of accomplishment regarding the parts of the project that involved them. Everyone has great hope for the prosperity and good work this new product will bring in the future. This is a good time. Heather Andrus, Altitude's General Manager often tells her team, "Whew. That was another great delivery. I hope the parents take good care of it".

Despite the handoff, Altitude's work is not done. True to its Relationship Platform, Altitude remains involved as the project works its way around the inner reaches of the client company. Need some help explaining the value of the product to a finance VP? Altitude will attend the meetings. Need to teach the sales group how to sell an item that's a little outside their normal product scope? Altitude will come along. Altitude will consult with manufacturing about how to manage the production processes, and it will help the marketing department understand the branding, naming and placement of the product.

Building a Resilient Culture

The first time I entered the large work area that houses Altitude's employees, I was curious about why everyone was walking around carrying boxes. This seemed like a positive exercise since there was more than a little socializing going on. Then I found out it was "moving day". That is the day every six months that all employees pack up their personal and work stuff and leave their desks to go work at another desk until the next moving day. This gives each employee new scenery and perhaps a desk near a window. Everyone wonders who will be the lucky one to get a desk next to Brian's office. More importantly, it gives everyone new neighbors. At Altitude, there are no permanent work clusters, and the professions are not segregated. So, engineers don't sit together. Nor do designers, researchers or any of the internal disciplines. This allows a designer to lean over to the next desk and ask an engineer a technical question quickly and without going through department heads or any other bureaucracy. It prevents these Creative Platform employees from having favorites, and it causes everyone to support the Relationship Platform by ensuring that everyone knows what is being done for each customer.

Altitude's culture is powerful, perhaps "cult-like", and not everyone can fit in. Said Gregor Mittersinker, Altitude's Vice President of Design and Strategy, "It is difficult to hire new people. They need to be technically skilled, dedicated to our work, and comfortable with Altitude's creative processes. They need the ability to work across disciplines. This is an unusual person." There are other reasons a person might not fit in. Altitude's process of thoughtful collaboration is everywhere. So, people who have opinions that are too strong or unyielding don't fit in, especially during the brainstorming sessions. Those who have no opinions don't' fit. Nor do those who are easily injured or offended when the group greatly modifies the person's suggestions, or discards them altogether. And, those who seem not to truly care about the final product don't belong at Altitude. This is a powerful culture, rightly pointed in the direction of this firm's Hybrid Relationship Platform and Creative Platform.

Constitutional Component of Culture

Altitude's resilience-supporting corporate culture begins with its Constitutional Component. This is the beginning of the "religion" of creativity and deep relationships found everywhere at Altitude. The spoken and unspoken DNA of Altitude's environment is evident from all this chapter has said about this firm, thus far. These bright people are masters of the Creative Platform and they deliver this creativity through their competent use of the Relationship Platform. Everyone at Altitude knows this. They all pursue creativity every day. They all gain knowledge about the client, and seek to render something special. These things give every employee a basis to understand the spoken and unspoken rules and assumptions that guide behavior at this firm.

Not only do all of these folks know how to conduct themselves according to this hybrid platform, they know the subtle nuances of their platform. So, when I asked one person whether Altitude simply tries to create new, cool products, the answer was, "No". It seems that there are many cool products that do not add value and do not represent the next step in technology. They're just cool. Altitude avoids this and seeks to invent new technology that supports the client.

Value Component of Culture

Brian explained how the mission and values of Altitude have become so well-defined by saying that if one were to tell a good story many times over for 17 years, the story would get better and stronger. So it is with this firm. Brian has given a name to Altitude's core guiding principles. He calls it its Avatar.

The word Avatar was first used by the Hindu religion to describe a god or deity that comes to earth in a person's body. The person is said to represent that deity, and to have its supernatural powers. In our modern society computer users have used the term Avatar to mean a three dimensional or two dimensional graphic figure that represents the personality of the sender. It is viewed to be the person's own trademark, and is especially popular in computer games. So, at Altitude new employees are told about the mission and core values of the firm. They are given the central concepts of dedication to creativity, thoughtful collaboration, relationship with customers, and sustaining the environment. Then they are asked to be an Avatar. Be a representation of this mission and these core values.

INTERPERSONAL COMPONENT OF CULTURE

When I suggested to a group of Altitude's staff that some Creative Platform day-to-day environments can be unconventional and even funny, one of the engineers said that this was not so much the case at Altitude. He said that they are all dedicated to the work and that there are some days that are quiet. Then I heard snickering in the group. The others reminded him that he is the one who made a toy helicopter that could actually fly, brought it to work and launched it. Unfortunately, he had not perfected the remote controls so it crashed into the back of the general manager's head and got tangled in her hair. They also told me about hillbilly golf and races with broken wheelchairs in the parking lot.

This is a diverse group and Brian has worked to keep it so. In my first meeting, I met people from England, France, Austria, India, Korea and all over the U.S. They have various interests, hobbies, as well as racial and ethnic backgrounds. Outside interests are valued because they enhance the collective knowledge of the group. To a great extent, these people all get along with each other. They put in long hours and then socialize with each other on the weekends.

The group's heroes are well known, like engineer Alex Tee who was described as the glue between groups and designer Phil Leung who is smart, willing to work long hours and eager to help the design mesh with the other disciplines. The artifacts of this culture are the sample products that can be found everywhere at Altitude. And, the most typical ceremonies consist of thanks given to the entire team that creates a new product.

Like most Creative Platform environments mistakes are tolerated at Altitude, and this is not an environment where a failed technical experiment ends a career. In contrast, behaviors that violate the core values of the firm, like being rude or condescending to a client, overbilling, or lying are not tolerated. These are more than mistakes. They are severe violations of Altitude's culture.

I was surprised to discover Altitude's relationship with money. I have worked with many consulting firms, and I have observed that some apply tremendous pressure for team members to generate bills. This is not the case at Altitude. Once it wins a flat-fee bid, Altitude's employees feel rather free to take the time they need to get to know the client firm. Altitude rarely asks for charge-backs or modifications to its bids, and rarely charges more than the initial fee. Brian could recall one case where Altitude had spent nearly double the bid, and simply explained this to the client, and asked if in time it would be willing to help pay any further expenses. The client voluntarily did so, and continued to work with Altitude on future projects.

Altitude's history with its suppliers is very consistent with both Creative Platform and Relationship Platform enterprises; it seeks to build partnerships. One such supplier is Scott Models in Cincinnati. Theirs is a 25 year relationship of hard work and mutual trust. Scott Models is freely given all pertinent information about a project, and is highly trusted. In return, Scott has never let Altitude down. Once, Scott made a scale model of a project that was so delicate that it was afraid to ship it by any conventional method. So, at its own expense Scott rented a truck, carefully loaded the model, and drove it from Cincinnati to Boston. It seems that Altitude finds partners who are built on both the Creative and Relationship Platforms too.

Resilient Strategy

Altitude's strategy is the collection of its client-facing activities that are produced by all that this chapter has said so far. Altitude's strategy uses its collection of competencies to study the client firm, its customers and its customer's competition so deeply that it truly understands the firm's products, services, and branding. It comes to understand the client's place in its market and it comes to know how that market is being absorbed by the competition. Because of this deep knowledge of its client firm, Altitude is able to engage all of its internal creative processes effectively. In the end it produces a unique product for the client that is valued. In the end, the client values Altitude as well.

Altitude takes a disciplined approach to its strategy. Competition is fierce in the design field, and desperate competitors can always offer a lower bid. So, Altitude seeks to gain client loyalty through its artful combination of its Relationship Platform and Creative Platform. Its website says, "We know what keeps you up at night."

Altitude has not limited itself to one industry or one market segment. It is just as likely to design children's toys as it is technical devices for satellites. It knows a lot about home theatre, mechanic's tools, and medical testing equipment. It knows about kitchen appliances and x-ray devices. It knows a lot about a lot of industries. And with each industry it has served in its 17 years, Altitude has accumulated a treasury of knowledge-assets.

Because Altitude has worked horizontally across many industries, it can use its broad knowledge of these diverse fields to serve not just the clients in those fields but clients in other fields as well. It has a keen understanding of overall market trends and shifting consumer values. All of this allows it to develop not just a product, but also a marketing strategy for that product, and this allows the client firm to extend its brand image.

How does Altitude select its clients? Its favorite way is to first seek the client firm, and then ask about which technology needs work. This is in contrast to some design firms who first attach themselves to a technology and then seek the clients.

Altitude's strategy is to use its broad base of knowledge to create innovative products, based on its knowledge of the client firm. Altitude's strategy is about building long-term, loyal clients.

Altitude Wisdom

Like any entrepreneur who begins with nothing more than an idea and a desire to do things his own way, the Altitude story is an inspiration to us all. Brian knew he didn't like working for his former employer. He knew that he wanted to build a consultancy on the premise that every one of his bright employees would have something important to contribute. He wanted a creative environment that would establish deep relationships with its clients. He started with a lot of ambition, little money and a poorly chosen partner. He has ended with a mid-sized design firm that is well respected in its profession and has his signature on it. This has required Brian to build the Creative Platform and Relationship Platform one day at a time.

Like all Resilience Builders, Brian knows that resilience can be lost by bad luck, fate, or by allowing the firm to become too comfortable. Says Brian, "Loyalty is forever inexperienced, and resting on our laurels is lazy. We have to be vigilant about who we are and how we are perceived."

Meanwhile, the gifted folks at Altitude continue to build deep relationships with every new client and seek opportunities to invent, create, or improve each new product they touch.

CHAPTER 8

CULTURE AND RESILIENCE

The United States Army Special Forces, or Green Berets, is greater than its total number of highly trained small teams. It is greater than its inventories of specialized technical equipment. And it is greater than its national and international prestige. After all these qualities are examined, there is one more source of its greatness; its powerful culture.

The requirements to become a member of the Special Forces are substantial. Candidates undergo the most grueling training the Army has to offer, and to pass daunting physical, emotional and psychological hurdles. Many are required to learn foreign languages. The majority of these highly qualified candidates either quits or fails the training along the way. Once graduates enter the Special Forces, they know they have joined the world's most elite combat fraternity.

The Army Special Forces is now a well developed organization, but it had a rocky beginning. It was started in 1952 during the Korean War. In its early days the nature of this organization shifted about as each new leader tried to define the program differently. During that time its members had to sneak to wear the green beret because it was considered an unauthorized uniform. It was President John F. Kennedy whose esteem for the Special Forces gave strong approval for this group, and legitimized its beret. His connection to the Special Forces was permanently etched into the American psyche when a Special Forces sergeant took off his green beret on television and placed it on President Kennedy's coffin in 1963.

The culture of the Green Berets can be examined at three levels. It begins at its very deepest level with how each member defines the

Special Forces. Each man knows that his mission is to be the best at reconnaissance, unconventional warfare, assault, and counter-terrorism. They all know the purpose of this organization is to operate in small teams, often behind enemy lines, and sometimes to act as a "force multiplier" to depose oppressive dictators. They know they must maintain their skills to be effective and efficient in all these things. This is the "religion" upon which the organization is built. There is unanimous agreement about this and this guides everything that follows.

The second level of the Green Beret culture has to do with the spoken and unspoken values by which they all live. Again, there is unanimous agreement here. These motivated troops value stealth, self-reliance, quick action, and the ability to work in effective teams. All are prepared to place their own personal needs, including their lives, second to the mission.

The third level of this culture has to do with the bond that develops between these men, especially between the members of small operational teams. They trust each other. They care about each other. They need each other.

Notice that the culture's deepest level defines the constitution of the culture, the second level defines its values, and the third level describes its interpersonal nature. We will see that in industry a resilient firm's corporate culture is built of the same three components. There are many enterprises today that have the same kind of intense, clear, and precise culture as the Army's Special Forces, and all of the great Resilience Builders from the past created this type of culture, at least for a while.

What is Corporate Culture?

When I begin to assess a firm's culture I often ask a group of employees a hypothetical question, "Imagine your kid brother just got a job at this company. He comes to your house the night before his first day and asks you what it's like to work here. What do you tell him?" In response to this, the employees begin saying random things like, "You should always keep your truck clean because the old man hates dirty trucks." "We get to go home early on Fridays if it's slow." "You can get promoted easily if you are willing to move around." "The pay is only OK but we have a lot of fun here."

All of these things describe the firm's culture, but as the conversation continues I listen for any statements that define the firm's platform, like,

"Participate actively in brainstorming sessions, don't just sit there quietly." "Take plenty of time to get to know what the customer wants in a project before offering a plan." "Mistakes are OK, but be ready to use them to teach the rest of your team what you have learned."

The more clearly their statements describe a competitive platform, the more well-defined the culture will be. All of these statements guide employees and set the standards for acceptable and unacceptable behavior in the workplace.

I listen for statements that show in which Quad of the developmental frame the company finds itself now, like, "We are number one in our market and nobody can touch us." "Just show up, don't screw up, and you can ride this thing to retirement." "Your supervisor will give you production goals, but nobody ever meets them."

Culture is the collection of all the spoken and unspoken rules in the workplace. Of greatest importance are the rules of conduct that emerge from the firm's competitive platform and its place on the developmental frame.

THE IMPORTANCE OF CULTURE

Resilience Builders have a strong and unanimous belief that corporate culture is capable of exerting a powerful influence on the smooth running and financial performance of their organizations, and they're right. However, culture is a vastly misunderstood concept, and less adept managers might see it as soft, irrelevant, or something that follows the organization rather than being a product of their own leadership. Some leaders complain about "the way things are around here" as if this is not their responsibility. In contrast, Resilience Builders are active, not passive, in their approach to corporate culture.

Culture creates the unique identity of the corporation or organization. Every company has a culture, but some are ill-defined and reveal no unifying characteristics or coherent traits. In those organizations culture can be described as "Around here we each do things our own way, but we get the job done", or "Each location runs its own shop and things change every time there is a new general manager", or "Some of us think we are sales-based but others think we are R&D-based".

A resilient organization has a strong culture. But even more, it has a strong culture that is pointed in the right direction. Some of the brightest business authors have talked about some cultures being "strategy-supportive". 1 I suggest that culture must support more than just strategy. It must support and be congruent with all three of the other essential elements of resilience. Wherever there is a strong culture, it is readily identifiable to both insiders and outsiders. Here, all individuals and pockets of the organization define and describe the organization in the same way and in concert with the leader or founder. Resilience Builders are remarkably skilled at defining and developing their corporate cultures.

Cult-Like Cultures

Some firms, like Southwest Airlines, Inc., give culture a place at the same table as strategy and operations. Southwest hires people who already seem to have the values of the organization (recommendations from current employees are encouraged). It has a department of corporate culture, and has had culture representatives at airports. Southwest Airlines embraces a culture of working efficiently while having fun. Once its famous founder, Herb Kelleher, hid in an overhead bin on a plane to frighten an unsuspecting flight attendant. Southwest gives awards that support its values, like the Winning Spirit Award, and the Positively Outrageous Customer Service Award. The folks at Southwest know who they are, and they know what life is like at SWA. Southwest has a strong, coherent, and clearly defined culture.

One book stands out as having made a substantial contribution to culture that can actually help the front line manager. In *Built to Last* authors Collins and Porras say that the very best companies have "cult-like cultures". 2 They say Hewlett Packard, IBM, Disney, and Merck all have this. These cultures can rise to religious levels. In each of these firms culture is so strong that a new employee may or may not choose to remain with the company just because of the culture. In your own enterprise, consider this. If every new person you hire can stay and be happy then you do not have a powerful culture. In contrast, if some people seem compatible with your firm's ways and others do not, then you have a strong culture.

THE PROFESSIONAL LITERATURE

Unfortunately, much of the professional literature on corporate culture is of little help to the Resilience Builder. It is a fragmented literature in which each author or researcher offers a unique definition of corporate culture. Each author also offers a unique collection of labels and typologies. Authors have made very little effort to integrate or build on the work that has gone before. Some authors have suggested culture types such as networked, communal, and mercenary. Others have used labels like self-actualizing culture, dependent culture, sociable culture, and even e-culture. 3

More importantly, it seems that most of the literature has described corporate culture as the collection of social or interpersonal interactions within the corporation. So, there is said to be a strong culture if everyone goes out for a beer on Fridays or plays in the company softball tournament.

The culture literature has largely ignored the lifecycle of an organization, or what this book calls the developmental frame. At times culture has been confused with job security. So, an embattled company that has gone through layoffs might be said not to have a culture.

Nowhere is there a theory that gives credit to the platform on which the company is built. Certainly it is different to work for Efficient Platform Wal-Mart, than a Marketing Platform company like L'Oréal, a Creative Platform company like DreamWorks, skg, or a Hybrid Relationship and Creative Hybrid company like Hallmark Cards. Everything about life inside these four companies is different, including their written and unwritten rules of conduct, the topics of their formal meetings, casual conversations, and how they address their markets. Promotions are formulated differently, different acts are viewed as heroic, and each culture has a unique relationship with money. Life, survival, and success are uniquely different in these different environments.

RESILIENT CULTURE IS PRODUCED
BY PLATFORM AND FRAME

I suggest that in resilient companies, culture not only matches the firm's competitive platform and developmental frame, it is created by them, and the very nature of the culture is determined by them. Platform is the primary determinant of culture, because platform determines the characteristics of the firm. Frame is the second major determinant, because each time the firm shifts from one Quad to another the firm's culture is affected.

This Chapter

In this chapter I further suggest that a powerful corporate culture consists of three components, not simply the social interactions within the organization, and Resilience Builders are remarkably skilled at using these components to their advantage. They are the First Level Constitutional Component of corporate culture, Second Level Value Component, and Third Level Interpersonal Component. I will discuss how moving through the different quadrants of the developmental frame change culture and thereby challenge resilience and require special adaptation. The ability to skillfully integrate these two abstract variables, platform and frame, into a third variable, corporate culture, is one of the remarkable skills that sets Resilience Builders apart from all others. The chapter will look at how resilience is affected by subcultures. Then it will examine culture and mergers and acquisitions.

Resilience and the Three Components of Corporate Culture

Resilience-supporting corporate cultures are about more than how sociable or pleasant coworkers are to each other. They are about more than having a company-sponsored Christmas party in which children are given free toys. They are about more than growth, downsizing, or lay-offs. Even at Southwest Airlines the culture is about much more than fun, pranks, and practical jokes. This book proposes that resilient companies have strong cultures and these cultures are built on three levels.

First Level:
The Constitutional Component of Culture

Resilience-supporting corporate cultures begin with the firm's competitive platform and its developmental frame. Cisco Systems has a culture based on its Creative Platform and its changing location on the developmental frame. This is where its culture begins. The same could be said of Wal-Mart, PepsiCo, and IBM. This is why life is characteristically different in resilient Efficient, Relationship, Creative, and Marketing Platform companies. This is why it is so different to work for a company in Quad 1 Growth than Quad 3 Degeneration, for example. This is why it is vastly different to work at Cisco than Wal-Mart. Their cultures are based both on their clearly defined platforms and their skillful adaptation to their location on their developmental frames.

Resilient cultures start here. The Constitutional Component of corporate culture is created by the intersection of two powerful forces, platform and frame. The Constitutional Component is the genetic alphabet, the DNA of the firm. It is generative, and in a resilient organization it creates all that follows. This is the primary determinant of culture and it forms the nature of the organization. It determines the material of which the culture is made and establishes its boundaries. Like animal chromosomes, it determines whether the organization swims, crawls, walks, or flies. It also determines the spoken and unspoken rules and assumptions of efficient, relationship, creative, and marketing cultures. In all resilient firms the Constitutional Component of culture creates the uniqueness of the environment. It answers the question, "What are the spoken and unspoken rules of conduct and behavior around here?"

Resilience Builders are exceptionally skilled at building this Constitutional Component of culture. This component determines the degree to which an organization knows who and what it is. It determines whether the organization will ever have a clearly defined image in the eyes of employees and outsiders. Therefore, it is here that the ability to establish congruence begins. And, once the Constitutional Component becomes well established, it creates the remarkable stability that is so typical of the powerful cultures of resilient companies.

The Constitutional Component is often unheralded and transparent. It, however, is also like the air we breathe. It sustains life as well as the nature of each of the four platform groups even though in many ways it is invisible. No one ever stands up and announces, "We are an Efficient Platform company. Therefore, when we travel we will only rent compact cars." If the organization is in a state of resilience and the entire enterprise has congruence with the Constitutional Component, then these behaviors and attitudes seem to be there automatically. They are inborn characteristics like the color of its eyes and the tone of its skin.

Constitutional Components of Efficient Platform Cultures. Everyone in a resilience-supporting Efficient Platform culture knows that the character and personality of the company is all about doing things faster, better, and cheaper. It is about avoiding steps, layers and procedures. Every process, piece of material, supply chain element, distribution channel, customer, department, and employee is openly talked about in regard to cost, benefit, and contribution to efficiency. In these environments success equals efficiency, as does the survival of the organization and one's chance at promotion. There is a special language around efficiency, and the word, "cost", is part of the cultural fabric. There is a constant awareness of time and supply limits. Often there is little option to improve the bottom line without lowering costs. This is the basis of everyday life at these firms.

Constitutional Components of Relationship Platform Cultures. If resilience is achieved at a Relationship Platform company, all interactions, transactions and events are viewed with an eye toward how the receiving party might feel or respond to the event. All of the characteristics of the Relationship Platform described in Chapter Four create the foundation for how business will be conducted and how buyers, sellers, and employees will be treated. The language here includes such words as caring, response, react, and satisfied. Even relationships with suppliers are treated as delicate. The DNA here is all about the relationship. This is what determines the nature of the culture.

Recall from Chapter Four, the currency exchanged in resilient Relationship Platform companies is attachment. It is so within their culture as well. Unspoken but powerful assumptions move the company to be so relationship-oriented that the receiver of the interaction will feel a need to stay with this company, whether it is the customer, supplier, or employee. There is a drive to persuade them that they need this company, and that they will be treated well. Every interchange is more than a transaction.

Not long ago, Hallmark only sold cards in Hallmark Gold Crown® stores or under the Ambassador name. Unfortunately, few people knew that Ambassador was a Hallmark product and only a small percentage of the populace was shopping at the Gold Crown stores. To reach a wider and more diverse population, in 1997 it decided to sell Expressions From Hallmark® cards in grocery stores, pharmacies, and big-box discount stores. There was extensive internal discussion about how to do this without offending the independent owners who ran the free-standing Gold Crown stores. These people had been good to the company, and now it was time for their good work to be remembered. Hallmark decided the relationship could be preserved (and profits could be made) by upgrading these licensed Gold Crown stores to become broad-scale gift stores in addition to card shops. This would differentiate them from the discount stores which would have less selection. Hallmark leaders met with the independent owners and even sent representatives to their stores. It is difficult to imagine an Efficient Platform company having a culture that would expend this much energy on preserving these good relationships.

Constitutional Components of Creative Platform Cultures. Resilience-supporting Creative Platform cultures are made out of a strong desire to contribute something unique, to formulate the impossible, and to generate something new or improved. Resilient Creative Platform companies have unique cultures. In these cultures mistakes are tolerated and even celebrated. People are allowed and encouraged to be different and unconventional. The culture is all about leveraging talent and knowledge, and building the next generation of ideas and products. The cultural linguistics include words like cool, wow, and "I didn't know we could do that". One also hears questions like, "How did you do that?" And, "How can I capture that?" The generative piece in this culture is all about creativity. This sets the tone of the culture and it is from this that all else comes.

Recall from Chapter Four that resilient Creative Platform companies have a culture of openness with their suppliers. There are many projects they cannot do alone, so they disclose the entire plan, resources, formula, and strategy to certain suppliers.

Constitutional Components of Marketing Platform Cultures. Resilient Marketing Platform companies tend to have a culture and a basic personality like no other. Looking at the common denominator of these firms, one will conclude that the constitutional component here is all about two things; energy and an unusual kind of intelligence. These are vibrant cultures, and the people involved are smart, but, it is a different kind of intelligence than is found in any other platform. It is both outgoing and analytic. They reach out to markets and market segments in an energetic and extroverted way, while also retaining a studious focus on numbers.

A look at the very basic constitutional component of this group reveals another important fact. All of the money poured into market studies, focus groups, and examining which market segments are growing serves a greater purpose. Sales. The sales culture is perennially erupting with energy. They have sales meetings that resemble high school pep rallies. Sales groups are broken down into competing teams and prizes are awarded for meeting goals or beating each other. Everyone's numbers are put on display for all to see and every person attempts to do things on a grand scale.

Implications. Notice how central to each platform these characteristics are. While we cannot say that all firms in a particular platform share all of these traits, we can say that some traits are quite characteristic of each platform. This is what Resilience Builders do best. They build companies on a specific platform, and the First Level Constitutional Component of the culture is the product of the chosen platform. In a resilient company every employee knows the nature of the company.

SECOND LEVEL:
THE VALUE COMPONENT OF CULTURE

The Second Level Value Component is a little less subtle than the Constitutional Component. While the Constitutional Component is pervasive but understated, in resilient companies the Value Component is quite visible and easily detected by all internal and external observers. This is because it consists of mission and core values. Powerful mission statements and compelling core value statements emerge among people who have a shared history and an accumulation of problem-solving experiences. Mission and values create the ability to build consensus regarding a vision of the future. While the Constitutional Component was global and generative, now we see some very specific and obvious traits develop. In resilient organizations, these traits are visible and enduring. They build the second level of the culture.

The importance of having a clearly stated mission is well documented. There are many Creative Platform companies. They invent, but how and in what manner? This is determined by the second level of culture. This begins with mission. Mission determines whether the Creative Platform company makes microchip circuitry, designs airplanes, writes computer code, or is an independent research lab in the land of big pharma. This selects the industry, and it selects one's place in the industry. Nevertheless, mission is still fairly general. A mission statement might say, "We make technical and educational films." But mission is not synonymous with strategy. Strategy is much more specific and it is the engagement of mission with the external world. So the same film company's strategy might be to make training films for surgeons, less expensively than the competition, within 60 days of a new medical development, which have only famous doctors in the films, and are exclusively distributed by the AMA. And, while mission remains quite stable, strategy is adaptive and flexible. In response to competition this company may alter strategy by deciding to license its films to training teams who do hands-on teaching along with the presentation of the films. For resilient companies, mission begets strategy, but mission and strategy are not the same.

Mission's influence on culture does not stand alone. Resilience-supporting cultures are strengthened when mission is in partnership with strong core values. A mission statement says what the firm does and the core value statement says in what manner. Some core values clearly support the platform on which a resilient company is built. "We offer our customers a bargain every day," is a good value for an efficient company. "We enrich our customers' lives and businesses every day," certainly represents a Relationship Platform company. "We put technological gain ahead of profits," is the central theme of the Creative Platform. "We provide our beauty products to every racial, ethnic and age group without discrimination," is a Marketing Platform value. These core value statements are good snapshots of each platform.

But what about these value statements? "We maintain absolute honesty and integrity." "We provide high quality services, and we are always looking for ways to improve our quality." "We support continuous learning." "We contribute to our community and we are good to the environment." These are all good values which provide clear guidance to all employees. They help orient new employees about the nature of the company, and surely reflect the values of the founder or leaders. However, they are irrelevant to the platform on which the company is built. They can be the values of a company built on any platform.

In order to achieve resilience the core values of an organization must have some statements that match platform, frame, or strategy. These are necessary for culture to be congruent with the other essential elements of resilience, but they do not prevent the ability of other core values to exist. Other important values may be present even though they are irrelevant to platform, frame, or strategy. The Second Level Value Component of corporate culture is different in its nature from the First Level. The First Level is all about the platform on which the firm is built and the location on the developmental frame. In the Second Level Value Component there is a greater allowance of some values that do not represent the platform, frame, or strategy of the firm. That's acceptable.

Consider Tyson Foods. BusinessWeek called it the Wal-Mart of meat. 4 Tyson knows who and what it is. It is all about building efficiencies. Like all efficient companies, it demands efficiencies from its supply chain. It has control of large mass-produced chicken farms and has created great savings through its aggressive contracts with cattle ranchers. It is remarkably efficient. One of its core values speaks about investing in processes. This is certainly an Efficient Platform value, so this core value strengthens resilience. Another of its core values is "We strive to be a faith-friendly company." Sounds misplaced? It isn't. Tyson can have this or any other core value that defines a unique characteristic of the firm. The "faith-friendly" core value does not relate to congruence. Culture is congruent only when there is a match between the particular core value as it is compared to platform, frame, and strategy. The more congruent these elements are, the more likely it is that resilience will be achieved.

Implications.   Some core values must match the firm's competitive platform and others might just be values that are unique to the founder's and leaders' values. Both sets of values are quite acceptable, but resilience is enhanced only by the former.

THIRD LEVEL:
THE INTERPERSONAL COMPONENT OF CULTURE

A few years ago an employee of a remarkably resilient company underwent heart surgery. His initial recovery was prolonged and he remained hospitalized week after week. On the windowsill next to his hospital bed was a white bud vase with two carnations and a small card signed by the CEO of his company and his wife, Don and Adele Hall. As winter began he spent his days slowly recovering at home. His coworkers sent meals and casseroles daily, along with cards and small gifts. One afternoon some women from the plant stopped by, rang the doorbell, and of course, brought more food. Then they asked the employee's wife for her Christmas card list, because she had been well known for always sending cards that had been carefully hand-addressed. The women addressed all of the cards and prepared them for her signature. As this was going on some men arrived with pick-up trucks and ladders. They rang the doorbell, asked for their Christmas lights, and put them up. In a matter of a few hours, their work was done and they were all gone, leaving behind a well-lit house, several stacks of addressed cards, cookies, and two stunned and grateful coworkers. What company was this? Hallmark Cards, Inc. It always cares enough to send its very best.

It is tempting to conclude that Hallmark is so nice to its employees because of its powerful mastery of its Relationship Platform. However, this would suggest that companies built on other competitive platforms are not supposed to, or are not able to, be this nice to their employees. The fact is that being good to your employees will strengthen any firm, regardless of which competitive platform chosen. Acts of kindness are equally available to all enterprises.

If the Constitutional Component is the genetic code and substratum on which the culture rests, and if the Value Component creates the character traits of the organization, then the Third Level Interpersonal Component renders the social personality of the company.

Common Interpersonal Elements. The president of any firm can eat lunch in the factory break room every Friday. Any firm can create a climate where employees show pictures of their children's dance recitals, and where everyone's birthday is celebrated. Any boss' door can be open to all employees.

Birthday celebrations, dance recitals, and open door policies are equally available to all four platforms. They create a nice workplace. While it might be hypothesized that some platforms, like the Efficient Platform, are less friendly, this is not so. Recall the kindly QuikTrip culture from Chapter 3. Further, consider the fact that Efficient and resilient Southwest Airlines is ranked highly among former employees as having been a great place to work. Despite its efficiency, its employees know they had fun and were respected and appreciated.

Specific Interpersonal Elements. In crafting a corporate culture, one should not stop at simply creating a positive work environment. Resilience Builders develop cultures which are congruent with platform, frame, strategy and the first two levels of culture. This is why Wal-Mart executives sleep two to a hotel room when they travel. This explains why the president of Hallmark travels to the local plants to attend almost all 20+ year anniversary ceremonies. This is why Bill Hewlett and David Packard shared recognition and money with engineers who created breakthrough technologies. This is why Marketing Platform Starbucks has started a farmer-support program for environmentally friendly producers in Costa Rica. These acts are congruent with the platforms on which these firms are built.

Almost all authors have written about culture as if it only consists of the Third Level Interpersonal Component. Their view has been that culture equals the interpersonal relationships within the firm, or the social context of the workplace. They have not considered how platform, frame, and strategy relate to the deeper levels of culture.

Artifacts. Much of my discussion of the Interpersonal Component of culture is taken from anthropology, the strongest discipline to study culture. The Interpersonal Component of culture attempts to transmit the values of the firm through artifacts, rituals, ceremonies, and heroes. Artifacts are those physical elements of the environment which are unique to the company or which typify its culture. Resilience-supporting cultures have artifacts that are relevant to the firm's competitive platform. The spartan offices at Wal-Mart's Arkansas headquarters are artifacts of its efficiency. The elegant architecture of Abbey Road recording studios in London speaks to the creativity that goes on inside. The powerfully imposing New York City headquarters of Goldman Sachs tells a client to expect a strong and secure relationship. The displays of antique advertisements and marketing memorabilia at the New World of Coca Cola in Atlanta are artifacts of a Marketing Platform company. Those are all congruent artifacts, and their congruence strengthens resilience. They are relevant.

Rituals. Rituals are the habits of daily conduct that reveal the nature of a culture. An expense report that is rendered daily rather than weekly or monthly probably reveals an Efficient Platform. A production manager who spends the first 45 minutes each day going over whether the previous day's special runs uniquely satisfied each demanding customer is probably in a Relationship Platform firm. Wadding up paper and having paper snowball fights during work hours is most likely a ritual of a Creative Platform culture. And obsessively reviewing sales per market segment is a ritual of Marketing Platform companies.

Ceremonies. Ceremonies are the collections of predictable behaviors that occur when something big happens within the culture. Some are actually called ceremonies, like retirement ceremonies, and others are not, like the way terminations or plant closings are conducted. Again, one can look for congruence and whether these events are resilience-supporting elements of the culture. For example, at a retirement ceremony, do those who speak kindly about the person tell their stories in context of platform and frame?

Heroes. Heroes are part of every culture. Deal and Kennedy described them as people whose actions "personify the culture's values." 5 That's true, but not everyone who personifies the culture's values is regarded as a hero by those inside the culture. In anthropology, heroes are described as those who personify the values of the culture, and help the larger group achieve what it needs (usually survival) by some form of self-sacrifice or personal risk. So, an efficient production manager who stands up to a menacing new vice president and risks his job by refuting the new inefficient bureaucratic paperwork and wins him over is a hero. However, a young manager who stands up at a meeting and calls the overbearing new vice president a jerk might represent the sentiment of the group, but is not a hero.

Implications. In this third level Interpersonal Component of culture, look carefully at the degree to which the elements are resilience-supporting. This comes from the degree to which congruence is achieved. Of course there will be many extraneous interpersonal pieces of the culture, and that's all right. The parts that support resilience should be congruent with platform, frame, strategy and the first two levels of culture.

RESILIENCE, CULTURE, AND FRAME SHIFT

In order to achieve resilience, the enterprise must survive or adaptively avoid at least one significant challenge. The challenge can come from a frame shift, a change that happens when the firm moves from one Quad to another on its own developmental frame. This section addresses how culture is challenged as a result of frame shift.

Imagine life inside Microsoft during the early 1980's. What a thrill! Bill Gates, and Paul Allen were at the helm and had strong hands on the wheel. These young men were out to build a very big Microsoft, create open systems, and make computers useable to the whole world. These were intense, heady and self-absorbed days. There was great work to do, and Microsoft did it very well.

Imagine what it was like to be part of this grand achievement. Early members of Microsoft viewed themselves as the smartest and coolest group of techies around. So did the rest of us. We should also give credit to their management achievements. By 1989 they had all of their people working in task teams, with parallel milestones and timelines so the programmers could all meet at the same endpoint, rendering a new product called Microsoft Office®. This was a lot like having two crews build railroads from the East and West and meet in the middle. Or, more accurately, dozens of crews coming from dozens of directions. And they did it. When it first released Office in 1989 Microsoft had 30,000 employees. It now it has 96,000.

These people were participating in the beginning of something great. Just being there was an adventure. As a result, the money came rolling in; enough to make many of them millionaires and Bill Gates the richest man in the world.

In the beginning we loved these geeky kids who defined an era. Then suddenly it all seemed to change. Having so many employees made Microsoft a real employer with rules and policies. Producing so many new software advances required it to vigorously protect its intellectual property rights. Bill Gates got a pie in the face in a public meeting. The government filed antitrust papers. Sun Microsystems and others publicly declared Microsoft the enemy. Eventually competing systems emerged that would cost consumers little or nothing, like Linux.

What happened here could best be described as a frame shift. This company moved from Quad 1 Growth to Quad 2 Steady State. Inside Quad 2, Microsoft was building the culture of an established corporation. In July 2000 Fortune magazine ran an article entitled, "I Remember Microsoft", in which it claimed that many smart Microsoft programmers were leaving the company to start their own small firms because they wanted to recreate the autonomy, enthusiasm and innovation that had described Microsoft's early environment and was now lost. Microsoft's culture had changed. 6

Strategically, Microsoft had signs of complacence as well. In 2000, before Google was a household name, Microsoft had developed a system that could steer Internet advertizing and pop-ups according to the content of a search, just like the process that created Google's success, but it didn't deploy the system. Also, Microsoft waited until 2003 to develop a user-friendly search tool and 2007 to aggressively market it. It waited until 2009 to ink a deal with Yahoo. All of this slow movement created a wonderful space in the market for Google to fill. Microsoft paid the usual price for its strategic complacency. It also paid the price of incumbency, where its market clout became viewed by others as abusive and exploitive. Most importantly, all of this caused a culture shift at Microsoft. As it moved from Quad 1 to Quad 2 it became a very different place to work.

So what are the culture shifts that come with frame shifts all along the developmental frame? And how can leaders resist, steer, or influence these shifts?

CULTURE IN QUAD 1 GROWTH

There are three snapshots of how a firm's culture can shift as it moves through Quad 1.

First Snapshot. The first culture snapshot of early-stage Quad 1 Growth is a buoyant group that struggles to create or keep up with demand, likes each other, and has the impression everyone shares the same mission and values. This is a positive experience. In this Quad we find enthusiastic energy and life here is both fun and frustrating. It is fun because the whole group believes it is having a unique impact on the world. The group owns a new place in the market. It is frustrating because of the ups and downs in the sales cycles associated with growth, the need to decide everything for the first time, and the clumsiness with which things are executed.

The culture here includes many under-experienced people doing tasks that are poorly defined. Some team members have a feeling that, "We are faking it." There is a sense among these novices about how cool it is to have their new and challenging jobs. In new organizations there exists the thrill of discovery. We are discovering a job, product, market, set of competitors, and mostly, we are discovering each other. Internal relationships are fresh and without the burdens of past struggles, and there is a false belief that we all share the same values. This is false because those values have not yet been tested.

The Resilience Builder must realize that these group characteristics are the product of the firm's location on the developmental frame, and that this climate cannot be sustained forever. Things are about to change.

Second Snapshot. A second snapshot occurs a little later in Quad 1 Growth. The work here is about establishing a culture that supports the platform on which the company is built. How will the leader build the culture around these strengths? And, as the leader tries to establish the platform, will internal groups protest or attempt to disrupt the progress? While it is still considered a good place to work, it seems the honeymoon is over and a more realistic approach must begin to settle into the culture.

Oddly, thus far culture has consisted of the Third Level Interpersonal Component of culture. However, growth is not a culture. Enthusiasm is not a culture. So, if asked to describe their new culture, these people would render an accurate description of a Quad 1 Growth start-up organization. They would talk about long hours and being willing to miss their son's soccer game or their daughter's birthday party, in order to land a big contract. Somehow this seems OK if it saves the day and helps the firm survive. They might describe sandwiches left on desks, and half empty cups of coffee, never to be finished. They might reveal a roller coaster of customer orders, making everyone excited, followed by a drop, leading to group depression. And while they might confuse new growth with culture, the fact is that growth is not a culture. Growth influences culture. Quad 1 influences culture. So do the other Quads.

This is the time when platform, mission and values need to be addressed in both obvious and subtle ways. There is a shared history and a common task, and the group has some sense of what it is about. But if one were to ask 20 employees about mission and values in their young firm there would be shockingly disparate answers. This is a leadership point which separates Resilience Builders from other leaders. It is time for the Resilience Builder to have a profound influence on the group as he or she becomes more directive and less compromising about what values and behavior will be required in order to support the competitive platform.

Third Snapshot. The third snapshot of culture is taken in late-stage Quad 1 Growth. It gives a picture of an optimistic culture that is dealing with new issues that the group does not understand.

Up to this point in Quad 1 Growth, most of the people who have failed in this firm have been those who couldn't do the job, couldn't tolerate the growth pace, or did not accept the platform, mission or values. They didn't belong, and the stronger the culture, the more apparent it was that they didn't belong. Now, however, the firm consists of a cadre of true believers and they all belong. So any infighting is not in support of developing the organization. It is personal or turf-protecting, and it is destructive to the organization. Departments may be seen as not supporting each other. Rivalry creeps into the culture.

While this may seem to suggest that a disorganized culture and a nasty climate are inevitable here, it does not need to be so. It just shows that the Resilience Builder is once again at a choice-point and that the cultural impact of this choice will be substantial. To succeed at this location on the developmental frame, the Resilience Builder must ask the group how every issue relates to the platform, mission and values. This allows the group to use shared beliefs and philosophies to solve problems. It reduces the ability of strong personalities to rule. It makes it less likely that the firm will now wander across strategies, platforms, and values. It gives the Resilience Builder a way to decide things on a basis other than impulse, circumstance, or favoritism.

The Shift from Quad 1 Growth to Quad 2 Steady State

The shift from Quad 1 to Quad 2 rarely happens abruptly. Typically there is a slow and insidious drift towards Quad 2 Steady State and then towards complacency. There are two developmental snapshots that define culture as the firm moves through Quad 2 Steady State:

First Snapshot. At first Quad 2 Steady State seems like a happy culture. Every member of the organization is confident. Times are relatively good, and the company begins to be seen as a caretaker of the employees rather than vice-versa. Complacency creeps into an organization when any of life's frustrations are good reasons to take a day off, when increased benefits are expected, production mistakes are common, excuses from sales are accepted, and there is slow or nonexistent development of products or services. It enters when employees don't worry about what they would do if the company were to fail.

Second Snapshot. If the teeter-totter in Quad 2 Steady State is allowed to tilt toward complacency, a paradoxical thing happens to the culture. Nearly everyone becomes unhappy. This occurs despite the fact that the company develops the posture of a caretaker and renders ever greater benefits to the masses. Healthcare, pensions, vacations and all of the standard awards emerge in Quad 2. Unfortunately, the recipients of these benefits may see these things as entitlements and come to believe they are owed to them. Some firms also allow time off for community activities, birthdays and company softball tournaments. The suggestion box might overflow and awards are given, even to suggestions that are never implemented. Big performance bonuses are given, even to those who didn't contribute to the new achievements. Tuition is reimbursed, daycare and elder care might be provided, and the local hospital might set up shop in-house once a quarter to give wellness checks. Benefits and rewards no longer relate to performance or the financial health of the company. They are viewed as entitlements or gifts.

This is not an impasse. This is just one more leadership crisis that separates Resilience Builders from all others. The leader has reached a point where he or she must decide either to do nothing or to act upon this comfortable organization. Resilience Builders have a remarkable skill at detecting complacency creep and reversing it. They confront even the smallest hints of complacency directly and publicly. But their primary way to resolve this is to begin anew to ensure that the competitive platform is clear and agreed upon. Then they aggressively pursue growth. This brings a climate of earning rather than entitlement. This is an intricate issue and readers are directed to an important book by Judith Bardwick, *Danger in the Comfort Zone.* 7

SHIFTING FROM QUAD 2 STEADY STATE TO QUAD 3 DEGENERATION

Unlike the slow platform shift from Quad 1 to Quad 2, the shift into Quad 3 Degeneration can happen either gradually or abruptly. The speed and extent at which the frame shift occurs determines the impact of the culture shift. A gradual decline into Quad 3 Degeneration happens when a formerly competent firm has entered a posture of continuous harvest, and has come to believe that the well will never run dry. Here we find companies like Polaroid and Kodak. Polaroid was an American icon with its instant picture development. Kodak couldn't imagine a world without film. Polaroid went bankrupt and Kodak now is in the midst of a competent but painfully slow recovery. Both companies were guilty of lingering too long in Quad 2 until they became bogged down by a culture of complacency. Edwin Land, founder of Polaroid, likened his firm to Utopia. And Kodak gave bonuses to employees every March, even after prosperity had dissipated. Some employees called it "St. Kodak's Day". In both cases the culture of complacency brought about Quad 3 Degeneration. 8

Abrupt declines happen to strategically complacent companies who are unprepared for a market shift. For example, independent local radio stations' entire industry underwent a rapid consolidation in the U.S. following the Telecommunications Act of 1996. In the five years from March 1996 to March 2001 the number of new radio stations increased 7.1% while the number of radio station owners declined 25%. In 1996 the largest radio station conglomerate owned 65 stations. In 2001 Clear Chanel Communications owned over 1,000 stations. More shocking though was the report by the FCC that by 2001 in America's cities the largest two radio broadcast companies owned an average of 73% of the community's radio advertising revenues. Firms who were not ready to adapt went through drastic Quad 3 Degenerations and their internal cultures were hit hard. 9

There are two snapshots that describe culture as the firm moves through Quad 3 Degeneration.

First Snapshot. The first culture snapshot of Quad 3 is marked by an organization in disbelief followed by surprise. During the disbelief, most employees lag behind the Resilience Builder and remain complacent. The Resilience Builder has become aware of the decline and the gloomy outlook, but most of management as well as the employees remain complacent. As bad news piles on more bad news, it becomes clear how severe this is. And then everyone is surprised, like a wounded soldier who is stunned that it could actually happen to him. Interestingly, this is the point of strategic hesitation, the pause. There have been downturns before. At first, the employees can't believe it and meanwhile the leadership group does nothing.

Second Snapshot. If things do not improve, the second culture snapshot of Quad 3 Degeneration contains far more suffering. As the group begins to fear the future, a need to assign blame emerges, and this blame is assigned to the leader whether or not it is accurate. Desperate people do desperate things. Anger fuels much of the organization, and this anger looks for someplace to go. This is the point at which subgroups begin to form which offer support to their members by joining the resistance.

Internally, this is the time when several of the leader's most trusted key colleagues do things that leave him or her feeling betrayed. These are the people he or she has nurtured, developed, laughed with and confided in without reservation. He or she has viewed them as partners and discussed the competition and the company's weaknesses. They are among the select few who know the firm's secrets. The leader has told them about his or her personal life. And now they use this intimate knowledge against him or her. They join the chorus of those who blame him or her personally for all of the current difficulties.

The internal discontent, of course, is a psychological defense on the group's part, intended to prove that they themselves have no blame or responsibility for the current pain. They have a primitive desire to regress to the good old days when Quad 2 Steady State was heavily weighted down by extreme complacency. Most likely, the leader's efforts to remedy the crisis will receive little internal support. He or she is now viewed as different, somehow strange, or less credible. In some cases even his or her outright gestures of kindness are viewed with suspicion. Normal efforts to supervise or improve basic quality or processes are perceived to be personal criticisms or insults. Every new strategic or tactical directive is secretly put to an informal vote, and the outcome is always the same. The group votes down his or her initiatives. The leader begins to lose influence and has been pushed to the sidelines; marginalized.

All of these cultural changes are a challenge to resilience. The influence of platform is weakest here, because the platform is viewed to have failed the organization, so most leaders allow the firm to become ill defined. In their efforts to survive, leaders allow the platform to drift or become lost. Its loss begets a fragmented company where each subgroup can do things its own way. The erosion of platform allows an erosion of the previously tightly defined culture. Employees don't know the rules of day to day conduct now.

THE SHIFT FROM QUAD 3 DEGENERATION TO QUAD 4 CONVERSION

Entry into Quad 4, Conversion has an unmistakable impact on culture and resilience. Once again culture can become resilience-supporting. This is the Quad that truly separates the Resilience Builder from other leaders, and this frame shift is the most significant of all.

There are two developmental snapshots of culture in Quad 4.

First Snapshot: Internal Resistance. The first culture snapshot describes the early days of Quad 4 Conversion, which this book calls Internal Resistance. Psychologically, most of the group is still under the dark cloud of Quad 3. The culture is still rife with criticism and anger. There hasn't been good news, and there doesn't seem to be a clear way out. Mistakenly, employees think there is no reason to believe things are better.

However, while fear remains menacingly present, things are different now because denial is noticeably absent. Honest discussions about the true realities start to happen. These discussions include the firm's responsibility for how it failed to anticipate the changes involved in its competitive platform and frame shifts. These talks also begin to openly examine how to respond.

A competitive platform is selected once again. This gives the Resilience Builder something to say and something to do. Rebuilding the firm around this new platform is also how Resilience Builders work on culture now, because the new platform once again guides day to day conduct. If the firm is at Quad 4 in the developmental frame, then there have already been several frame shifts. So, it is time to convert the organization.

Perhaps at this point it might be easy to conclude that Quad 4 Conversion is a negative and strikingly unpleasant experience. It might be unpleasant in the beginning, but we should expect it to improve as the Hope Bearing Plan begins to work. Remember there are two phases of Quad 4 Conversion. First there is Internal Resistance. Then comes Internal Recovery.

Second Snapshot: Internal Recovery. It is the second snapshot of the culture in Quad 4 Conversion that begins to reveal a rebirth. Whereas the first phase of Conversion was called Internal Resistance, this is Internal Recovery. This happens when the Resilience Builder pursues the Hope Bearing Plan. As this plain-spoken statement of how the firm will recover is communicated throughout the organization, a crusade to win true believers begins to attract followers. It represents the beginning of a process in which the plan will be continuously examined and adjusted. Internal Recovery is considerably strengthened by reports of good news and small victories. The Resilience Builder is on a crusade to present these victories to everyone from employees to lenders.

Once again an old motivator returns to the culture; risk. Usually the Hope Bearing Plan involves bet-the-ranch financing and the possibility of failure is great. This risk is different than it was in late Quad 3, because there everyone believed they were headed for certain death. Here, there is a chance that if we all do it right, both success and failure are possibilities. So now as the organization begins to go through Internal Recovery it is as if there is a competitive platform for the first time, and it seems that only now does a positive culture reemerge. This culture shift is the first visible sign of renewal.

The Hope Bearing Plan gives strength to the new platform and recreates a clear culture. Employees can once again explain why the firm is successful. They can begin to develop the core competencies and skills needed to support that platform. They know the nature of their work environment and they understand the spoken and unspoken rules of conduct that form its culture.

For those who haven't experienced a successful Quad 4 Conversion, it can be said there is nothing quite like it. One Resilience Builder told me it was as if one of his children had been terminally ill and after a long battle is now well. There is relief everywhere. The group congratulates itself and the Resilience Builder becomes a hero and an appreciated champion. People stop to talk to each other in the hallways and employees are unafraid to praise one another. Birthday lunches are back. The group has energy. It is a good time. The HBP has brought hope and the future looks bright.

There is another element of culture in this recovery. A lot of people are missing, and these are people we loved. Along the way they quit in frustration or fear, or the agenda changed and they rightly felt this was unfair. Perhaps the skills which created success for them were not adequate for the new agenda, or they caught on too late that there really was a new agenda. Some became dissenters, led the opposition, and resigned or were terminated. Others stayed too long in their efforts to hurt the Resilience Builder. In all cases they were once our comrades, partners, and brothers or sisters on this journey and they are gone. So while this victory is sweet, in some ways it is bittersweet.

RETURN TO GROWTH

The Resilience Builder establishes the Return to Growth by engaging anew the essential elements of Resilience; a sound strategy, the appropriate platform, a clear understanding of frame, and a strong culture. This is the point at which the culture once again becomes a resilience-supporting culture. This is the place where all three of the critical components of culture (Constitutional Component, Value Component, and Interpersonal Component) support the firm's new competitive platform.

Success here is defined as growth, and this might be slow, lean, and incremental or it might be dramatic and thrilling. Either way, there is something great about a Return to Growth.

If Quad 2 shifted into complacency and then the firm went through Quad 3 Degeneration, the culture was absorbed with itself and its selfish needs of indulgence or survival. Now the culture can focus outwardly on the enterprise. Those inside the organization can discontinue anger and blame and begin to share a common definition of the business, thus giving it a strong identity.

SUBCULTURES AND RESILIENCE

Subcultures exist in every organization. Some are barely noticeable and inconsequential. Others have great impact on the firm. Some are healthy subcultures and others are unhealthy. All exist for a reason. These subcultures can have a significant positive or negative influence on resilience.

A subculture is a separate entity within a larger culture and the subculture has distinct characteristics which differ from the larger culture in which it is embedded. In our American society, subcultures are everywhere and include religious, political, ethnic and immigrant groups. Some subcultures develop because of a unique history among a group of people, like VFW members. Others, like teenage skateboarders, develop because these people feel that the larger culture does not represent them, and that their input and influence has been restricted. Subcultures develop their own rules, including behavioral norms, dress, and language. Compliance with these norms and rules is required for continued inclusion in the subculture, and just like the larger culture, group incumbent members automatically enforce these rules.

Healthy and Unhealthy Subcultures

Overall, the literature looks at subcultures as unhealthy and destructive. I suggest that there are both unhealthy and healthy subcultures.

Unhealthy subcultures. I encountered an unhealthy subculture once when a company (name omitted) had two plants located in the same town. One was large, with about 600 employees and it had been in place for fifty years. The other plant made niche products and was about 10 years old. The niche plant was small, with about 80 employees. Then the company decided to close the smaller plant. No one was laid off, and everyone kept their benefits as they moved over to the larger plant. However, in their new location the employees from the small niche plant closed their group to the other employees. They all ate together in the cafeteria, socialized together and remained tight-knit. In addition they were angry, because although they kept their seniority when they moved to the larger plant, none had enough seniority to matter. If a job became open on a new and desirable machine, or a spot became available on a better shift, no former employee from the niche plant could win the bid, because the most senior employees in this group had only 9 or 10 years tenure. In their old plant the 9 and 10 year employees could win every bid. Consequently, they were resentful, huddled together, and shared some common beliefs about how unkind and unfair the employer was. The last time I spoke with any of these employees was about 10 years after the small plant had been closed, and the resentment remained. Certainly, this was an unhealthy subculture.

Healthy subcultures. There is great resilience-supporting power in understanding, enhancing, and allowing healthy subcultures to flourish in an organization. Healthy subcultures are groups within an organization that differ from the larger organization in at least one of the essential elements of resilience, but still support the organization's efforts to achieve resilience. In order to call a subculture healthy, it must support either platform, adaptation to the developmental frame, strategy, or some elements of the organization's first, second, or third level cultural components. Look for a healthy subculture to contribute to resilience.

An Efficient Platform organization might decide that its sales department should use a Relationship Platform and therefore allow it to become a healthy subculture, even though this will reduce the efficiency of sales. Similarly, a Marketing Platform company might determine that its production units should use an Efficient Platform model and therefore become a healthy subculture.

Cereal maker, Kellogg, is a resilient company and an American icon. Theirs is a mature industry, the field is crowded, and profit margins are thin. Kellogg employs a hybrid model of Marketing and Efficient Platforms. Do you want happy children? Then you must buy them Frosted Flakes®. Tony the Tiger says, "They're Great!" Internally, the company focuses on lean manufacturing, efficient supply chains, and effective distribution. So the whole company adheres to this Hybrid Marketing and Efficient Platform model. Well, not the whole company. Kellogg's R&D unit employs scientists and technicians who create new products and look at technical issues like increasing freshness and shelf life. The laboratory is a Creative Platform subculture within the larger company.

Wisdom and Subcultures. Some organizations become so zealous about their competitive platform that they create a culture that requires every person and every department to excel at the chosen platform. A wise Resilience Builder would examine each department or function to decide whether it needs to operate on a different platform. If so, it should be evaluated differently than the rest of the firm and its rules of success should fit its own platform.

MERGERS, CULTURE AND RESILIENCE

Mergers and acquisitions can be effective tools to promote growth and achieve resilience. There has been great focus on the role of culture as an explanation of why mergers sometimes add value and more often destroy it. In this section, I will often use the term merger for both mergers and acquisitions because in both types of transactions the typical sequence of events involves one organization purchasing the assets of a company of lesser value. In the end, the purchaser is the dominant power.

When one firm buys another, it is unlikely that the two companies are located in the same Quad in the developmental frame. The two firms might be built on two different platforms. The success or failure of a merger is largely determined by how similar or different the two firms are on these essential elements of resilience. If we could find two firms that have the same platform, are located at the same place on the developmental frame, and have similar features of the three components of culture, the merger would have a superb possibility of full integration and post-combination success. Inside both companies the rules of success, conduct, competing, relationship with money, use of IT, and methods of selling would be the same. Does this ever happen? Yes, and it when it does, the mergers seem to succeed beautifully. This is why same-industry mergers have a high rate of success. Here we find the mergers like the 2001 merger of Chevron and Texaco, or the 2005 merger of phone company SBC Communications with AT&T.

Platform and Merged Cultures. Platform match has a powerful influence on post merger culture here. Cross platform mergers are filled with pitfalls that produce incompatible cultures and can damage resilience. This was the case in the acquisition of U.S. Trust by Charles Schwab Corporation in 2000. U.S. Trust was a highly respected and admired firm that quietly managed the money of very wealthy people, including many of America's most famous and well-heeled families. It was founded in 1853 and could have been described as steady, trustworthy, and having maintained an intimate relationship with its clients. It provided trusts, investment guidance, and personal financial advice to its millionaire and billionaire families during times of crisis such as deaths and divorces. It came to know the intricate details of these families well, and gave sound advice based on that knowledge.

The Charles Schwab Corporation was incorporated in 1986 as a mass market discount brokerage, and it became successful because of its $29.95 trades, eschewing commissions and hidden fees. It was skilled at the efficient and rapid-fire handling of high volumes of trades at low cost. Charles Schwab Co is a discounter which created a competitive response to the high commissions and self-indulgences of other brokerages. Like U.S. Trust, Schwab is good at what it does.

Both U.S. Trust and Charles Schwab Co. were in a state of resilience in 2000. Both offered financial services. Each had a history of success. Therefore, it was expected that their merger would go well, but it didn't. From the time of the merger until 2004, the pretax profits for U.S. Trust fell 80%. Margins fell to 6% compared with around 40% for its competitors. There was a major exodus of senior managers, and with them went long-term clients. What went wrong?

Both sides of this merger did a lot of things right. That's what went wrong. U.S. Trust was a Relationship Platform company and it did this right. Schwab was and is an Efficient Platform company and it continued to do this right. But the marriage of these two fine groups was ill-fated from the beginning due to their near perfect skills at their own platforms and the internal cultures those platforms created. Schwab, in true Efficient Platform style, called the U.S. Trust consumers, "customers". U.S. Trust made an issue of this and insisted they be called clients, thus suggesting it was a relationship, not simply a transaction. Efficient Platform Schwab was preoccupied with cost, but this mattered little to the relationship-oriented U.S. Trust. Predictably, Schwab greatly reduced the massive bonuses U.S. Trust officers were accustomed to receiving. Schwab had developed substantial IT and data processing functions. U.S. Trust still kept paper records in file cabinets. In fact, the management of U.S. Trust nearly blocked the merger, in fear that Schwab would interfere with its long-standing relationships with its clients, so Schwab allowed U.S. Trust to remain a separate operating unit. But the separation was not great enough. Finally, Schwab sought synergy, expecting that its own super-wealthy clients would switch over and let U.S. Trust manage their affairs. Of course Schwab's wealthy, hands-on clients liked managing their own portfolios and were not interested in this. The synergy never came about.

The real problem? U.S. Trust was a Relationship Platform company and had a Relationship Platform culture. It conducted itself fundamentally differently in every way from Schwab's Efficient Platform culture and operations. Schwab sold U.S. Trust to Bank of America in July 2007. 10

Developmental Frame and Merged Cultures. Merging firms should look for differences in location on the developmental frame to influence culture. In 1999 the very old AT&T purchased the young Mediaone Group in an effort to get into the broadband and cable markets. The idea made sense, but too little attention was given to the notion that it would be difficult to integrate this young firm into the culture and practices of this old business icon.

Cross-Quad mergers create an extra challenge to resilience. Some old cultures would best be described as complacent, known for layers of decision-slowing bureaucracy, with perhaps too much sense of comfort and self-importance. When these firms purchase a young company that has a culture based on underdeveloped financial controls, impromptu decision making, and a narrow focus on expansion a formula for disaster begins. Requests for reports or approval from the senior company are misinterpreted by the junior group as unnecessary intimidation, silly, or harassment. The two cultures have distinctly different relationships with money; the older reflexively conserves it, while the younger burns through money to support growth and then seeks more money to burn. Unfortunately, the younger firm usually is absorbed by the older one, rather than being allowed to remain a freestanding subsidiary. So, the acquirer's culture attempts to impose its own rules on the culture of the acquired firm, resulting in tight policies of conduct, formalized budgeting, and slow approval processes. The dramatic risk-taking that is characteristic of young firms is discouraged. The two firms have two different ways of doing business, and therefore two different cultures.

Compatible Cultures. When we see a merger go smoothly and render synergies quickly we can believe it is because more than the stars were aligned. It is likely that there is good alignment of the essential elements of resilience. It is also likely that the two firms' cultures were similar on all three levels. In 2005 Proctor & Gamble bought Gillette Co. for $54 billion, and immediately the united entity's profits as well as its stock price benefited. It is regarded to be one of the most successful mergers in recent times. The two firms had great similarities.

Gillette's history creates an image of a nice fit with Proctor and Gamble. Gillette was founded by King C. Gillette in 1901 who wondered why the razor blades of those days were so thick and why people had to tolerate the never-ending task of sharpening them. So, he developed and sold new disposable razor blades. At first, his invention was a flop. People wondered why they should buy his disposable razor blades when they had a perfectly good blade already. So, he became a marketing pioneer by offering razor handles so cheap, or free, that the consumer could not resist the sale. Once they had the handle, they felt compelled to buy replacement blades, again and again. This method has been imitated many times in the business world. Just ask how your printer can be so inexpensive and why the ink replacement cartridges cost so much. Or, look at your cell-phone contract. The service provider gives you a phone for free if you sign a multi-year contract to use its service. Recently, as Gillette's patents expired it began creating more complex arrays of blades including the five-bladed Gillette Fusion. It added other lines that required R&D, like the remarkable advances of the Duracell battery, Braun, and Oral-B products. So, this firm was a Marketing and Creative Hybrid firm, a lot like P&G. In addition, like P&G it was an old firm that had a history of remaining in Quad 1 Growth.

A closer look at culture shows that the Hybrid Marketing and Creative Platforms of both companies make up their first level Constitutional Component of culture. They are all about creating and marketing products. They look at numbers. They exploit market segments and they market product lines. How did the acquisition of Gillette strengthen P&G's Marketing Platform? P&G had recently added women's beauty products and by acquiring Gillette it got an instant launch into men's grooming products. Both firms have similar second level Value Components even though Gillette had less formal decision-making processes than those of P&G. Both firms' third level Interpersonal Components reflect kindness and courtesy. Both reward the same conduct of performance-accountability of products and individuals. In short, because these two firms were built on the same platforms and were at the same location on the developmental frame, they were cut out of the same cultural fabric. So, of course the merger worked.

Incompatible Cultures. What about merger failures? Much has been said and written about the culture conflicts between merging companies. However, it seems these discussions have generated more heat than light. For example, we have heard about the famous culture clashes between Daimler CEO Jürgen Schrempp and his subordinates at Chrysler after their merger in 1998. Articles abounded about how this European moved into Chrysler's Detroit headquarters, dismantled the smoke detectors in his office so he could smoke his cigars, and that he was perfectionistic and demanding. 11 The popular press claimed the failure of this marriage happened because of a culture incompatibility due to cross-oceanic geography, and a stuffy air of superiority among the Daimler group. Of course, it's not that simple.

Now we can view that failed merger in retrospect. Daimler bought Chrysler in a $38 billion stock deal in 1998 and sold 80% of its Chrysler stock to Cerberus for the low price of $7.4 billion in May 2007 after nine years of trying to create synergies. However, the discussion of cultural incompatibility described in the previous paragraph suffers from exactly the same weaknesses as nearly every merger and acquisition discussion. It uses the third level Interpersonal Component of culture as a full explanation of this failed merger. The discussion is largely about how these people treated each other. The theory proposed by this book suggests that the Constitutional Component of culture begins with the firm's competitive platform. Let's look at how this component contributed to the merger's failure. 12

All automobile companies today are built on a Hybrid Efficient and Marketing Platform. That is the overall industry's competitive platform. At Daimler Benz every employee can say with pride and confidence that their products, especially Mercedes cars, are built efficiently and flawlessly, and they address a specific segment of the market by being prestigious and expensive. These employees sincerely believe that Mercedes is the best car in the world. This suggests that Daimler's Efficient and Marketing Platforms build the foundation on which this firm stands. It is clearly identified, and the powerful Daimler culture begins here. At Daimler, all employees know how they fit in, what value they are expected to bring, and how they are to behave in order to create this value.

Chrysler is also built on the same two competitive platforms. However, although it was proficient enough to be called an Efficient Platform firm, its Marketing Platform was weak. If one were to ask Chrysler employees to describe their products during the Daimler years, they would have given a variety of answers. Some might have said Chrysler products were muscle cars because it brought back the old hemi engines, some could have said they serve all market segments, some might have said they were family cars, and others might have said they didn't know. Because of this, the identity of the firm was unclear and poorly defined. The Constitutional Component of culture had a shaky foundation on which to stand, and Chrysler was unable to communicate its rules of competition and conduct to its employees. So, employees would have been confused about how they fit in, what value they should bring, and how to behave in order to bring value.

If Daimler had wanted to create culture synergies, it should have strengthened Chrysler's Marketing Platform and created an identity for its products as well as its employees. This identity did not have to be the same as Mercedes, it just had to be strong, clear, and well-defined. In the absence of this, Chrysler had a weak identity and a weak culture. This merger failed because these two cultures were incompatible and the Chrysler culture was never repaired.

BUILDING A RESILIENCE-SUPPORTING CULTURE

Look closely at your work environment, and be aware that your firm does have a corporate culture. It may be poorly defined and fragmented, or it may be a strong culture that is pointed in the right direction, but be assured you do have a corporate culture. Know also that the responsibility for the nature of this culture goes to you, the leader. You are charged with building the culture and you are charged with building resilience. If the culture is not where you would like it to be, how do you go about changing it?

There are many consultants who will promise to change your culture for you, but you should view them with some caution. Many seek to impact the group by influencing the social interactions in the workplace. They might advise you to install better benefits or increase pay, and they are likely to set up town hall meetings between the senior managers and everyone else. These are all nice things to do, and sometimes they are appropriate. But at best they might have an impact on only the Third Level Interpersonal Component of culture.

It is important to remember that culture is shaped by the everyday experiences of the group. Your employees know what is important in the workplace and what is not. If you have placards in the hallways stating what the firm's core values are, but they are not a true reflection of your real values, then the group's collective understanding of what's important trumps what's on the placard. If you say that your firm gets to know everything about its clients before advising them, but in fact you render the same cookie-cutter advice to all, your employees will know. If you preach that you stay on the cutting edge of technology, but your IT system is obsolete, they will know. Therefore, begin to shape your culture by "walking the walk", not just "talking the talk", and get all of your managers to do so, too.

Then ask what the basic nature of your firm really is. What is your competitive platform? This book has uniquely proposed that there are four platforms, and that your choice of platform should be clear, strong, and communicated relentlessly to employees, customers, suppliers, and the public. Please believe that life inside an Efficient Platform company is different than life inside a Relationship Platform company, and so on. If you promote your platform like a zealot, it will influence everyone's relationships with time, money, technology, customers, and each other. It will influence the day to day behavior that makes up culture.

As you do this, closely examine where your firm is located on its own developmental frame. There is different work to do in each of the four Quads. Believing you are in one Quad when you actually are in another will cause you to make too many wrong decisions and it will render a confused culture.

If you do this, you will be able to use these two elements (your competitive platform and your place on the developmental frame) to define your firm, and to build your First Level Constitutional Component of culture. You will have built the DNA of the firm.

Then seek to build the Second Level Value Component of culture. Gather your senior people together and ask what the firm's mission is. Engage a consultant for this. Ask what's important around here. What are your core values? There should be some core values that relate to your competitive platform, and there should be some that are there just because they are things you value. Use these values to teach, preach and indoctrinate your employees. Use them as the basis for annual performance reviews. Use them in the everyday language of the firm.

Carefully study the Third Level Interpersonal Component of culture. Look at how your employees feel about you and their supervisors. A 360° feedback program will help here. If they feel that their opinions are not sought or valued, or that their hard work is not appreciated, only you can change this. Look at the social context of the firm. If an employee is sick or hospitalized, do coworkers call, visit, or send flowers? Do supervisors? What happens if there is a death? Do you have birthday celebrations? Look at the rituals that occur every day. Look at the ceremonies that celebrate milestones and accomplishments. Ask whether they occur in the context of your platform (Jane has marketed our cosmetics to an entirely new segment) and your core values (Jane has exceptional honesty and integrity). Last, observe the heroes in your work environment. Make sure they are the right people who support your platform and values.

If you do these things, you will build a healthy culture that is the product of your platform and frame. You will build resilience.

CHAPTER 9

THE CREATIVE JOURNEY OF
APPLE AND STEVE JOBS

There is a popular story about the history and remarkable drama of Apple Computer Company (now simply called Apple). The story goes something like this: There were two geeky boys, Steve Jobs and Steve Wozniak (Woz), who invented the personal computer in a garage in California. They had built a better mousetrap so the world beat a path to their door. They were ahead of their time and made the PC interesting and useful. The world fell in love with the entire group of very young, very idealistic, new millionaire kids at Apple who worked 90 hours, slept on the office floor, and with very limited resources did what no one thought they could do. It was the American dream, come true. We all shouted Bravo!

The myth continues that in 1984, they improved their product by introducing the Macintosh, a powerful computer that was so simple anyone could use it. They became fabulously rich and their company grew. Then sharks in the form of businessmen came in and surrounded these innocent and idealistic kids. One shark became the new CEO, and he kicked both Steve Jobs and Steve Wozniak out of the company they had formed. Woz never came back, but eventually Jobs had a triumphant and spectacular return and now heads the company.

This chapter will show that there is much truth to this popular legend. Jobs and Woz did create some cool and innovative technology in a garage in California (as had several brilliant California inventors before them). The entire group often worked 90 hours, or more. They became fabulously wealthy. And we did shout Bravo! But some of the popular fable is inaccurate. They did not invent the personal computer. Woz was not kicked out. He resigned. Twice. Jobs' ouster was not capricious. And his subsequent return only succeeded because of the wisdom he had gained during the eleven years he was away from Apple regarding how to build true resilience on the Creative Platform.

The real story of Apple involves meteoric success, overblown egos, innocence, arrogance, betrayals, and genius. It also involves the creation of a remarkable company by remarkable people. Apple has given us easy user-interface, the mouse, the laser printer, and the current generation of smart phones. It created a computer revolution. And it lit afire the technical movement we are all in today.

The storyline that follows is as accurate as can be obtained. All of it was taken from reports, interviews, interview quotes, the popular press (e.g., *Time Magazine's* Machine of the Year article) [1], and some excellent books including *West of Eden* by Frank Rose, *iCon* by Jeffrey Young and Bill Simon, and *Revolution in the Valley* by Andy Hertzfeld who was on the original Macintosh team. [2, 3, 4]

In the early days, many of the people who worked at Apple did not understand what was happening to them or their company. They consistently used misapplied logic to explain the tumultuous sequence of events that occurred. When Apple struggled, when Jobs was ousted, when new products flopped in the marketplace, there was plenty of inaccurate blame to go around. They and the press blamed the new or old product, Jobs' purported abrasive personality, newly hired groups of engineers, and the market. My efforts to examine the history of this enterprise did not find any explanations that described good or poor platform fit, platform shift, or the expected internal changes that happen when a firm moves from one Quad to another on its developmental frame. Understandably, these terms are unique to this book, but even in synonymous terms, these explanations are absent.

This Chapter

In this chapter we will see that with more information, some facts, and a critical view of Apple's ever-changing developmental frame, platform, culture and strategy, this story becomes quite understandable and instructive. We will see that Apple was initially built on a Creative Platform and its high level of congruence between platform, frame, culture and strategy gave it tremendous forward momentum. However, even though Apple had a meteoric rise and by 1982 it seemed bulletproof, this was only accidental resilience. Steve Jobs had not gained the wisdom of the Resilience Builder and he allowed his firm to enter Quad 3 Degeneration and to fall hard. The subsequent mutiny resulted in Jobs being cast out of the company he had founded.

We will also see that Apple has now had one of the most remarkable revivals in modern business history, but only after it brought back an older and wiser Steve Jobs, underwent a Quad 4 Conversion back to Creative Platform, rebuilt a creative culture and strategy, and then as a result, experienced a Return to Growth.

Jobs and Wozniak: Two Different Creative Personalities

Apple's founders, Steve Jobs and Steve Wozniak, each had different sets of creative talent. Both were brilliant, and both were necessary to create Apple in the beginning. Woz was arguably the most renowned PC programmer in his day. He always surrounded himself with the brightest minds, and even they paid him homage. Jobs was brilliant, but not a genius-level computer engineer equal to Woz. His genius lay elsewhere. He was entrepreneurial and a master of design. Even as a young man he had remarkable insights about needs of the user.

The seeds of this enterprise were planted for Jobs and Woz in their youth. Jobs later said each piece of his life was a dot and the dots would eventually be connected, but he couldn't see how this would happen at the time. It was only clear in retrospect. The Steves became friends when both were teens, but Woz was 5 years older. Both were into circuitry and electronics. Both were socially sidelined, and both were antiestablishment rebels who wanted to change the world.

Woz. Woz had already built a hobbyist computer in high school and as a senior had designed sophisticated circuit boards. He was a dedicated student and a brilliant boy. Although he was shy, he was described unanimously as a nice person who couldn't say no to anyone. In order to offset his brainiac identity, he developed a lifelong skill at pranking others. In high school he placed signs on classroom doors, saying the class had been moved to another room. Then he watched the fun. At the University of Colorado he invented a TV-signal jamming pen which disrupted the viewing pleasure of his dorm friends. When the residence council decided to look into it, he joined the committee. As the group wandered through the residence halls, TVs mysteriously stopped working. He even interfered with the university computers on election day. Later he became known for kindly pranks on his friends at Apple and began donating time and money to worthy causes. He was brilliant, funny, kind, and quietly personable. He was very creative and a huge generator of Apple's Creative Platform, but he was not the kind of guy who could do battle with the whole world and win. That's where Steve Jobs fit in.

Jobs. Steve Jobs was made of different character than Woz, even in the beginning. In high school Jobs attended classes when he wanted to. He was strongly counterculture, self-centered, demanding, and impulsive. He was a scrapper and had a sense of grandiosity about himself. For example, when he was a teen he was looking for some electronic parts and called Bill Hewlett, who was the founder of Hewlett Packard and was 41 years his senior. More importantly, he was seductive enough to entice Hewlett to carry on a conversation, and he got summer job out of it. Jobs always was able to maneuver around obstacles. Also in high school he got free parts from Burroughs by misleading them that he was planning to sell new electronics and might use their parts. So, here it might seem we could conclude he was not a source of creativity at the company he and Woz would later form, but he was. His ability to anticipate user needs, create sleek internal and external designs has become legend. His genius simply used a different kind of creativity than Woz'. The two needed, offset, and complimented each other.

Two Very Different Creative Paths. Jobs went to Reed College in Oregon, a liberal and freethinking haven, and dropped out after 6 months. He stayed on campus, went to some classes anyway, but lived in dorm (or other) rooms for another year and a half, often when other students were gone. This drop-out-continues-to-go-to-school-and-live-for-free identity gave him great status on campus. He took a calligraphy class, learned about Eastern mysticism, refused to conform, and went hungry. He did not know it, but this was all part of his training in the Creative Platform.

He returned to California briefly, then went to India seeking spiritual insight with Dan Kotke who became a long time friend and coworker at

Apple. Overall, the trip to India was a huge disappointment. They were mistreated, got beat up, went broke, and Steve Jobs was hungry again. Despite all of this, the lure of eastern mysticism remained strong for him.

At first glance it seems these were failure experiences for Jobs: He failed at college, failed as a nonconformist, and failed his pilgrimage to mysticism. But these times fuelled the two primary themes in his life, creativity and hunger. Had he not been required to sleep on friends' floors, miss meals, and been poor at Reed College and on his pilgrimage to India, his relentless emotional hunger might have waned in later years. At a commencement speech at Stanford University in June 2005 he said if he hadn't learned about calligraphy while sitting in on "free" classes at Reed, he would not have had the creative insight to pursue the original typography and fonts developed at Apple. The creative formation of Steve Jobs was the creative formation of Apple.

The creative talents of these two young men were further formed by the Homebrew Computer Club, started by Gordon French, a well-known systems designer. Not surprisingly the club initially met in French's garage, but later moved on to more suitable settings. Woz often helped the others with problems. Club members shared designs, traded parts, and showed off their latest working models. This was an extraordinarily open group with little concern for that which was proprietary. This was an incubator for creative ideas, and it was exciting. It was here in 1975 that Woz presented a printed circuit board which used an affordable microprocessor and could drive a color display. Most of the group was only momentarily impressed, but this was the point in time when the creative genius of Jobs connected with the engineering genius of Woz. It was Jobs who knew there were hobbyists who would buy this. Jobs understood the circuitry, and Jobs also understood how far the technical acumen of Steve Wozniak could take them. It was Jobs that persuaded the man who couldn't say no to go into business selling these primitive computers. The Creative Platform at Apple had taken one more step toward formation.

THE EARLY DAYS AND QUAD 1 GROWTH

On April Fool's Day in 1976 they founded Apple Computer Company as a partnership. Jobs was 21 and Woz was 26 years old. Their base of operations was both Steve Jobs' parents' garage and the apartment of

Steve Wozniak and his new wife, Alice. Soon, the garage was a workbench assembly shop and to Alice's dismay the apartment looked like a computer parts garage sale. Jobs worked at Atari, and Woz at Hewlett Packard. They had jumped into Quad 1 Growth, built on a Creative Platform in a fashion similar to so many other new Creative Platform companies. They had no orders, but they were in the business of inventing and creating.

The Biggest Order. Paul Terrell's name is etched into computer history, because he was the man who placed the first order with Apple for his Byte Shops stores. He wanted computers with circuit boards the consumer didn't have to solder at home, and ordered fifty computers at $500 each, an order worth $25,000. Woz later said that in the history of Apple, this was the biggest order and the biggest single event. Unfortunately, they had no idea how to fulfill the order. Neither had any money to buy parts. Neither had ever started a company. Neither knew anything about business and neither had a college education. But they knew it would work out. Here again we see Steve Jobs maneuver beautifully. This long-haired, bare footed, antiestablishment young man went to the offices of one computer hardware parts vendor after another asking for 30 days credit. One by one they turned him down, until he met one vendor who called Terrell to verify that there was an order, and then said yes.

Selling the VW Microbus. Still, they needed money to get started, so they raised $1,300 by Jobs selling his Volkswagen Microbus and Woz selling his programmable calculator, both prized possessions. This was the moment they took the plunge. They sold what they owned to build an enterprise. They were committed. Soon, they delivered 12 circuit boards to Terrell, thinking the circuit boards were computers. (Remember that at the time there was no such thing as a "personal computer".) Terrell was unhappy, but accepted the boards. He wanted computers that were complete units. Woz and Jobs' response to this frustrating interchange was typical of resilience-building Quad 1 entrepreneurs. They adjusted their product to the needs of the market. They learned. So, Woz built the Apple I in 1976 and its design was far ahead of any competitor. The closest was the Altair 8800, but the Apple I was a fully assembled unit, built on a microprocessor with a single circuit board and ROM. In its time it generated almost $1 million for this fledgling company.

Although Woz had developed this computer on his own time, he still had a full time job at Hewlett Packard. Upon revealing his new machine to his supervisor, he was sent to the legal department. In what is known as one of the biggest intellectual property rights blunders of modern business, Hewlett Packard said it had no interest in ever developing a personal computer. So it gave Woz the property rights releases, thus securing his young enterprise.

That same year they had nearly completed the design for the Apple II, and proudly took a prototype to a trade show in far away Atlantic City. There, they were humbled. Their machine sat on a small table without an appropriate convention display booth, and they were unnoticed. They were novices with none of the marketing skills needed to promote their work. But they did note who was getting attention, and what they did to get this attention. They also observed that the field was seeking a small, powerful, useful machine. So once again, they learned.

McKenna & Markkula. Steve Jobs did two brash things next for a young man who had no money, a single product, few sales and worked out of a garage. First, he contacted the premier marketing agency on the West Coast, The Regis McKenna Agency. And, he insisted on seeing Mr. McKenna. McKenna was a famous man whose business card read, "Regis McKenna, Himself". Jobs was so persistent with McKenna's secretary that finally McKenna agreed to see this novice with an inflated sense of self-importance. Not only was McKenna impressed, but he agreed to work with Apple and this relationship lasted for years.

The second brash thing Jobs did was to find Mike Markkula, who had been a manager at Intel in its early days, had gathered stock options and had retired at 33 years old. He was even-tempered, technical, very wealthy, and understood the impact microprocessors could have on the new field of microcomputers (the early name for PC's). Soon thereafter the two Steves gave Markkula a one-third ownership of Apple for $91,000 in cash and his signature on a line of credit for $250,000. Markkula was an early source of inspiration and confidence for them by openly predicting that this could be a billion dollar, Fortune 500 company. This was flattering to Woz, and added even more fuel to the hard driven ambitions of Jobs. Markkula also persuaded them to hire a professional manager, so they brought on Mike "Scotty" Scott as president and paid him a salary of $20,000. Finally, it was Markkula who convinced them to incorporate. They did so in January 1977.

Growing Pains. This young company was moving along the developmental frame very quickly, so it had to grow up fast. Jobs and Woz had formed their enterprise only one year earlier with a single product. The new president, Scotty, did what he was supposed to do, manage the business. But that is what Jobs thought he was doing. So these two strong personalities collided frequently. Unfortunately, Apple mythology seems to have misrepresented what was really occurring here. These clashes were dubbed the Scotty Wars by insiders, and simply seen as a personality conflict. 5 In reality these were the growing pains needed by this fledgling firm, and since it was in such a rapid growth spurt, its growing pains were more severe than most. Recall that in Quad 1 any enterprise attempts to define itself, build a structure, establish a culture, and divide labor. This is never easy, but it is harder in rapid growth.

Odd Work Hours. As early as the Apple I days, the patterns of growth were so erratic the small firm had odd work hours. These people were creatives and they had little use for normal workplace rules. Woz programmed and designed around the clock. Jobs poured unimaginable energy into this project, and there was one fire after another to put out. They began to hire employees. As happens with start-up Creative Platform firms, credentials were far less important than skill and talent. Credentials also tend to raise the issue of affordability. One of Apple's early programmers was Randy Wiggington, a bright high school student Woz had met in the Homebrew Computer Club, who showed up at 3:30 am, programmed until he went to school, and then programmed until late into the evening for little more than minimum wage. Wiggington stayed with Apple for years, and was instrumental in writing Word for the Macintosh. He is also known for dumping a bowl of whipped cream down Steve Jobs' back in a restaurant on a bet.

The Apple II. Meanwhile Jobs and Woz were busy trying to implement all they had learned from the Atlantic City conference. Woz knew their next machine needed advanced technology and Jobs wanted ease of use and marketability. When they introduced the Apple II in 1977, it had all of this and more. It included a printed circuit board, an impressively powerful new microprocessor, its own power supply, keyboard, text capability, and graphics. It was built on BASIC programmed by Woz, 4K of memory, had 62 chips and integrated circuits, all in a very small box. Best of all, it was all contained in an attractive plastic case. The user still had to supply a TV as a monitor, but this machine was a giant leap ahead for the industry. It was cool.

The Apple II was Steve Wozniak's finest moment. He designed the circuitry, wrote the code, and ensured that it had plenty of speed. It could save data on audiocassettes and it was fun. It included games. Soon he created an interface using one of the computer's slots that could attach to an external 5¼ inch floppy disk for more storage and rapid retrieval. This feature stunned the technical world, and is still regarded with some awe. Most important, Woz included an open design using several expansion slots, so other software vendors could sell their own packages for use on the machine's operating system.

The Apple II was launched at the West Coast Computer Fair in 1977 with a splash. Apple's lavish display booth overshadowed the others, with 3 Apple IIs, projection screens, and demonstrations of all the exciting things this computer could do. It was a crowd-pleasing showstopper.

In and Out of Chaos. Behind the scenes, as is so typical of rapid growth in Quad 1, preparation for the show had been less than relaxed. There was a mad rush to make the machines work with the projection screens. There were no cases to put the machines in until the last minute, and when they arrived, they were ugly and not what had been ordered. Jobs had begun to find his gifts with design and would not dream of presenting this great machine in an ugly box. Under his direction, the group spent all night sanding and painting. Here was Steve Jobs coming into his own, creating exquisite design and presentation. And here was Woz the engineer, confirming his place in computer history.

Apple's competitive platform now seemed etched in stone; it was a Creative Platform firm. It had moved fast and far along the developmental frame. While still in Quad 1, the impudence of Jobs had paid off. His overreach to contract with McKenna brought about a super launch for the Apple II. The McKenna agency developed the Apple logo, a rainbow apple with a bite out of it. McKenna coordinated a national marketing campaign. He also created the myth that these two boys had invented the personal computer, which was not true. SRI, Micral and Commodore had all made PC's previously. McKenna made Steve Jobs the face of all young tech upstarts. And behind it all was Mike Markkula, building a business, creating stability, and steering finance.

Life Threatening Crises. Like all rapid-growth Quad 1 companies, there were lots of chaos crises. The first occurred when they outsourced production of the Apple II case and due to manufacturing problems, the supplier could not supply the cases. At this point, Apple Computer was operating on a shoestring. In response to this crisis, Scotty tried to delay paying other suppliers and to press retailers to pay quickly. The problem was that if Apple couldn't get the cases, it couldn't provide the machines, and it would go bankrupt. What was needed was a man with an over-inflated sense of self-importance, a belief that he could promise the world anything, that the rules didn't apply to him, and that despite all of this, it would always work out. They had just such a man; Steve Jobs. Despite the fact that they were essentially out of money, he called the case supplier and offered a $1,000 bonus for each week ahead of schedule Apple received delivery. It worked. 3

Securing the cases was one thing. But securing appropriate financing was another. This went beyond Jobs' skill set, but it was a perfect task for Mike Markkula. So Markkula loaned Apple $200,000 of his own money and found venture capital money. They were back in business again. This company was squarely in Quad 1 Growth, and Quad 1 is not for the faint of heart.

The second chaos crisis occurred soon thereafter. Apple could not yet afford its own storage so it used a mainframe time-sharing service. Panic struck when young Randy Wiggington discovered that six weeks of his programming work had been accidentally erased by the time-sharing service. The programming work was simply gone. When Wiggington asked the contractor to run a previous backup tape so he could retrieve the bulk of his work, the contractor refused because Apple was several months behind on paying its bills. Jobs calmly began to negotiate with the contractor and told him to come over to Apple immediately and pick up a check for the entire amount. When he agreed, Jobs asked if the contractor could run the previous backup before he headed over to Apple, so Wiggington could get back to work. He agreed. Wiggington got the backup and left the building, knowing what was soon to transpire. When the contractor arrived for his check, Jobs informed him there would be no check, now or ever, on the grounds that his service had erased weeks' worth of Apple's work. He could forget it. 5

This episode required courage for the 22 year old Steve Jobs, but more importantly it was a display of some of the basic survival skills needed in order to give birth to a young enterprise. This was pure Quad 1.

Creating a Culture in Quad 1. The Apple II began to sell. In fact, it started out with a bang and sold well for many years. It became the cash cow that supported the company through good times and bad. So, these young entrepreneurs hired employees and built an organization. They created a culture in their enterprise that reflected their own personalities and also was the product of Apple's Creative Platform. Creating this organization was not easy. Everyone knew they were defining their company and marking their own place in it, so there were power struggles. Most of these people were antiestablishment California techies. They were ambitious and very smart. They tried to create a workplace that had no regulations, no dress code, and loose working hours. They would have said there was no corporate culture. In fact they would have been offended for anyone to have called them corporate at all. But in the process of being so antiestablishment, they were creating a very strong culture. IBM and HP still had formal attire. The concept of flexible work hours barely existed in 1978. And while they claimed to have no rules, they had formed a group with very powerful rules. The attire was informal, but it was not dress-as-you-please. More rigid attire did not fit in. They all wore blue jeans and T shirts. It was a uniform. Barefoot? Expected. Long hair, beards and moustaches were de rigueur. One technician grew a big moustache to get promoted to engineer. It worked. Eventually they needed titles and business cards, so their official job titles became Hardware Wizard, Software Wizard, Trailblazer, and Boy Guru. Because of their long and weird working hours, they played nerf tag in the office, built cardboard forts, and had spontaneous sing-alongs, complete with musical instruments.

More than any other culture characteristic, the one thing all of these early Apple people shared was the fact that they cared. They cared about the technology. They cared that their computer would be the coolest. They cared that they were doing things that smart people like computer science professors would have said could not have been done. They cared that they were doing more and more with fewer and fewer chips. Mostly, they cared about each other.

Apple reinforced its antiestablishment roots by declaring war on the establishment. The technology company that was most established, had most of the market, and had the most rigid dress code was IBM. It stood for everything the Apple team resented. Not only did these young inventors compare Apple's culture with IBM's, they compared its products, even in advertising. IBM could have gobbled them all up in one minute. So in declaring IBM the enemy, IBM became a threat. This is a clever method of solidifying a culture and uniting people. Dictators of small countries do this. They announce that a world power is out to destroy them, and in doing so, the people unite with each other and with their leader. So it was with Apple. This was a tight group. The leader was Steve Jobs. All of these influences created a very well-defined and powerful corporate culture.

CHARACTERISTICS OF APPLE IN QUAD 1 CREATIVE PLATFORM

Defining Characteristics: Jobs and Woz were in the business of inventing things. They had learned how to leverage their own talent in order to succeed. Slowly they began to leverage the talents of others.
Relationship with Money: They started with nothing, sold the microbus and calculator and then had some money. Unfortunately, soon we will see them run out of money before making a fortune.
Motive: At this point, Jobs and Woz cared about two things: First, doing more than could be imagined with the fewest number of circuits in order to build a very impressive computer. Second, succeeding.
Growth Method: New growth would come with the next innovative product, and they knew it.
Relationship with Customers: So far their customers were computer hobbyists. Their next product, the Apple II, would change all of that, but already Apple's design focused on the needs of the end user.
Relationship with Suppliers: Apple demanded quick payment from its customers (Byte Shops) and paid its suppliers slowly. Suppliers were getting tired of this.
Technology: They were about to shock the technical world with some innovative steps that are still impressive today. The genius of Wozniak gets the credit here.
Platform: This firm was clearly built on the Creative Platform, and was only beginning to learn how to produce and market its products.
Culture: There was a strong culture already. Jobs and Woz worked day and night, poured innovation into the endeavor, wore T shirts, blue jeans, and no shoes. They were friends and there was no corporate structure or bureaucracy. That was the culture.
Strategy: Apple's humiliation at the 1976 Atlantic City conference was a good thing. It was time to become more than just two guys in a garage. The industry was ready for sleek new design in a small but powerful computer. Their strategy was to build one and call it Apple II.
Congruence: At this point in its development Apple Computer Company had developed perfect congruence between its place on the developmental frame (it was a start-up), platform (purely Creative Platform at this point), culture (all of the employees shared the same beliefs and attitudes regarding their company), and strategy.

These young entrepreneurs did a good job of establishing a resilience-supporting culture. The first level, or Constitutional Component of culture, was solidly based on the Creative Platform. It allowed mistakes, experimentation, and unconventional thinking. The second level Value Component of culture was not spoken or written on a placard in the lobby.

They simply all agreed on the mission (to create cool new technology for the general public) and their values (nonconformist, progress-seeking, innovative technology where everyone works hard to change the world). The third level Interpersonal Component of culture portrayed a clear personality of this group. During the 1970s and early 1980s everyone knew about those bright and devoted kids at Apple.

BUILDING ACCIDENTAL RESILIENCE

Despite the above chart, the story of early Apple is a perfect example of building accidental resilience. As we see, Jobs and Woz had correctly put all of the pieces in place on all four of the essential elements of resilience. It all looked good. Apple was the premier personal computer company in the world, built on the right platform, remaining in Quad 1 Growth despite some struggles, establishing a solid culture, and using its creative competencies as the basis of its strategy. Everything was just as it should be, except one thing. Steve Jobs did not yet have the wisdom of Resilience Builders. Accidental resilience occurs when the leader does the right things, but lacks the wisdom to understand why his company is so successful, and therefore is unable to deliberately do those things, or require others to do those things. He knew how to build a company on the creative platform, but he did not know how to maintain that platform, nor did he know how to prevent his firm from going through Quad 2 and right into Quad 3 Degeneration. He was a young novice at the helm of a major corporation. He was about to get some heartbreaking lessons that would eventually add to his wisdom.

MOVING TO QUAD 2 STEADY STATE AND COMPLACENCY

The Apple II gave Woz and Jobs solid credibility in the technical community. The McKenna Agency's campaign to make Steve Jobs the persona of the computer generation was working. The product was selling nationally, and the money rolled in. Apple was an immediate success. In 1977 it generated $770,000 in sales. In 1978 this figure was $7.9 million, and in 1979 it went to $49 million. By 1982 Apple would become the first personal computer company to generate one billion dollars per year. Today Apple holds the record as having made the fastest rise from start-up to membership in the Fortune 500. These were good times. Too good. The fear of failure gave way to a sense of overconfidence. During all of this, Apple was growing. Woz and Jobs now had people working for them they didn't know. In fact, new hires were hiring new hires. Their laid-back work environment became just that, laid-back. Some of the new hires were installed to create new processes, and predictably, the old timers didn't like them. Many of the originators were not educated. The new folks were. The entire group felt things were secure enough to begin infighting. Why not? Orders for Apple II would continue to come in.

Divisiveness. As early as 1978, serious divisiveness began to emerge. The old timers as well as some of the trusted vendors gave names to the new crowd, the Bozo Brigade, or the Bozo Explosion. Internally they got blamed for engineering problems on new products, execution and shipping errors, and most mistakes. The real problem was that new orders for Apple II came in despite the complacency of the company. And when Apple added Visicalc, an excellent early spreadsheet program, the orders only came in faster.

This was a frame shift, from the earning and performing mindset of Quad 1 to the comfort zone in Quad 2 Steady State. Apple was a wonderful place to work, and clearly everyone hired there had a right to see themselves as being as bright as those at IBM, Hewlett Packard, or Intel. They were the best and Apple would continue to succeed simply because it was Apple. The scales of Quad 2 Steady State abruptly tilted toward complacency.

At this point in his development, Steve Jobs was good at managing the design and architecture of the machines, but not the design or architecture of his company. He knew that software programs would continually get bigger and Apple II would gradually be unable to run them because of its speed and memory limitations. He also knew that Apple was at its best when it was designing and kicking off a new computer. So he began to plan the Apple III. When it was launched in 1980 it had twice the memory of the II (128K) and twice the speed (2MHz), but there were problems. Quickly it became clear that this machine was a failure. Jobs went too far with product design and appearance, so the box was too small to fit all of the components. He thought a cooling fan would be unattractively noisy, so the Apple III didn't have one. This caused the chips to overheat and the hardware to fail. Although the III had a good launch, the company had to replace 14,000 machines almost immediately. Not only did this reduce Apple's credibility as being able to produce serious computers, it killed the sales of Apple III. There were two revised versions of the III, but they didn't spur sales or credibility. The Apple III was removed from the market after selling only 65,000 units. Meanwhile, Apple II was still selling, and surprisingly, the overall tenor of the company remained complacent.

Overconfidence. By 1980, not only was Apple's credibility beginning to deteriorate, so were both the reputation and the credibility of Steve Jobs. He was the face of Apple. This decline was small but present, and it was the result of both complacency and arrogance. This was a group that believed it was so brilliant, that if Apple built it, the world would come. But in creating the Apple III, these bright people adhered poorly to their own Creative Platform. All previous work had successfully matched new technology to the needs of the consumer. All previous work had produced reliable durable computers. And all were introduced with anxiety. In contrast, the Apple III was produced too quickly for a machine with its capacities and it missed the needs of the consumer. Worst of all, it was launched with great confidence. All of this revealed not only a loss of this team's previous competency at the Creative Platform, but also that they had become too comfortable. Apple was in a bad place on both platform and developmental frame. And this could only predict disaster.

The disaster had a name, Lisa. Apple had a history of secretly code naming the computers in its pipeline using names like Annie, Sara and Lisa. For unknown reasons this product kept its code name as a final product. It has been speculated that this was the name of the daughter of one of the engineers, or that it was named after Jobs' daughter. Whatever the reason for the name, this was the disaster that complacency had been brewing.

Lisa was intended to take on IBM and its hold on the business market. Unlike the Apple III project, Apple would not act hastily here. Lisa was given four years and $50 million of development. From the beginning Apple had openly talked about taking on the establishment, declaring war on the suit and tie crowd, and taking away IBM's business-application market. Lisa was a frontal assault on IBM. It had a $10,000 price tag, much higher than the IBM PC. Unfortunately, the huge operating system overworked the 50 MHz processor so it was slow, and the floppy drives were unreliable. Few were sold and it was discontinued after a surprisingly brief 2 years.

Loss of Credibility. Once again, the credibility of Apple was in decline but this failure did not shock Apple employees out of their complacency. Failures rarely do. Only a Return to Growth or a fall into Quad 3 Degeneration breaks complacency.

While the senior team was busy looking at whom to blame for Apple's decline, they overlooked their own weaknesses. Everyone in the entire group, including Jobs, was unskilled at assigning the right amount of resources to new tasks. They undernourished the III and over-nourished the Lisa. They had not learned how to operationalize the creative process. They allowed the healthy creative arguments to become out of control ego-crushing blows. Regarding strategy, they didn't see what was right in front of them. They were a personal computer company and they made great computers for individuals. Their computers were small and creative and exciting. Their efforts to challenge IBM in the business market only diluted Apple's brand. They had become complacent and they were allowing their Creative Platform to erode.

The Visit to Xerox PARC. In December 1979 Jobs, engineer Bill Atkinson, and a few other Apple employees spent a day that would change history. They visited the prestigious think tank research facility owned by Xerox Corporation, called the Palo Alto Research Center, or PARC. Even then PARC had already used Xerox's fabulous wealth to develop laser scanning and printing, storage of video images, and unique uses of imaging materials. Along the way PARC scientists had asked questions about whether documents could be shared from one desk to another, or whether workers could have a small printer on their desks, rather than getting up and going to a common copy machine. As a result, by 1979 PARC had already invented the office of the future. PARC had personal computers, personal printers, word and publishing programs, an Ethernet system between work sites that allowed easy transfer of files, and more. Its screens had a prototype of the Graphic User Interface (GUI) we know on all PC's today, with little icons and a mouse to move a cursor around. It all worked, and all of this was just sitting in their labs, unsold and unused.

Try to imagine the reaction of Steve Jobs to this beautiful and elegant system. He was ecstatic, and the Apple team asked relentless questions. They asked about the operating systems, how the GUI related to the programming, and how every element worked. It was clear they intended to put this to commercial use, and wanted to do so as soon as possible. They would have to re-invent it all because Xerox wasn't selling it. But still, they saw the future that day. Their mastery of the material was so great and their enthusiasm was so strong that Larry Tessler, the PARC scientist who gave them the tour, quit his job at PARC and went to work at Apple.

So Steve Jobs was bubbling over about the future and now had a clear vision of the way to move out of Quad 2 Steady State directly back to Quad 1 Growth. Unfortunately he was working every day in a company that was complacent. He took his newly gained insights to the Lisa engineers, and they resisted. There was a lot of fighting back and forth, but in the end it was Jobs that lost these battles. He was becoming marginalized in the company he had founded.

The Macintosh Team is Born. Meanwhile, there was a small band of extremely bright, motivated, creative Apple programmers who had started their own research project in September 1979, headed by Jef Raskin. Jef had been a professor at U.C. San Diego prior to joining Apple. He gathered together a collection of Apple people whose names are now famous, Burrell Smith, Bud Tribble, Joanna Hoffman, Brian Howard, and later Andy Hertzfeld. Bud Tribble was in medical school when Jef convinced him to take some time off to help program the Macintosh. Burrell Smith had started at Apple as a low paid service technician, and began working on the Macintosh for fun. He was so talented that he is given credit for inventing the new and innovative digital board for the Mac. Andy Hertzfeld was so bright that while he was still assigned to the Apple II he volunteered to participate with the Mac team and in one long marathon session, he single-handedly brought its images onto the screen.

New Excitement. While these were truly gifted programmers and designers, there was more to what was going on here than just a group of brainy people. Photos of this early group reveal that while Jef Raskin was middle aged, all of the others were very young, and they certainly had the innocence to go along with their youth. They were not in this project for the money, most were paid modestly. They were in it for how cool the new technology could be. They fed off of each other's creativity, and that made them all more creative. Steve Wozniak later praised the original Mac team, saying this was one of those historical events, impossible to anticipate, that shape the lives of people for hundreds of years. He also said the motive in this case was not money, but the personal excitement of doing something great. Woz further said that all computers today are essentially Macintoshes. 6 These people were absorbed with the project and thrilled with their own imaginations, unconcerned with normal working hours and willing to pour themselves into the work. Inside the larger Apple organization, this little team had remained in Quad 1 Growth, had retained its Creative Platform and had the culture and strategy to match.

That was the climate of the Mac team when Steve Jobs discovered it at the end of 1979. Soon he co-headed the project with Jef Raskin, but Raskin left the team in the summer of 1981. Jobs had learned from his early days and from the failures thus far. He encouraged the Creative Platform including the crazy lifestyles, weird hours, and unusual people. Bud Trimble usually came in to work about 10:00 am and stayed late. Everyone knew that Bud had put in a marathon night if he didn't come in until the afternoon. Burrell Smith could be bribed into working late with pineapple pizzas. And everyone liked to play games with each other and on each other.

Jobs got input from everyone, and it was on the Macintosh that he perfected his mastery of sleek design, perfectly integrated circuits, minimal chips, and ease of customer use. He stole ideas from the Lisa group, which was attempting to use the Graphic User Interface Jobs had seen at PARC. He took staff to off-site days or weekends to develop ideas or to decide about implementation. Once again he solidified his group by declaring the rest of Apple as the enemy (at least at first, latter it would once again be IBM).

Pirates. He was at his best in the start-up phase and he loved to be counter-culture, so once at an offsite meeting Jobs wrote on the board "It's better to be a pirate than join the Navy." A few weeks later, Steve Capps and Susan Kare secretly made a big pirate flag using an Apple logo for an eye patch. Capps climbed onto the roof after hours, and attached it to a makeshift pole. He thought that in the morning this would be seen as a prank and it would be taken down. But it wasn't. Steve Jobs loved it. A couple of months later the Lisa team stole the flag and took it to their building, and Capps had to pry it out of the hands of a frightened secretary.

So why did this feel so good to Steve Jobs? It is unlikely that he could have answered this question in 1979 or 1980. The fact is that Apple had become Quad 2 complacent organization whose Creative Platform had been eroding. Apple no longer felt like the creative, cutting edge, innovative company it had been. Hiding here in the midst of all of this complacency was a pocket of Creative Platform happily working in its own Quad 1 Growth. Members of the Mac team were innovative, sincere, and proud to be working on the most exciting project in Silicon Valley. They were happy. This was where Jobs belonged. As his story progresses we will see that he is only happy and productive when he is in this kind of environment. He just didn't know it yet, because he was about to become distracted by his own wealth and would soon lead Apple even further away from its Creative Platform and resilience.

1980 – 1984: Complacency and a Divided Apple

In December 1980 Apple underwent an Initial Public Offering (IPO) of stock, and it hit Wall Street like a tidal wave. Within an hour of the offering the coffers of Apple were full and so was Jobs' bank account. Steve Jobs was worth over $200 million. Suddenly the notoriety he had experienced up to this point was eclipsed by worldwide fame. He was only 25 years old and he was as famous as any rock star. This kind of money gave him leverage in all things, from influencing the creativity of the Mac team to his ability to make demands on suppliers, to getting to know celebrities, and he did all of these things.

The culture at Apple was also impacted. Overall, the culture became distracted by this money and began to struggle. However, there was some serious dissention about who did and who did not receive stock options. Bill Fernandez, Randy Wiggington, and Chris Espinosa had been there since the beginning, and were excluded. The list seemed to make no sense, and Jobs got the blame. In contrast to all of this, Steve Wozniak felt compassion toward those who were slighted and started what authors Jeffrey Young and Bill Simon called "The Wozplan". 3 He gave away his own stock options to friends, family and long-time founders like Wiggington and Espinosa. Was this an example of the nice Woz who couldn't say no, or perhaps just his effort to do the right thing? Either way, the episode showed how these extreme riches affected these two men differently.

Plane Crash. Only two months later another event would influence Steve Wozniak and the ability of Apple to maintain its Creative Platform. On February 7, 1981 the small plane Woz was piloting crashed soon after takeoff, injuring him and his three passengers. One of the passengers was his fiancé, Candi Clark. Woz sustained serious face and head injuries and for five weeks lost his ability to store and retrieve new memories. He resigned from Apple, got married to Candi, and eventually enrolled in U.C. Berkeley. In fact, in order to have some anonymity he registered under a pseudonym, Rocky Clark, but his identity was soon discovered. On graduating, he was called, "The student most likely to have succeeded." 7 His creative influence at Apple was now absent. No one could replace Woz.

Bloated Bureaucracy. The popular press began to attack Apple, calling it a bloated bureaucracy and saying that Apple executives acted as if they, rather than the shareholders, were the real owners of the company. 8 So only days after Steve Wozniak's plane crash, Scotty called together a large gathering of Apple employees and told them there would be a layoff. By the end of the day he had eliminated 41 jobs. Once again, the names that were and were not on the list made no sense to most people. This day has since been called "Black Wednesday" at Apple.

It is a shame that Scotty didn't have the wisdom to understand Apple's place on the developmental frame or how to begin the process of moving from Quad 2 back to Quad 1. Executing people does not improve morale or make them more productive. This occurred about 5 months after the Apple III had first shipped, and by this point it was clear this machine was failing financially. So some staffers speculated this could be the rationale for the layoffs. Others thought it was simply the product of office politics. There was an uproar among the employees, and soon Scotty was demoted, then resigned bitterly. He claimed Apple was a culture of "hypocrisy, yes-men, and empire builders." 9

The complacency at Apple is further documented by author Frank Rose who says that the overall tone of executive and staff meetings was harsh. "Unlike the vice-presidents of most American corporations, who are constrained by mortgages and college expenses and hope of advancement from being too forthright about their feelings, these people didn't give a damn what they said. Why should they? Apple had made them rich. Most of them were worth $10 million or more…They could walk away tomorrow and spend the rest of their lives happily managing their investments. So they tended to be frank with each other – often too frank." 10

THE ILL-FATED SHIFT TO A MARKETING PLATFORM

Even worse, Steve Jobs had just wowed the stock market and had come to see himself no longer as the anti-conformist who accidentally succeeded, but rather as an astute and skilled businessman. Scotty had been a good start-up president but he was gone and they needed new leadership.

The Man From Pepsi. Jobs pursued John Sculley, then president of Pepsi-Cola Company. Scully was as different from the Apple culture as could be. He had attended East Coast upper crust schools and his family had lived in Brazil, Bermuda, and Europe. He had received an MBA from the elite Wharton School. He was poised, sophisticated, and skilled in the boardroom. He wore suits and ties, and rode around New York in a limousine. But more than any of this, he was a marketer.

Pepsi, like all soft drink companies, was and still is built on the Marketing Platform. Its products are commodities which are differentiated by their market segmentation and their alluring advertising. Sculley had participated in the long-running Pepsi Generation campaign - If you want to be young, join the Pepsi Generation and drink Pepsi. So Jobs began a crusade to win over John Sculley. The fact that Sculley was not technical and didn't think like a disciple of the Creative Platform didn't seem to matter. To Jobs, he looked like just what Apple needed. At 44, he was older than most of Apple's employees so he would have the experience and courage to fix Apple's internal problems. Best of all, he would have the marketing skills to make their computers, especially the upcoming Mac, household names. So, Steve Jobs asked Sculley the famous question, "Do you want to sell sugar water for the rest of your life, or do you want to change the world?"

John Sculley became president and CEO of Apple in April 1983. In the beginning it was clear that Sculley and Jobs were partners. Inside Apple people noticed their obvious camaraderie and ability to complete each others' sentences. Sculley and Jobs talked privately with each other to discuss strategy and organizational changes, excluding other appropriate input. In a meeting, Sculley exclaimed that he was grateful to have the opportunity to work with a brilliant mind like Jobs. Nothing was said about Woz, who had returned to Apple after his plane crash or any of the other bright contributors. All of this went on while Apple remained strategically too comfortable and while Sculley instinctively operated on a different platform, the Marketing Platform.

Failed Platform. John Sculley operated on a Marketing Platform at Apple from the day he arrived, but neither management nor employees followed. Like all good Marketing Platform mangers, Sculley began to divide customers into segments. Apple had long courted educational users, small business owners, and home users. So under Sculley each was marketed differently and separately. This resulted in high overhead and duplication. The consumer became confused about how to buy differently when each machine seemed the same. We now know the same computer can be used at work, home, and in the classroom; it is the software that makes the difference.

Internally, Apple resisted this shift to the Marketing Platform, because these were creative people who had succeeded by using the Creative Platform. So the internal functions of Apple were incongruent with each other and with the new platform. More importantly, there had been no platform shift in the larger personal computer industry. So in seeking a Marketing Platform, Apple was grossly incongruent with its industry.

QUAD 3: DEGENERATION AND THE LOSS OF RESILIENCE

It seemed that everyone from Tandy to IBM to Timex was making a PC. Some were better and some were worse, but suddenly the market was crowded. At the exact time that Apple was struggling with the Lisa, a shakeout began in the industry. Osborne, a respected industry leader, declared bankruptcy. Texas Instruments lost money. Then, market capitalization for the entire field began to evaporate as Wall Street dumped computer stocks.

It soon became Sculley's embarrassing task to announce the first quarterly loss in Apple's history.

Bad enough, but inside Apple the rumors were rampant. The engineers were not comfortable with Sculley's Madison Avenue approach to their science. Under him, long-standing projects were ignored. It was generally felt that the Lisa was a great machine which had been hung out to dry because of poor execution. Competitors were encroaching on the Apple II and profits were eroding. Many Apple people were wondering how much longer Apple would be in business.

This tale shows just what it takes to put a company in Quad 3, Degeneration. Some companies swing back and forth into profits and then losses without ever moving into Quad 3 or losing resilience. For Apple employees, it was a matter of contrast. They had been so comfortable, so smug, and so confident that the world would beat a path to their door that this quarterly loss on top of a failed Apple III and a failing Lisa was all it took to shock them into a panic. How could this happen to them?

The Famous 1984 Ad. What did Steve Jobs and John Sculley do with the fact that their company was falling into Quad 3 Degeneration and losing resilience? There was a moment of pause. This was the calm before the storm, and a momentary sense of disbelief. Then what? Like so many leaders, they did the wrong thing. They did more of the exact things that got them into this mess. They pursued their Marketing Platform ever more intensely. They prepared to launch the Macintosh, using a TV commercial that was so intense and so memorable, that it is now one of the most famous ads in the history of advertising. It was shown as a paid advertisement only once, during the Super Bowl in January 1984. Then news stations and TV talk shows showed it for free everywhere else. It showed a dark dungeon-like room with masses of oppressed-looking people. In the front of the room was a giant screen displaying the face of a man with a frightening scowl. A brightly clad attractive woman in a running outfit then ran forward and threw a sledgehammer at the screen which shattered into pieces. Then there was a voiceover and script on the TV which said, "On January 24th Apple will introduce Macintosh. And you'll understand why 1984 won't be like 1984." The implication was that Apple would be taking on Big Brother, which was Big Blue, IBM.

It is a shame the initial focus of the Macintosh was this strange TV commercial and its attack on IBM. The Mac was an amazing new computer built on a Creative Platform by brilliantly creative people. Since its inception it has survived as one of the icons of personal computing and it still exists today. In 1984 it had an advanced processor, running at 8 MHz, fast for its day, and came with Mac Write and Mac Paint, both ahead of their time for word processing and color graphics. It had a mouse. And best of all, it had the Graphic User Interface (GUI), those little icons on the screen that we all use today. Simply drag, click, and enter the programs. It was the prototype of today's personal computers and it made computers easy for the general public. The history of technology will show that the Macintosh was the single machine that had the biggest impact on our daily use of computers. It is a shame no one would have been able to tell this from Apple's advertising. The Marketing Platform was dominating Apple, but it was marketing its attack on IBM rather than the features of its wonderful computer.

More Decline. About three months after Mac's successful launch, sales began to fall. A more seasoned company might have been patient in supporting a new product, but Jobs' grandiosity had gotten the best of him, and published reports now indicate he had predicted sales somewhere between 425,000 and 500,000 Macs the first year. [11, 12] This would have been $1billion in revenue from the Macintosh alone. It just didn't happen. There were problems with the original Mac. It needed more memory, did not have a hard drive, was not expandable, and there were few software programs available. This was all resolved nicely with the Macintosh Plus in 1986, but that was too late. A serious resilience crisis developed in 1984 and 1985.

Because of Jobs and Sculley's grand predictions of Mac's sales, a huge organization was created. A state-of-the-art manufacturing facility in Freemont California, which was intended to handle high volume production was also built. Instead, it had to be shut down several times when its "Just in Time" suppliers sent defective parts. Retailers became afraid they would be unable to get Macs. Then, when sales cooled, the plant kept producing machines and generated a huge oversupply of inventory.

Apple's competitive field had changed quickly. The industry shakeout had left too many competitors standing, and as often happens, it simply had brought pain to the field. Apple was still surrounded by competent rivals, and it was losing the fight it had picked with IBM. Apple was squarely in Quad 3, Degeneration and resilience was eroding fast.

Internal Struggles. Internally, the entire Apple organization looked just like a firm in Degeneration. It was buzzing with rumors and a need to blame. Who would be the first candidate to receive this blame? Who had put himself up as a poster child for Apple and the entire personal computer movement? Who had been impossibly demanding, uncompromising, and irritating? Steve Jobs. The blame became focused directly on him. In addition, as predicted in Chapter 6, there was a pervasive desire to return to the good old days. Oddly, this desire existed among long timers as well as those who were not present in the old days, and good people were resigning to go to work for competitors.

By this time there was open tension between Mac people and the Apple II group. Historically, the II had developed a strong line of computers, each generation an improvement on the previous. It was the single steady source of revenue for the company, and it was II money that had supported all of the failed new products. However, Apple II computers did not have the icons nor was there a mouse to drag and click. Users had to give it commands in linear code. So, when the Mac arrived, the II group naturally felt upstaged and threatened.

Apple put together a big-event rally at the Moscone Center in San Francisco which was followed by heavy use of TV and magazine ads as part of a $15 million campaign. John Sculley took the stage. His speech marked a turning point in the competitive platform of Apple. Despite the wonderfully creative achievements of the Macintosh and the new Apple IIc, Sculley's focus was solely on the Marketing Platform. In his speech, he said that marketing is what Apple is all about. He said, "Apple is going to become not just a great product company, but a great marketing company. McDonald's and Burger King are great marketing companies in their industry, just as Pepsi and Coke are in theirs. The Apple challenge is built on firm foundations – that product innovation and marketing innovation can play a major role in shaping this dynamic growth industry. If we are right – and we believe we are – Silicon Valley will never again be the same." 13

In retrospect, we now know how wrong he was. Apple should not have been viewed as similar to McDonald's, Burger King, Pepsi, or Coke. Those companies were impressively competent at the Marketing

Platform, and champions of commodity products. Apple had done well as a start-up because it was so purely Creative Platform. Now it was losing its way. The more lost it became, the more Sculley pushed the Marketing Platform, and the further it moved away from a state of resilience.

The Loss of Wozniak. This was followed by a very public insult. The annual stockholders' meeting in January 1985 was once again a big event. However, its focus was the Macintosh and the continued image-making of Steve Jobs. Sculley offered no praise or support for the Apple IIc, the II team, or Steve Wozniak. This was the breadwinner for the company and now it was being publicly pushed aside. Not only was Woz hurt, but so was the II team. He began to think about resigning from Apple.

In February 1985 Steve Jobs and Steve Wozniak went to the White House to receive the National Medal of Technology from President Ronald Regan, along with America's most brilliant scientists and engineering pioneers. Imagine how odd it must have seemed for both Steve's to receive this award, knowing that their company was in Quad 3 Degeneration, so many of Apple's most recent products had been cancelled or were struggling, and their personal relationship with each other had declined.

A grim milestone occurred in February 1985 when Steve Wozniak resigned from Apple. This was different from the resignation he had tendered after his plane crash. That was obviously for personal reasons and Apple was ridiculously prosperous at the time, so that resignation didn't hurt Apple or Steve Jobs. This 1985 resignation was calling it "quits". This one did not bode well for Apple. After having been slighted at the January meeting, Woz knew that he had been discarded and he was not capable of watching himself or his engineers continue to suffer as a result of all of this. This did not bode well for Jobs either. Here was his cofounder resigning out of frustration. From the beginning, they both knew that their paths at Apple had diverged. Woz was a brilliant technician, but for some time he had been unhappy with how far the Apple II team had been pushed aside. And now, rightly or wrongly, Woz openly criticized all of this to a Wall Street Journal reporter and then he resigned. 14, 15

CHARACTERISTICS OF APPLE'S
QUAD 3 DEGENERATION

Defining Characteristics: Apple was collection of creative people who had a Marketing Platform superimposed on them. It wasn't working.

Relationship with Money: Like most Marketing Platform companies, Apple had entered the media business. It even had placed one of the most expensive ads in history, the Super Bowl ad.

Motive: Apple seemed motivated to embarrass IBM.

Growth Method: Apple was failing to teach members of various market segments about how each product meets their needs, then patiently support those products for a long time.

Relationship with Customers: As a result of Apple's ill-defined place in the market, its customers were confused.

Relationship with Suppliers: Apple was still a new company and a series of suppliers came and went. New initiatives, like the just-in-time program for Macintosh production did not go smoothly.

Technology: Apple's technology was still impressive. Woz was patiently advancing the II family. Macintosh was the first large-scale commercially available use of the Graphic User Interface.

Platform: When Apple was in Quad 1 and Quad 2, marketing was quite secondary to creative technology. Now this was reversed.

Culture: Squabbles were attributed to power struggles, but internal groups were actually pursuing different platforms. So the culture became fragmented, depressed, and anxious. Were the Marketing gurus the new heroes of this culture or were the creatives still the heroes?

Strategy: Apple had done well when it was simply the most creative group around. Now it was taking on IBM. Later this would be replayed with Apple versus Microsoft. Apple needed to just focus on producing cool, exciting, creative, artistic, fun, products that would be easy to use.

Congruence: Congruence had been lost. It was now a Marketing Platform company, but the employees were creative people and the products were innovative. It was in Quad 3 Degeneration, despite launching some wonderful new products. The culture was ill-defined and discouraged, and the strategy seemed to be that Apple is an opponent of big players. Apple was no longer in a state of resilience.

MUTINY

Woz' resignation was more than just the loss of a brilliant man. Woz had been the symbolic icon of the Creative Platform at Apple. Every culture has heroes that personify its values, beliefs and assumptions. With Sculley dialing up Marketing Platform and dialing down Creative Platform, Woz' departure was the symbolic representation of the loss of the Creative Platform at Apple. The platform had shifted.

Blaming. The blaming and finger-pointing now focused on Jobs and Sculley. Most employees blamed the guy who seemed to be taking too much credit for the achievements of Apple, Steve Jobs. Some believed he was too demanding and overly focused on every machine's appearance. But Jobs had a different interpretation of the problems. According to him, the trouble was Sculley. Sculley was a failed leader who allowed factions and subgroups to squabble and to refuse to cooperate. Sculley needed to take control, and he wasn't doing it. Meanwhile, Sculley was becoming openly frustrated with Jobs and excluding him on major decisions. It is a shame that no one attributed the Quad 3 Degeneration to their inappropriate advertising focus, poor execution, products cannibalizing each other, loss of Creative Platform, and an inappropriate effort to turn Apple into a Marketing Platform company. So, they blamed Jobs and Sculley, who blamed each other.

Exiling Steve Jobs. Then, while at a retreat for the executive staff in 1985, Mike Murray, the Marketing VP, Regis McKenna, and Sculley had a meeting of their own. It has been said that Jobs saw them going off to their meeting and asked to be included. Their answer was, no. This was a very odd thing. He was the cofounder and Chairman of Apple. But even more, he had recruited each of them and they were his friends. They had shared all of the joy and pain of these years together. He knew their wives and families. The four of them were the inner circle at Apple. The purpose of the secret meeting was to discuss removing Steve as the head of the Macintosh Division. Then, in a Board of Directors meeting in April 1985, with Jobs present, John Sculley proposed that Steve be removed from the Macintosh Division. The board actually asked Jobs to step out of the room so they could discuss it. Steve was the target of a mutiny.

Sometimes the best defense is a good offense, so Jobs began to organize a mutiny of his own. He networked among Apple managers to strengthen his position and to seek the removal of Sculley. Wisely, Sculley chose to network among board members. These were very emotional times, and the palace intrigue was intense. There were tears, mixed with fear and panic. Every key player was asked to openly declare loyalty to one or the other. Jobs hoped to go to the board with a plan and the support of the masses. But he did not get much real support and in the end the board would not be persuaded. They viewed Jobs as a motivational leader and a visionary, but poor at operations and execution. On May 31, 1985 the board met and decided they would allow him to remain at Apple, but he would have no operational role in the company. He was to do nothing. They gave him an office in a remote building all by himself that he called Siberia. At first no one even went to visit him there. Eventually Mike Murray spent some time with Jobs at his new outpost, but there was nothing to do. No reports, plans, updates or financials were sent to Jobs. Nothing. So, on September 17, 1985 he resigned.

THE SCULLEY ERA

Mutinies never produce the happy new chapter that is sought. Under Sculley, Apple failed to thrive. He never returned Apple to a Creative Platform, and simply strengthened the Marketing Platform model during his tenure. He further divided his customer-base into smaller and smaller segments, resulting in a proliferation of categories, each with its own cost structure. Of course, the computers he attempted to sell to these segments offered little difference from one another. Customers remained confused about which one to buy, or whether to buy an Apple at all.

More than any of this, Sculley's place in the history of the personal computer field has to do with a disgraceful strategic blunder. A little known fact is that Microsoft had helped with Macintosh's development. Bill Gates understood the events happening at Apple, and he had a keen eye on where the field was going. So after Jobs was defeated by Sculley, Gates persuaded Sculley to license the coveted Macintosh Graphic User Interface (GUI) to Microsoft in exchange for Microsoft's continued support of the Mac. From that point on, Microsoft had the GUI and the ability to supply it to any computer maker that Microsoft supplied with software. Due to a loss of its own Creative Platform, and a marketing rather than creative emphasis, Sculley was blind to the value of this treasure. He gave away Apple's greatest competitive advantage. Sculley was removed from his post by the board in 1993 with Apple still lacking both congruence and resilience.

JOBS GAINS WISDOM AT NEXT

After he left Apple, Jobs started NeXT Computer. He smartly observed two things. First, PostScript language was new and exciting, so he developed a very convenient PostScript display. Second, object-oriented programming (OOP) was now good enough to be marketable, so he created an object-oriented toolkit. This object-oriented programming was remarkable because it created clusters, or objects, inside the software program, each relating to its own type of data. Objects could send messages to other objects. Using these objects, programmers could manipulate self-contained modules without rewriting all of the code line by line. This made programs more flexible and easier to tailor to big and unique problems. It would make his product customizable. Using it, he could further pursue a Creative Platform and sell to scientists, research labs and universities.

He developed the NeXT Cube and called it a supercomputer. It had a huge (for that time) 8 MB of RAM, a powerful 33 MHz Motorola processor, e-mail graphics, Ethernet, a built-in synthesizer, and a display that was bigger and had more clarity than the competition. He thought the new wave would be computers that had no hard drive, so he didn't include one. Instead he used a Cannon Magneto-Optical Drive. All of this made the NeXT Cube a showstopper. It was reviewed favorably by the technical industry and it gave NeXT and Jobs renewed credibility. NeXT was a growing company, but not a resilient one.

Overreaching. Steve Jobs had still not gained the wisdom he needed. For him, some of his greatest personal strengths seemed to go too far and tended to become weaknesses. This began to happen again. His deepest passion was for perfection in design. So he made the NeXT Cube look futuristic and put it in a laser-cut magnesium case. Simply, the elaborate cosmetics made the computer too expensive. Then came more bad news. The cube's massive software programs made the original computer irritatingly slow. The drive was unreliable at first, thus temporarily eroding NeXT's reputation. So, by trying too hard to be different, Jobs had created the NeXT Cube's own shortcomings.

Looking Inside the Box. As this story unfolded, however, Jobs was able to take a detached and objective look at his product. He began to see that the real treasures were hiding inside the boxes. This insight came from two places: First, the customizable programming made available by the OOP. This made the computer a hit. The scientist customers loved it. They could write their own programs in relatively few lines and fine tune their applications. Tim Berners-Lee was working on development of the World Wide Web at that time. He used the NeXT Cube as the first web server.

When asked why he didn't use a different computer, he said it would be like trading in your sports car for a truck.

The second insight was that the NeXTSTEP® operating system was the most valuable asset this company owned. In all the excitement about the new computer (the box), the market power of the underlying operating system had been overlooked. Jobs began to see that the real source of creativity was the software and the operating system. In 1993 the company produced its last machine. That year he changed the name to NeXT Software Inc.

NeXT Software Inc. ushered in an era of prolific creativity which further developed all of NeXT's software, created applications, and allowed customers to use the software on Microsoft products. He was in the business of selling software and an operating system instead of a "closed systems" box. His firm was able to maintain unimpressive but steady profits. Clearly, after trying a lot of things and learning from the market, Steve Jobs was nicely placed deep in the Creative Platform once again.

As it turned out, all of the struggles during his days at NeXT turned out to be an important part of gaining a Resilience Builder's wisdom for Steve Jobs. He had learned how to maintain a firm in Quad 1 Growth in a rapidly changing marketplace. He had become a competent manager of creative people and processes. He had come a long way.

THE CREATIVE INFLUENCE OF PIXAR

There was a second story line that went on during the same time as NeXT. In 1986 Jobs bought Pixar Animation Studios. Pixar could best be described as a meteor that hit Jobs so hard it altered the trajectory of his life. Before Pixar, he was already a creative person, but Pixar's standards of creativity were about to give him some real clarity.

The development of Pixar's Creative Platform began in the 1970's when Ed Catmull was at the computer sciences department at the University of Utah where he and others were pioneering computer graphics. He made advances in texture mapping and helped to develop a method called Z-buffering. His advances allowed computers to achieve 3D effects by determining which surfaces were behind an object and therefore needed to be moved, hidden, or shaded when a forward object moved in a scene. The computer was said to "render" an image, and the process became known as rendering. From the beginning, Catmull was both technical and creative.

Star Wars. In 1979 George Lucas invited Catmull's group to move from New York to California to work on his Star Wars movies as part of Lucasfilm. He gave them enormous money, unfettered freedom, and wonderful opportunities to develop their creative skills. There, Catmull developed a small group of powerfully talented artists and computer graphics animators. Surprisingly, these exciting advances were largely unnoticed by companies who sold computers to the public, like Apple.

So when Steve Jobs walked into the computer graphics division of Lucasfilm in 1985 he had an experience similar to the one he had experienced at Xerox PARC. The advanced creativity and abilities of this special effects and animation group were astounding. He had discovered something that could have great application but was being overlooked by the larger markets. The department at Lucasfilm was a small group that was somehow akin to Jobs himself, wearing blue jeans, sweat shirts, and keeping odd hours. The more he learned about them, the more he discovered that he was in the presence of artisans who had a deep passion for what they were doing. This was a culture and climate he could understand and love.

This time Jobs did not go home and try to replicate what he had seen, as he had done after the Xerox PARC experience. He didn't have to. George Lucas put the division up for sale, and in 1986 Jobs bought it for $10 Million. This was one-third the asking price, and Jobs' ability to wait for the best terms and price revealed that he had reached a new level of professional development. He named the new company Pixar, or Pixar Animation Studios.

Pixar was different. It was pure Creative Platform. At first the people there didn't even know how to sell their services to the market. They were an in-house department of a successful movie studio, so there was no need to sell. Then they did some computer animated TV commercials, but the entrepreneurial piece of this group was low. They just created artistic stuff. And Steve Jobs was different now; growing in wisdom. He let Pixar be the creative enterprise it needed to be.

Lessons Learned. One thing was eerily the same as at Apple. John Lasseter had worked there since 1984 and was the creative genius who was able to make the animated figures seem so life-like. John Lasseter was his new Woz. He understood both the technology and the content of the animation. Even today, Lasseter is a legend in this field, because of what he accomplished early on with some very primitive tools.

Jobs could have turned the group upside down and insisted they do all of their work his way, but this time he didn't. He could have outshone Lasseter as happened with Woz, but not this time. Not only has Lasseter been remarkably productive, but despite many outside job offers, he remains at Pixar today. Jobs had learned from the pain of the past. Rather than steer the Creative Platform, he supported it.

Jobs wisely sought a cash cow to sustain Pixar as the Apple II had done for so many years. However, he still had some strategy lessons to learn. On his arrival, he attempted to put all of this good technology into a big computer and sell the imaging capabilities to whoever would take it. He was still trying to sell the computer as a machine and he was still focused on pushing his technology at the customer. He targeted the medical community with the Pixar Image Computer or PIC, but it was expensive, difficult to use, and too far ahead of its time. It sold poorly and it was out of step with the Pixar crew. This was not a watered-down version of Apple. These people were interested first in their special effects software and secondly in the hardware. Little did Jobs know the cash cow was sitting right under his nose; or perhaps right inside the machine.

Pixar's talented programmers had developed their own rendering program, called REYES, or "Renders Everything You Ever Saw". Under Steve Jobs this software became a marketable product and Pixar began licensing it to other studios under the name, RenderMan®. In traditional Jobs fashion, it was delightfully user-friendly (to the skilled technicians who do animation computer graphics), created the next step up in technology, and it was very popular. It allowed for special effects far beyond anyone's wildest imagination, and it sold its 100,000th copy in 1995. Jobs had found his cash cow. He was applying many lessons learned from his long journey, and all of this allowed congruence between Pixar's culture, Creative Platform and its strategic move away from hardware toward its software products.

Toy Story. Pixar's artists could not be happy living on software alone. Pixar needed to continue to pursue its own animation projects, beyond the shorts and the commercials it was making. So, in a multi-picture joint project with Disney in which Disney paid all of the production costs and provided the distribution channels, they released Toy Story in 1995, featuring Tom Hanks as Woody and Tim Allen as Buzz Lightyear. This was a work of art, joy, and perfection, and, the man behind the perfection was John

Lasseter. He made sure objects blurred as they moved faster, softened the crisp lines that the edges of objects have in traditional animation, changed colors as objects' surfaces curved, and he even ensured that the sketches of doors and baseboards had scuff marks. The technology behind this was massive. Completed scenes were sent to Pixar's "render farm" of 117 Sun Microsystems servers to be transformed into photo-like animation. One frame might take as long as 20 hours to render. 16

The creative result was a cartoon that looked like a real movie. The business result was a blockbuster; it was the most successful film in 1995 even though it was released on Thanksgiving. It grossed $362 million in six weeks. The professional community recognized this team's great work on Toy Story with a Special Achievement Oscar for John Lasseter, An Academy Award for four members of the scientific and engineering team, and two Golden Globe nominations. But the best praise of all came from the fact that the public was amazed and delighted with the wonderful creativity of these skilled animators and programmers.

There were two other things going on behind the scenes that allowed all of this success. The first was a Pixar software program called RingMaster®, used for tracking creative schedules, coordination of project milestones, interaction of teams, and timelines. In RingMaster, Pixar had learned how to get all participants talking to each other. And, in RingMaster, Steve Jobs had learned how to operationalize these creative processes without the loss of control, rush-to-deadline and ego crushing that had been known at Apple. The second thing behind the scenes was pure Lasseter. He developed Pixar University where every animator had to learn the creative doctrine of Pixar. He even included acting lessons so the technicians could put themselves in the place of their subjects. Clearly, he wanted artists, not just technicians. This was the Creative Platform at its best.

Flawless Hits. The result of all of this has been magnificent. Pixar has flawlessly created one hit after another. To date, its productions have generated more than $3.5 billion. This has moved it from Quad 1 to Quad 2 on the developmental frame. Pixar adapted well to this frame shift. Its greatest growth spurt happened when it moved quickly from a staff of about 40 people when Jobs arrived to 375 in 1997 and 600 in 2001.

So impressive was Pixar's performance that in 2006 Disney bought it from Jobs for 7.4 billion. And to sweeten this great offer, Disney gave Steve Jobs a seat on its board of directors.

Steve Jobs had learned how to deftly protect his Creative Platform. He learned how to shepherd his group through the stages of the developmental frame without injuring the organization. He learned how to interact with a creative culture in ways that allowed each person a little more creativity. And he learned to stop pushing his hardware onto an audience that might or might not want it, but rather he let his customers define his strategy. Steve Jobs had learned the subtle nuances of how to establish congruence between platform, frame, culture and strategy.

QUAD 4: JOBS' TRIUMPHANT RETURN TO APPLE

In 1996 Steve Jobs was still at both Pixar and NeXT. Pixar was setting box office records with Toy Story and selling its RenderMan® software. It was ablaze with success, recognition, and pride. Profits at NeXT, however, remained modest.

Back at Apple, new CEO, Gill Amelio, was the captain of a sinking ship. Apple had lost its self-declared wars with IBM and Microsoft. During this time the entire computer industry was experiencing steady 15% quarter after quarter growth, but Apple's revenues were declining. During fiscal 1996 Apple had $9.8 billion in sales, which was an 11% decline from the year earlier. Its product line was stagnant and unexciting. Its recent efforts to build a new operating system had ended in failure, and Amelio knew that the only thing that could revive Apple would be a new and viable operating system. NeXT had just such an operating system. So Amelio went to visit Steve Jobs in December 1996. Not only did Amelio offer to buy the NeXT corporation, but he also wanted Jobs to return to Apple and resurrect the enthusiasm and vitality he had once given it. So, Jobs sold NeXT to Apple for $400 million and in 1997 he returned as leader of the company he had founded so long ago. He also remained CEO of Pixar.

Frozen in Time. The Apple Steve Jobs returned to was somehow frozen in time. While he had gone on an amazing voyage of his own during the eleven years since his departure, it was as if Apple had not moved at all. It was still stuck in Quad 3, Degeneration. Its Platform was poorly defined as it tried to be a Marketing Platform company in a Creative Platform industry. The culture had eroded at all three levels. There was no foundation built at the Constitutional Component level of culture, since Apple had chosen the wrong competitive platform. The second level of culture, Value Component, failed to materialize as programmers and engineers struggled to be creative, unsupported by the senior management group. And the third level of culture, Interpersonal Component, could best be described as demoralized and discouraged. Finally, Apple's strategy had produced a series of boring tagalongs like the Mac Plus, and the Mac 2 as well as some flops like the Newton and the original Powerbook.

It was clear that Jobs needed to be a Resilience Builder here. He had to move the company through a Quad 4 Conversion and then a Return to Growth. Apple needed a Hope Bearing Plan. Jobs needed to look at the four possible platforms and decide which one should be his primary platform and which of the others to dial up and which to dial down. He needed to define the organization around the primary platform. It was time to rebuild the culture around the platform and frame. Most important, all of these factors needed to intersect with strategy in a way that pleased the end-user. He needed to do every one of these things.

Strange as it might seem, now Jobs was prepared to do all of these resilience building steps because he had been kicked out of an ailing Apple eleven years earlier. His successes and failures at NeXT had prepared him to respond well here. His deep plunge into the Creative Platform at Pixar was an excellent education in the power of a clear platform. The lessons learned from early Apple taught him that he was a great campaigner. He was a great motivator. He was brash enough to think he could do anything, and to demand everything from his team. He knew what congruence felt like at his early Apple days as well as NeXT and Pixar. But he had learned other things at Apple, like the fact that Degeneration is not just bad luck, it is the product of making the wrong moves. He knew what it was like to build a strong culture and then watch it erode because of a confused platform. He learned at NeXT that consumers would give him clues and he must let them lead him (e.g., away from hardware to software). He also learned at NeXT that there must be a balance between attractive design and cost (e.g., the magnesium cube). So, this was an older and more seasoned Steve Jobs. His journey had tempered him and taught him well. He had gained the wisdom of the Resilience Builder.

Hope Bearing Plan. Jobs' return was greeted with crazed enthusiasm among the employees at Apple, even those who had never met or worked for him. He was just what they needed and they knew it. His Hope Bearing Plan was more than just two words, "I'm back." In fact, the Hope Bearing Plan he outlined had three elements. First, Apple would make cool stuff (and therefore once again be the Creative Platform company it was born to be). Second, it would introduce products ahead of the competition. And third, it would be efficient in its manufacturing operations.

Resurrecting the Creative Platform. Jobs' plan met the needs of platform, frame, culture and strategy. With some humility, he did not guarantee instant recovery. In fact, he predicted that establishing a healthy and sustainable recovery would take about two years. So, he began where any Resilience Builder would begin, with platform. Apple's Creative Platform had been lost and had to be reestablished. He had learned how to operationalize the creative processes at Pixar, and he put this to work here. He started with the computers themselves by creating the most eye-catching easy-to-use machines in the business, and he wasted no time. The iMac was introduced in 1998 as a low cost computer that made the Internet easy and it came in a revolutionary "Bondi Blue see-through case. The PowerMac G4 Cube (yes, a cube again) was introduced in 2000. It had an 8x8x8 inch computer, Harmon-Kardon baseball sized speakers, a slot on top of the cube for CDs or DVDs that worked like a toaster, an optical mouse, the best graphics in the business, and plenty of power. Because of its elegant design this computer was placed in New York's Museum of Modern Art in 2001.

He introduced the iLife suite free with every Mac that included the iMovie video editing program to make home movies, iDVD for recording movies and slide shows, iPhoto for making and editing pictures, the GarageBand music mixing package, and iTunes for downloading music. In addition, Apple's computers were no longer seen as permanent products. The iMac was first released in August 1998, quickly revised with 5 new colors in January 1999, and then further revised in April 1999 with a bigger processor. The iMac was to be a sequential family of computers. The same was true of the PowerMac line which underwent continuous revisions. So under Jobs, the Creative Platform was dialed up, way up.

Then he considered the Marketing Platform element. Under John Sculley, Apple had been marketed like a soft drink. He began marketing less like a Madison Avenue marketer and more like the Creative Platform Silicon Valley promoter that he is. No longer would the world be divided into a long list of market segments. Apple's brand identity would be as a smaller firm that made cooled stuff. The advertising campaign, "Think Different" was installed, and included pictures of Einstein and Picasso. This placed Apple in the great strategic posture of not competing on the same terms as Microsoft, Dell, Compaq, or Hewlett Packard. It was different.

It was creative. It was artistic. When asked why he was not pursuing the corporate PC market, he said that big companies wanted cheap PCs rather than innovative computers with creative features. He knew the only corporate markets for Apple would be artists, graphic designers and advertisers. Under Jobs, the Marketing Platform was dialed down to an appropriate level, and it revealed Apple's unique artistic personality.

Little needed to be done with the Relationship Platform at Apple. Wisely, Jobs stayed out of consulting while all of its rivals including highly efficient Dell Computer wandered in. His competitors saw the profits IBM was making from its consulting arm and tried to imitate. Few had any success. Jobs had overreached platform before and wasn't about to do so now. He had learned. Relationship Platform was dialed down to a minimal level.

Dialing up the Efficient Platform. Then there was the Efficient Platform component. Because of its unrestrained spending habits, Apple had been known as the least efficient of the major PC producers. Most manufacturing was still in-house, suppliers preyed on the company, and distributors were uncontrolled. It was time to run Apple like a business. So Jobs dialed up the Efficient Platform component for the first time in Apple's history. Recall from Chapter 4 that when Resilience Builders select a strong Platform, they sometimes pick certain internal functions to operate on a different platform. Jobs picked manufacturing, purchasing, sales, and distribution to operate on the Efficient Platform. He also put them on the same two year turnaround time.

The result? Jobs reduced overall expenses from $8.1 billion in 1997 to $5.7 billion in 1999. He outsourced half of manufacturing, created a web store to sell Apples, and cut his confusing array of distributors down to only two. When he arrived in 1997, there were 15 separate product lines, each uniquely designed and manufactured. He reduced these to only a few, and they all shared the same technology. This caused an immediate 15% loss of revenues, but gave the company a smaller menu of products to rebuild. In 1997 Apple had 70 days of inventory under its roofs. By 1998 this was down to 30 days. Then he said he wanted to be more efficient than Dell. So, Apple cut its suppliers down to only a handful and had them set up shop next to manufacturing. This cut inventories on hand down to less than a day. The point of all of this was simple. Apple could no longer allow its noncreative components to behave like its creative components.

By doing all of this, he dialed up the Efficient Platform, but only where it was appropriate to do so.

Culture and Strategy. All of this created a culture shift. This shift developed at the same pace as the Quad 4 Conversion, which lasted from 1997 to 1999. In 1997 the culture had consisted of a group of discouraged and lost people, operating at survival-level. Remember that they had had their mutiny in 1985 when Jobs was ejected. Since then, financial improvements were brief and fleeting. Nothing Apple had tried had worked. It was being outdone by Microsoft and the PC behemoths of IBM, Hewlett Packard, Dell and even Gateway. The Quad 4 Conversion had to do with the three elements of the Hope Bearing Plan. First, Apple would make creative and cool stuff. Second, it would lead the technology rather than follow the competition. And third, it would have efficient manufacturing. By 1999 the Quad 4 Conversion had occurred and the culture was shifting. By that time, the spoken and unspoken norms of this culture required the same creativity, performance, and efficiency that formed the Hope Bearing Plan. This established an unusual collection of culture heroes, like designer Jonathan Ive, responsible for the configuration that added color and light to the iMac, and Tim Cook, whom Apple recruited from highly efficient Compaq to streamline purchasing and the entire supply chain. The culture offered clear second level values to guide daily work and collaboration, and this success supported a more positive third level interpersonal environment. Apple's culture was productive, creative, positive, and healthy.

Strategy became an obsession at Quad 4 Apple. Jobs knew Apple had long pursued a failed strategy of taking on the giants. He knew this because he was the one who had initiated it in the beginning. In 1997 Apple was failing at its attempt to be "Microsoft Junior". Apple had to stop trying to be all things to all computer users and focus. Surprisingly, to accomplish this, he asked for help from rival Bill Gates. He asked him to continue supplying Internet Explorer and Microsoft code to the Macintosh line so Apple could be compatible with other Windows users. He looked at the Microsoft help as a temporary way to keep cash flowing while he went back to the drawing board on his own products. Contrary to expectations, Apple did not expand research and development, but cut R&D spending from about $600 million in 1997 to about $300 million in 1999, and discontinued work on all irrelevant projects. Instead, all R&D was to focus on products or product improvements due within one year. The strategy was to focus on what Apple did best, a friendly user interface, making the Internet easier, and allowing personal creativity like graphics, iLife and iMovies. The remarkable iPod was launched in 2001 and the iPhone in 2007. All of this was consistent with Jobs' efforts to convert Apple to an organization of true believers in the Creative Platform. [17]

Return to Growth

The results of Jobs' Resilience Building move through Quad 4 Conversion has produced what the Wall Street Journal called a striking revival. Its January 13, 2005 article heaped accolades on Jobs and Apple as it more than quadrupled its earnings that quarter, compared with a year earlier. [18] The Return to Growth did not stop there. Apple has continued its stunning revenue growth quarter after quarter since. Looking at the bigger picture provides an even more breathtaking view. When Jobs was invited back to Apple in 1996 its stock was selling at $5.21. Today it hovers around $140. Revenues have risen from $9.8 billion to $33.7 billion. Best of all Apple has a strong culture, thrilling new products and a sense of identity and pride.

Building True Resilience

At this time Apple is in a state of resilience. This is not the accidental resilience of the early 1980's. Steve Jobs has gained the wisdom needed to manage all four essential elements of resilience. This is true resilience. Being in a state of resilience gives this company enhanced ability to withstand or tolerate shocks to its economic and internal systems. It aligns internal and external interactions to enhance adaptability, and in doing so it renders tremendous value to the organization. But it is never time to rest. Just when iPod sales had seemed to peak in March 2005, BusinessWeek said Apple might have a six month competitive advantage. [19] Seven months later Apple announced video iPod and a new video/TV compatible remote controlled iMac. In 2009 technical reviewers wowed the latest version of the iPhone and said it will once again dominate the market. [20] That same year Apple's iPhone became so popular that this firm announced it was having difficulty making them fast enough to fill all of its orders.

Apple Wisdom

I can think of no story that better exemplifies the power of choosing the right competitive platform, the destruction of prosperity caused by its loss, and the value of its recovery better than Apple. Here we saw Steve Jobs build accidental resilience, lose that resilience, and then build true resilience; all in a short time.

As I write this, controversy abounds regarding Job's overall health and recent liver transplant. The question is asked repeatedly, "What will Apple do if it loses Steve Jobs?" The answer depends on how well he has indoctrinated his firm on the Creative Platform and how well Apple will continue to dial up or down the other competitive platforms. It depends on how well he has trained his successors regarding Apple's place on all four of the essential elements of resilience.

Job has chosen a difficult platform to maintain. It requires running at full speed, anticipating consumer desires, as well as being able to invent and produce the next technology ahead of the competition. It is easy to falter at any one of these steps. But now Jobs knows what makes his company great and he does these things on purpose. He has gained the wisdom of a Resilience Builder.

CHAPTER 10

STRATEGY AND RESILIENCE

The most compelling challenge facing the Resilience Builder today is finding and proficiently executing a strategy that will give the firm the ability to sustain growth despite the inevitable shocks it will experience. All of the economic and strategic theories that have stood the test of time are as sound today as they were the day they were written. There is an invisible hand guiding the markets, as Adam Smith proposed more than 200 years ago. 1 Joseph Schumpeter correctly theorized that industry structures shift over time, with incumbents being ousted by entrepreneurs through the process of creative destruction. 2 And, the crown jewel of resilient strategy is to create an organization that has the ability to offer products and services that are so distinct, they give the firm what Michael Porter called a sustainable competitive advantage. 3 Successfully navigating the pathways these founding fathers prescribed was once all that was necessary to establish a resilient strategy. Today they are necessary, but not sufficient. That's because the requirements of resilient strategy have changed.

Not long ago successful firms were surrounded by many layers of safety and once they established a winning strategy they had the ability to exercise great influence over their own markets. In contrast, now abrupt start-ups routinely become instantly huge. Because they are new ventures, they are nimble and impressively adaptive to the requirements of every new market. What was once called the incumbent's advantage could now be called the incumbent's disadvantage.

Until recently every business knew its competitors, and its competitors' strategies. Not so today, because now strategic competition can come from anywhere. Competitors located across the globe affect even companies that intend to stay local or regional. Firms that attempt to go global must learn how to align the core competencies of their outsourced partners with those of their own organizations.

An increase in buyer power has made it ever more difficult to choose a resilient strategy. Using digitally supplied information, consumers easily compare products and services across companies. Price, scope, and quality differences are neither hidden nor proprietary. This has created a much steeper competitive landscape and has eroded resilience for many firms. In addition, the process of disintermediation is in full swing. Here, consumers can buy directly from manufacturers, eliminating the need for storefronts, wholesalers, distributors or brokers.

Resilient strategy is harder to achieve now because product lifecycles have shortened dramatically. Until recently a company could produce a new product or service while the enterprise was only skilled enough to gain a strategic foothold. The firm would then be allowed enough time to gain mastery of new competencies, abilities, and unique market requirements before being crowded by competition. Now, every new advance is quickly copied or surpassed by very capable competitors and the lifecycle of a competitive advantage is often reduced to months or weeks. For example, in the 1970's JVC's VHS technology beat out Sony's Beta Max and gave JVC a 30 year advantage. In 2008 Sony's Blu-ray Disc triumphed over Toshiba's HD-DVD format. But in today's marketplace we can expect this competitive advantage to be short lived as new digital distribution methods emerge and make the advantage progressively less relevant.

Despite all of this, we find ourselves in the presence of many exciting and robust leaders who know how to choose the right strategy in these new conditions. Today's Resilience Builders understand exactly which strategic responses will create a sturdy enterprise and which will not. Unlike the past, today's Resilience Builders know what they're doing from the very beginning, they are allowed less time to experiment, and they are closely followed by capable competitors. Of course, present-day Resilience Builders begin their work by mastering the essential elements of resilience this book has discussed so far: platform, frame, and culture. Now I address the last essential element of resilience: strategy. Strategy is the final piece of wisdom that separates Resilience Builders from those who are transiently successful.

Resilience Builders Know What Strategy Isn't

In response to today's business challenges, we have seen nearly all enterprises go through a sequence of misplaced strategic efforts which were intended to establish resilience. This collection of efforts has been a series of initiatives, each of which could most honestly be described as giving a business a tune-up. In the 1990's many leaders enthusiastically "re-engineered" their corporations. Usually this meant they reduced headcount by installing the new technologies of the digital age. The net result was more effective firms, but no increase in competitive advantage for any one firm because all competitors did this simultaneously. What followed then was an offshoot of re-engineering, called process improvement. In this trend, a business was divided into distinct sequences of events, called processes. So, order taking, purchasing of raw supplies, manufacturing, and distribution might all be called "order fulfillment". The executive in charge of ensuring the smooth execution of this process was called the "process owner". This reduced barriers between departments and improved efficiency, but it did not render any competitive advantage to the company because, again, everyone was doing it. Add to this the quality movement which included six sigma, total quality management, and continuous improvement. Like re-engineering and process improvement, this gave a temporary advantage to some firms. Eventually all of these methods, including quality, became the required price of admission into every field. All of today's companies are well engineered, all have effective processes, and they all produce goods and services of very high quality. These things are entry requirements. They are not strategic because they do not give one firm an advantage over another, so these things are not sufficient to achieve resilience. They are like standing up at a rock concert. It gives you an advantage as long as the people in front of you don't do the same thing. 4

Creating Resilient Strategy

What creates resilient strategy? The two most common views of strategy can give us insight here. The first occurs when one creates something new which thereby starts a new competitive field. Examples would be the inventions of the telephone, television, air conditioner, or personal computer. In each case, a firm creates demand that did not exist before, and thereby creates a new market. In the early stages of this strategy, we don't even ask where a firm is positioned relative to its competition because there are few if any competitors. This approach relies on what is called "influenceable demand" because the creation of the new product or a significant alteration of an existing product influences the level of demand for that product.

The second concept of strategy is that which occurs within an established competitive field. Here, strategy is best defined as a company's method of producing goods or services that are so distinct from all others that consumers feel compelled to seek them. How this is done can sometimes be complex, but this definition of strategy is simple: growing by being different. Michael Porter's theory offers three ways to be different: be least expensive, be differentiated (high cost and special), or fill a niche. So here one might produce expensive televisions with better color in order to be differentiated and unique, or one could devise a new distribution method, like cable TV in the 1980's which offered 100 channels inexpensively. All of this builds good strategy, but not necessarily resilient strategy.

We already know a lot about the basic fundamentals of what makes good long-term strategy. It is good strategy to understand why your company is successful in the first place, and to strengthen this competitive advantage as days and years pass. It is wise to prepare for the impact of changing tastes as age or ethnic changes gain influence in the market. It is essential to be keenly attuned to technology changes in our world and embrace them. It is good strategy to be a market leader, the first to successfully mass market innovations, skillfully reinvest profits, have a cash reserve war chest in case of an economic downturn, develop a strong talent pool, build a powerful brand image, and establish competency in all of the company's functional areas.

While these things can create good long-term strategy they do not create resilient strategy. Most leaders do well at the above list of strategic and managerial skills, but they are not Resilience Builders.

So, when does good strategy become resilient strategy? What do Resilience Builders do so much better than other leaders? What skills do they have that produce this magic? Their secret is that in order to establish resilient strategy they answer three strategic questions that others either ignore or under-emphasize. These questions are: 1. Is this business planted in fertile ground? 2. Is our collection of strengths hard for others to imitate? 3. How mature is the overall industry? Resilience Builders integrate their answers to these strategic questions with the other three essential elements of resilience: platform, frame and culture.

THE FIRST STRATEGIC QUESTION: IS THIS BUSINESS PLANTED IN FERTILE GROUND?

This question relates to the issue of strategic viability. It is almost always fruitless to enter a failing industry with the intent of simply trying harder or working smarter.

The famous Resilience Builder and oft-times world's wealthiest man, Warren Buffett, has bought and sold many companies during his long career. At this time Berkshire Hathaway owns over 60 companies, but success didn't always come easily for Buffett. He regards his biggest mistake to have been when he bought Berkshire in the first place. It was a struggling textile manufacturing firm in New England, and he believed he could turn it around. There were some very favorable variables, like community support, employees willing to make concessions, and it was a firm with a great old reputation. But, in the years prior to his purchase of this firm, one venerable competitor after another had fallen and Berkshire Hathaway was the last textile firm of its kind still standing in the Northeast. Despite heroic efforts on his part, the company could not compete with low wage manufacturers in the Southeast US and abroad. It lost money and couldn't be revived. Here he gained the wisdom to stay away from businesses and industries that lack fertile ground and do not have strategic viability.

The concept of strategic viability does not address how long a company can last. It addresses how long a strategy can be continued in an industry. This involves some basics of resilience that might seem so simple that they barely deserve mentioning. However, a careful examination of industry conditions and the competitive landscape in any industry today reveals that most businesses would get a grade of C or even lower on their responses to these dimensions. In my own consultations I have observed that many business leaders are so obsessed with daily operations that they forget to examine the question of strategic viability. Of course, no business is perfect at each of these factors, but the higher the grade, the more resilient the strategy. Strategic viability is best understood by three variables: industry health, new industry, and shift in industry structure. Here they are:

Rick Tirrell, Ph.D.

Industry Health. The first resilience question to examine in order to determine strategic viability is whether the business resides in a healthy industry. When Boeing developed the 707 jetliner in 1957, rail companies responded by trying to make their Pullman cars more luxurious. The rail companies' attempt to revert back to earlier glory days destroyed the resilience of their own enterprises. Even being the "last man standing" in an unhealthy industry is not enviable. Look at Amtrak in the U.S., which exists only because it is chronically propped up by the government.

New Industry. Being in a new industry is better than being in an unhealthy one, but Darwinian life-threatening factors challenge resilience here. Dozens of Internet search engines all arrived at the same time, some now famous, but most forgotten. Some died before they were fully born. Despite this, there is room to thrive here, as have Google, Yahoo, and others. Often there is such wealth to gain in new industries that a rapid launch can be followed by some decline, and the firm can still maintain a resilient strategy, as has e-Bay.

Shift in Industry Structure. Porter's theory of the five competitive forces actually gives us five questions to ask regarding strategic viability. How intense are the industry competitors? Are there new entrants displacing incumbents? Are there new products that can substitute? Has there been a shift in supplier power? Has there been a shift in buyer power? Each of these forces has the ability to shift the location of profits in an industry. Wal-Mart is a good example. Prior to its rise, suppliers had powerful influence over the prices of goods, and most profits went to those suppliers. Wal-Mart was a new entrant that shifted this value away from suppliers to itself, and then passed these profits along to its customers. This created a shift from supplier power to buyer power in the industry. Knowing this, one can craft a resilient strategy. Being unaware leaves a firm bogged down in executing daily operations, persisting with an obsolete strategy, and simply "trying harder". History shows how resilience-enhancing it is to be responsive to changes in industry structure and how unsafe it is to be oblivious.

The Second Strategic Question: Is Our Collection of Strengths Hard for Others to Imitate?

In order to create a resilient strategy, it is not enough to just create a competitive advantage. Recently Delta Airlines announced that it would provide Wi-Fi Internet service its entire fleet, and outfitted 130 of its planes in only a few months. It was ahead of all of its rivals, but this gave it only a momentary competitive advantage. Virgin America, United Airlines, Southwest Airlines, and JetBlue immediately followed with similar announcements. Creating a temporary competitive advantage is not enough. To build resilience one needs what Porter calls a sustainable competitive advantage or what Buffett calls a durable competitive advantage. This "sustainability" is vital to resilient strategy.

Much has been learned about what makes a competitive advantage sustainable, but the single element where Resilience Builders surpass other leaders is Porter's concept of ambiguity. This is the secret formula that makes the resilient enterprise difficult to understand or seemingly impossible to imitate. It is the unique recipe that guides the company and all of its employees. It is the product of all of its procedures, methods, and internal norms. To those inside the company, this is their way of doing things, which comes so naturally, but is difficult to put into words. Ambiguity allows you to invite the competition in and show them what you do, and still they remain unable to perfectly imitate you. Because of ambiguity, one of your senior managers might leave the company, intent on imitating, but even he or she might be unable to build a team and establish the processes that replicate the magic.

Ambiguity is not usually achievable by one's supply of materials, because AMD has access to silicon, just like Intel. It is rarely the product of extra features, since Kia uses safe airbags, just like Volvo. It is not the product of add-on's, as we see the same video screens installed in Boeing and Airbus jets. Today most businesses have (or soon obtain) the same supplies, technology, and design capacities as their competition. Ambiguity is achieved by developing and then combining a company's core competencies in a unique way. This is how Resilience Builders apply their strategy, and this is why their methods are so difficult to imitate. A closer look at the strategic issues of ambiguity and sustainable competitive advantage will reveal three ways Resilience Builders do this.

First, Resilience Builders build strategy so it is congruent with the other three essential elements of resilience. This means they build it on top of a well-defined platform, use the developmental frame to make wise choices about their capabilities, and do all of this in concert with a culture that is congruent with platform and frame.

Second, they strengthen ambiguity by engaging platform as part of strategy. It is difficult to copy the way someone else addresses platform, because there are just too many variables that support platform. No company is a clone of another. How a company defines and achieves its platform is quite subjective and unique to that company. There are hundreds of decisions that go into building and maintaining a platform, and the ambiguity of this process makes the resilient company very hard to imitate. And, while every resilient enterprise is built on a platform, sometimes this platform is not a simple, single-strength, solo platform. Sometimes it is a Hybrid Platform, using two very strong platforms to create multiple strengths. As noted in Chapter 4, the business landscape today has come to require more and more Hybrid Platforms in order to achieve resilience.

Recall that while this book recommends that you pick one platform or build a Hybrid Platform, the remaining non-dominant platforms are not to be ignored. Every company has some greater or lesser skill level on each of the four platforms. This is the platform mix. It's like a sound mixer, able to dial up and dial down even those platforms that are not identified as the primary platform on which the company is built. Even though the remaining platforms are significantly lesser, they are not irrelevant. The best Resilience Builders know just how high to dial each one up or down in order to create their strategies. Wal-Mart was built on the Efficient Platform. But its platform mix was deliberate and skillfully chosen. During its loftiest days, Sam Walton did his marketing by driving around a small town himself, studying local competitors by walking into their stores, and then pasting his newspaper ads together out of copies old ads. He didn't ignore the Marketing Platform; he dialed it up only slightly, just enough to let the community know his prices were lower. One might think he completely ignored the Creative Platform, and in the strictest sense of this concept, he did. However, he was a first mover at applying the creative concepts of others, especially the use of point-of-sale technology involving low flying satellites and massive computer banks. And, he intentionally ignored Relationship Platform because customers were in his store so briefly that he didn't have time to learn personal things about them and then do something unique or special for each of them. So, although he built Wal-Mart on the single Efficient Platform model, the combination of the factors that make up the other platforms was intentional, not ignored, and not left to random chance. The many decisions that were made every day regarding how to execute Wal-Mart's platform mix made its strategy more ambiguous, and this made Wal-Mart more resilient.

Imagine how difficult it would be for someone outside of the Wal-Mart organization to imitate Wal-Mart's unique mix of all these variables. Many have tried and failed. This is why ambiguity is defined as combining your collection of skills in a way that is difficult for your competition to understand or imitate.

Third, ambiguity is strengthened when Resilience Builders integrate their platform-based strategy throughout the entire value chain, including suppliers, contracted services, and retail outlets. They do this in a way that the activities of each component of the value chain are congruent with the uniqueness brought by their own platform and platform mix. They strive to get all parts of the value chain to fit the strategy and the platform configuration.

Here, compare Pfeizer, Inc. with Teva Pharmaceutical Industries, LTD. Pfizer has been struggling. This is the world's largest pharmaceutical firm with $48 billion in sales and 87,000 employees worldwide. It was formed in 1849 by two cousins, Charles Pfizer and Charles Erhardt in Brooklyn, NY. In recent decades Pfizer achieved success by operating on a Hybrid Platform combining a Creative Platform (it spends more than $7 billion annually attempting to invent new blockbuster drugs) and a Marketing Platform (with the world's largest team of pharmaceutical marketing reps who go to doctors' offices). Its Creative Platform has been challenged by a prolonged dry spell of new blockbuster products and the expiration of big patents like antidepressant Zoloft, blood pressure medicine Norvasc, and allergy drug Zyrtec. Its Marketing Platform has been damaged by declining sales and a new CEO, Jeffrey Kindler, who is intent on making Pfizer more efficient. In 2007 Pfizer discarded 11,000 employees, many coming from its force of personal sales representatives. BusinessWeek decried this decimation of the sales force as the end of an era. 5 Also in 2007 it closed two R&D facilities, thus diminishing its Creative Platform. However, while this shows some erosion of resilience, all is not lost. Pfizer has deep pockets with $22 billion in cash reserves and is expected to right itself. What is clear is that this company's resilience was built on two solid platforms, and in the past all value chain activities were congruent with these two platforms. The company's decline paralleled the erosion of both of these platforms. So, what about ambiguity? When Pfizer was operating at peak-performance, it had a collection of skills that all worked nicely together and at that time it was hard for others to imitate this collection of competencies. In the early 2000's this strategic "secret formula" became less clearly defined.

In contrast, Teva is a 107 year old Israeli firm that makes and distributes generic drugs, and it sells bulk raw materials to the pharmaceutical industry. This resilient $14 billion firm is growing at a 27% annual rate, and is squarely built on the Efficient Platform. It is the largest generic drug company in the world and its size allows it great economies of scale. Most generic drug producers wait until a blockbuster drug comes off patent, then sue to gain the rights to produce an equivalent of that drug. Teva starts manufacturing these drugs even before they are off patent. Then it seeks court approval for the exclusive rights to distribute it. Once this approval is gained, the entire organization is capable of moving quickly and efficiently. Add to this its first rate competency of driving cost containment throughout its entire value chain as one more element of its low-cost competitive advantage. Teva understands that it sells commodity products, so early on it opted to grow rapidly in order to gain a worldwide first mover advantage. It now has 38 factories. Like other resilient Efficient Platform firms, it gets cost-contained pricing advantage from its suppliers and its own value chain. This has made Teva's products attractive to government plans, managed care organizations and the ever-frugal Pharmacy Benefit Management (PBM) programs. Teva has achieved resilience by strategically adapting to the current medical industry and by achieving a clear identity built on the Efficient Platform. What is ambiguous about Teva? Very few firms can develop a comparable set of core competencies driving efficiencies throughout the supply chain, being quick to respond, and making all parts of the enterprise match the Efficient Platform as well as Teva. That's why Teva's strategy and resilience are so hard to imitate.

The Third Strategic Question: How Mature is The Overall Industry?

In Chapter 6 I rejected the traditional view of a firm's life cycle, and replaced it with the developmental frame. It is important to note that the developmental frame only addresses the firm's own life cycle. There is another life cycle to examine, and its influence on resilience is profound. This is the industry lifecycle. As an overall industry moves from one stage of development to another, individual firms are required to adapt.

Unlike most business leaders, Resilience Builders are skilled at examining and interacting with the collective influences of this cycle. All managers will feel the influence of this potent force. Resilience Builders anticipate and prepare in advance to adapt to the shocks this cycle generates. First, let's review what we already know about industry lifecycle development.

Fragmented Industry. In the beginning, an industry forms around a new technology or a new revenue stream and the competitive field is said to be "fragmented". There are lots of players, some large and some small. Some are family owned or local companies, and the competitors may each have a different competitive platform, or even no platform at all. An example would be the automobile industry around 1900, when there were over 200 car manufacturers. As an industry develops, one player creates a successful methodology that allows it to operate more effectively than the others and this becomes the industry's dominant strategic model, as was the moving assembly line. In order to create resilience here, the lead company must not only perfect this strategic model but also promote it to suppliers, financiers, and customers. This further secures the method as the dominant strategic model.

Takeoff Stage. This is followed by a "takeoff" stage where others copy or improve upon the dominant strategic model, and essentially no one leaves the competitive field.

Shakeout. Then comes a "shakeout" stage where many of those firms that have not adopted the dominant strategy suffer or are forced out. Typically, this is where we see a peak in firms that try to integrate their activities vertically. Forward integration occurs when, for example, a manufacturer buys or establishes its own retail outlets. Here, think of automobile dealerships. Backward integration occurs when a firm attempts to own its supply chain, like when car companies owned rubber plantations.

Maturity. Subsequently the entire industry is likely to go through a comfortable stage of maturity. The time frame here can be brief or long depending on the intensity of the competition and the rate of technical changes impacting the industry. As the product or service continues to develop, it becomes clear that the supply chain is becoming more sophisticated and complex, so the supply inputs are better handled by specialty shops or suppliers, because the larger firm no longer has the expertise or desire to develop all of these various inputs. This causes an undoing of vertical integration and is replaced by vertical specialization.

Late Stage. The subsequent late stage industry development tends to be dreaded by all insiders. The survivors tend to be large and have good brand identity. The most secure survivors are the ones with the lowest cost structure. Products and services are more complex, and survivors usually have a broad scope. Incidentally, the small companies that were created by vertical specialization tend to become new growth industries that are substantial in their own right.

Rationalization. To the surprise of most industry participants, the overall industry begins to decline. However, this decline is not a random event. It is predictable and this stage is filled with activity. This is often accompanied by the final appearance of the one overarching set of product and process standards the industry will use. Those who are most competent at these standards will become the industry incumbents, and will have the best shot at retaining resilience. At this point we find that the collection of all competitors' trade "secrets" are no longer secret, and have become the standards. In this stage there are too many competitors for the new, leaner profits. So, there is an industry "rationalization" in which firms leave, merge, or acquire others in order to have fewer competitors. This is not necessarily a bad thing. Usually what follows is a smaller group of large players who have bought or defeated their competitors and who can enjoy the benefits of a mutually shared industry. Here, consider the present day rail freight industry in the United States. It has only a few big firms, but they all are comfortable.

This description of the industry life cycle is relevant because unlike other leaders, Resilience Builders use their understanding of the industry life cycle to guide their strategy and enhance resilience. Now, let's see how this relates to this book's theory of resilience.

INDUSTRY LIFECYCLE, PLATFORM SHIFTS, AND RESILIENCE

As we have seen, in the earliest stages of industry development, the rules of success are not yet established and individual companies tend to surge ahead, then fall behind or fail. The appearance of the dominant strategic model establishes not only a common strategy, but also an industry-wide competitive platform for all players. This gives the field some stability and a formula for how to build resilience. However, this comfortable playing field always changes when a new business leader modifies the industry's dominant strategic model. This, of course, can cause the entire field to go through a platform shift to a new competitive platform or to a hybrid platform. Resilience is built or destroyed by the leader's response to an industry-wide platform shift.

Ford Motor Company was Henry Ford's third attempt to start a car company. His initial failures occurred because the auto industry had not yet formed either a dominant strategic model or an industry-wide competitive platform and hence, there was confusion about what the rules of resilience would be. When Ford made use of the moving assembly line, he not only created the industry's new dominant strategy, he also established that this would be an industry built on the Efficient Platform. From that point forward, the only path to survival or success would go through the Efficient Platform. Of course this was met with resistance, as hand-made motorized carriage builders refused to degrade their artisan skills to the level of assembly line unskilled labor. But soon all of those resistors were either converted to the Efficient Platform or were extinct. This created not only the industry's strategic model, but also its first industry-wide competitive platform.

For years the auto industry remained solidly built on the Efficient Platform under Ford's leadership. But Henry Ford had only one platform, and he persisted in making cars more and more efficiently. They were plain, simple, and cheap. They were all the same. When MIT graduate and industrialist Alfred P. Sloan entered the field he established a new dominant strategic model and this created a platform shift. As president of General Motors in the 1920's he realized that the consumer had secondary needs that could be met by cars. These were needs for prestige, power and style, so he rank-ordered the GM family of cars from least to most prestigious. The order was Chevrolet, Pontiac, Oldsmobile, Buick, and Cadillac, and the American public bought into this marketing scheme completely. He also allowed affluent as well as non-affluent people to borrow their prestige by making loan programs available. (He called them inverse saving programs.) Ford opposed lending programs of any kind. Thanks to GM, one could be judged by the status of one's car. Sloan also used planned obsolescence for the styling of these cars, systematically replacing each one with a new, improved and more attractive model. He caused the auto industry to experience a platform shift from a simple Efficient Platform to a more complex Hybrid Platform which mixed Efficient Platform production with Marketing Platform's feel-good secondary identity benefits. This Hybrid remains the auto industry platform to this day. Each car must be made efficiently and must deliver modern fashion styling that tells the world whether the consumer is exciting like BMW, safe like Volvo, sensible like Toyota, or prestigious like Mercedes. And, like the fashion industry, if any car falls out of style, it instantly gets left behind on the showroom floor.

For most of the history of business, an established dominant strategic model might have changed only once, as seen in the auto industry. So, to remain resilient, one would have to adapt to the initial establishment of a platform, and then one platform shift. However, today the task of the Resilience Builder is much more complex. Look at how many new dominant strategic models have formed in telecommunications. We used to have different companies that provided us with our telephone, television, cable, internet, movie rental, and music. When did the lines of distinction between these product lines and industries blur? Other fields with multiple platform shifts include retail electronics, consumer finance, and the delivery of medical care. Building Resilience today requires gaining the ability to respond to more sequential industry-wide platform shifts than previous generations of leaders had to do.

Industry lifecycles create platform shifts, and the impact of this on resilience is substantial. Add to that the advantages of early adaptation to platform shifts and we are putting together a powerful force to build or destroy resilient strategy. Many successful enterprises have ended in failure due to their leaders' inability to anticipate these stages and the predictable platform shifts associated with them. Many others have anticipated these changes and built resilience.

Two Examples of Early to Mid-Stage Adaptation

In order to display the powerful influence the three strategic questions of fertile ground, ambiguity, and industry-wide lifecycle have on resilience, the stories of four companies will be told. The first two stories describe companies as they progress through the early and mid-stage phases of their industries. The third and fourth stories will examine how resilience can be maintained by strategic choices in late stage industry development. First is the compelling story of Sun Microsystems, Inc. as a tale of fortune and misfortune; resilience gained and resilience lost.

Sun Microsystems, Inc

In the early 1980's computers consisted of mainframes, minicomputers (small mainframes), and personal computers. Minicomputers were misnamed, because they were actually big, and personal computers were hobbyist's toys with too little power to be useful. So Stanford University graduate student Andy Bechtolsheim developed the first Unix workstation for Sun. The name Sun came from the Stanford University Network, and Sun Microsystems Inc. was formed in 1982. It created workstations that were more powerful and useful than PC's and lighter and more affordable than the other big computers. Workstations were initially used by only one person, and this solo user model freed up the mainframe for large jobs and allowed lots of people to simultaneously work on their own projects. Then, as workstations began to be linked to each other and to mainframes, Sun was in a good spot to be the early mover into Unix-based networking. Thus, they developed the slogan, "The network is the computer". Sun had found fertile ground and the field had strategic viability. Sun's first target market was engineering firms.

Creating the First Dominant Strategic Model

Sun's Quad 1 Growth position in its own developmental frame was classic. The early days were excitingly hectic and Sun's rapid growth caused chaos, followed by more rapid growth. The firm was built squarely on the Creative

Platform and developed a freewheeling, inventive, open culture to match. The strategy was focused, limited to workstations.

As the company moved into Quad 2 it began to show signs of complacency. In response to this CEO Scott McNealy seized the opportunity to restore growth by moving the company into servers. In many ways servers were the next natural evolution of workstations, linking large numbers of computers and systems together in ever-bigger networks. By sequentially creating these developments, McNealy skillfully moved the company back into Quad 1 Growth several times. At this point, the company was very well managed by McNealy. This Harvard economics major and Stanford MBA was making all the right moves to build resilience.

In the early 1990's McNealy triggered the first dominant strategic model in Internet technology, by creating the industry's software standard, Java. Java is a language based on the very technical and difficult C++ language. It took the best elements of C++ and made them more adaptable and more useful. This allowed Java to be used on any computer and for it to have universal compatibility. It became the language of the Internet. Meanwhile, Sun attempted to provide the industry's dominant strategic model for hardware by introducing its own powerful and elegant servers to build the Internet. It had also established that the server industry's competitive platform would be the Creative Platform.

A STATE OF RESILIENCE

Thus far McNealy had formed a collection of bright and innovative people into a company solidly built on the Creative Platform, moved it through Quad 1 Growth into Quad 2 and then back to Quad 1 Growth. In the process he built an exciting and engaging corporate culture in congruence with the Creative Platform, and his strategy matched the platform, frame and culture. Strategically, he had created the industry's first dominant strategic model using servers and Java. Sun was in a state of resilience.

Several more good things were about to happen. In January 2000, the Wall Street Journal published an article headlined "Sun Microsystems Basks in the Glow of Internet Aura". 6 The subtitle was "Computer-server maker profits handsomely at the expense of IBM and HP." By this time, Sun had become the default option in the minds of server customers, especially for those new upstarts selling everything on their Web sites. Sun

2

had changed its slogan to "We're the dot in dot com." These were heady times, and Sun's stock showed it by tripling from the previous year.

For that long moment Sun had won the tech wars. It sold servers equipped only with its own hardware and software, including its Sparc chips, and Solaris operating systems. Its servers were the most powerful, secure, and sought-after machines on the market. Sun had mastered the art of ambiguity, through its remarkable collection of core competencies and its inimitable servers. Critics scoffed at IBM and HP for selling servers using a variety of chips and operating systems. The world was coming to Sun, and Sun had established the industry's prevailing strategy in server software as well as hardware. McNealy was the Henry Ford of servers. Or, so it seemed.

Failing to Adapt to the Next Dominant Strategic Model

No competitive advantage can lock out a firm's challengers forever. Eventually they will imitate or surpass the incumbent's technology or skill sets. No one could see that Scott McNealy was about to experience a strategic failure. Like pre-windows IBM, Sun filled its machines with its own proprietary software, and sold the entire package as a closed system. McNealy did not see that his firm was in a niche in a much larger IT industry and the larger competitive field was establishing the second dominant strategic model, based on the efficient open systems of Windows and Intel. Sun's small piece of the tech pie could not outweigh the massive and powerful influence of Wintel. So here came the second dominant strategic model, based on Windows and Intel. McNealy would have to decide whether to excel at this second dominant strategic model or resist it.

Unfortunately, he was blind to the power of the new model and the platform shift that was happening in this industry's life cycle. Imagine what would have happened to Ford Motor Company if Henry Ford had permanently ignored or resisted the platform shift that accompanied the second dominant strategic model in his industry. Regrettably, that's what McNealy did. As IBM and HP were developing servers using a wide range of components and systems, Sun stubbornly insisted that its own closed and proprietary systems would prevail. And they did for a while, until they didn't. By the time the January 2000 Wall Street Journal article was written, both HP and IBM were developing servers that would run several languages including the free language of Linux.

Then came worse news. Microsoft entered the server wars with NT and Windows 2000, capable of managing complex server work. McNealy was undeterred. Sun was spending more than $200 million annually on R&D and he believed its servers were far more sophisticated than any of its competitors. Its products were just better. McNealy wasn't interested in having any Intel or Microsoft architecture on Sun servers.

Sun's profits fell sharply as the Wintel-based servers approached and then equaled the capabilities of Sun. The crowning blow for Sun was when Dell joined the fray, selling servers at stunningly low prices. By late 2002, large customers were replacing their $250,000 Sun servers with small collections of $4,000 Dell products. These Dell servers were considered to be so inexpensive that rather than spend a lot of money maintaining them, they were disposable and replaceable. Sun responded by adding impressive options and capabilities to its servers, most of which its customers didn't need or want. By 2004 its market share in servers had fallen to 12%.

The second dominant strategic model in the industry lifecycle had been established and he resisted it. This new model created an industry platform shift which was Hybrid Efficient Platform and Creative Platform. Although it is an exaggeration to call servers a commodity, they began to sell like commodity items. Dell and others were eager to provide servers as generic boxes, using others' technology and software, and sell them as cheaply as possible. Sun's secrets of success had been found out and surpassed. It had lost its strategic ambiguity, and with this came the fact that its competitive advantage was no longer sustainable. It had lost resilience.

Recall what happens to those who resist the industry dominant strategic model and an industry-wide platform shift. They are injured or they leave the competitive field. Within this new Hybrid Platform, the need to be bright, innovative and creative was not gone; Intel and Microsoft were brilliantly upgrading their products. But Intel and Microsoft's sheer size and market power allowed them to pay for those upgrades quite cheaply on a unit-of-sale basis, and this allowed them to constantly give the consumer more for less. Sun was unable to do this, and McNealy did not have the wisdom of Resilience Builders regarding this piece of his strategy.

Sun was using an obsolete model which involved backward integration. There was a long value chain required to create a server, and Sun had integrated the key parts of this chain into its own operations. It wrote the code for its servers and it built the chips. Meanwhile others were specializing in these key steps on the value chain and began to do it better. So, the industry process of vertical specialization began to occur. Eventually Sun could have bought better chips than it could produce for itself, at a fraction of the price, but it refused to do so.

DEGENERATION

In the early days, McNealy had responded well to Sun's location on the developmental frame in Quad 1 and Quad 2, by constantly returning the company to Quad 1 Growth. By the end of 2002 Sun was clearly in Quad 3 Degeneration and McNealy was not responding. From 2000 to 2002 Sun's stock price fell from $64 per share to around $3. Revenues declined from $18 billion to $12 billion. Internally, his senior managers began singing a loud chorus to McNealy, begging him to open his systems to Wintel products and other low cost and powerful alternatives. He refused. As often happens, this CEO began to focus his attention on his most powerful opponent in an angry, bitter, and sometimes personal way. It was during this time that Microsoft was under attack from the justice department and McNealy was Microsoft critic-in-chief, often seen on business news shows or in print acidly decrying how unfair was Microsoft's success. Of course, none of this negative energy increased his sales, stock price, or market share. As expected, this plunge into Quad 3 Degeneration derailed Sun's culture and internal climate. Because McNealy had been a revered co-founder and was such a strong incumbent, no overt mutiny would succeed. So, rather than attempt a coup, his senior people began to leave. Of course, a mass exodus is a form of mutiny. The most shocking defection was Ed Zander who had been his president and greatest cheerleader. Zander left in 2002 and became CEO of Motorola. That same year, five members of McNealy's senior team left and McNealy still refused to adapt to the new dominant strategic model or platform shift. As managers and scientists continued to leave, the business press labeled this a crisis. By 2004 BusinessWeek called it a "damaged culture" and said that this previously creative culture had become risk-averse and survival oriented. 7

Under all of this pressure, McNealy finally declared peace with Microsoft, settled two lawsuits, and in April 2003 announced Sun servers would begin running Windows. Gradually, Sun became an open-source system, but it continued to create its own Sparc microprocessors and Solaris operating systems, both of which absorbed a huge R&D budget.

THE SALE OF SUN

In April 2006, with Sun's stock hovering around $5 per share, and after having lost $200 million of market value since 2001, Scott McNealy resigned as CEO. The new CEO, Jonathan Schwartz, promised to innovate the company to success again. Three years later, in April 2009, Sun was purchased by Oracle Corporation for $7.38 billion or $9.50 per share. Sun Microsystems, Inc. would be no more. Oracle now owns Sun's Java software and Solaris operating systems. These allow Oracle to better manage its huge databases and to offer back-office service consulting to its customers.

This case is presented, not to point out the misfortunes of these bright and worthy scientist-entrepreneurs. Rather, it shows what happens when a leader fails to adapt to a shift in an industry's dominant strategic model and the accompanying platform shift, all of which is the product of normal and predictable progress of a competitive field along the industry life cycle. As competition improved, Sun's strategy was imitated and surpassed, and it lost its secret collection of core competencies; its ambiguity. These failures produced a dramatic loss of a previously remarkable competitive advantage. Finally, absent had been a Quad 4 Conversion for Sun, even after Sun began to allow open systems on its servers. Unfortunately, this left its products somewhat ill-defined. They weren't the cheapest like Dell, and they weren't stunningly high-option like IBM. They were a little of both, so Sun was attacked from both ends. All of this led to a loss of resilience. Return to Growth could have occurred only if Sun had pursued a new strategy that was fully adaptive to the industry's new platform.

So, how would another Resilience Builder have proceeded differently? There are many examples from which to choose.

THE WALT DISNEY COMPANY

Although he was in a different business at a different time, like Scott McNealy, Walt Disney built his enterprise on the Creative Platform. In the early stages of his enterprise, this young artist thought that all he had to do was make great cartoon figures. Some painful business lessons came his way, but he grew in wisdom each time. Eventually, he shifted platforms as his industry changed, and became a great Resilience Builder. The Walt Disney Company became the premier source of family and children's entertainment and won 48 Academy Awards during Walt's lifetime.

INVISIBLE FRIENDS

Walt Disney was born in Chicago in 1901, the fourth of five children, and spent part of his early childhood on a farm in rural Missouri. His father, Elias, has been described as a harsh man with a tendency to mistreat the children. As a result, the two oldest brothers ran away from home, and without their labor the farm failed. Their painful departure was traumatic for young Walt. The family moved to Kansas City where Elias became a newspaper distributor, enlisting the help of the two remaining boys, Walt and his older brother Roy. History repeated itself when Roy left home as a result of his treatment by Elias. It is believed that Walt's mother, Flora was a supportive and pleasant woman, and this theme of harsh versus kindly authority figures, found so often in Disney's work, traces back to these early days.

To contend with his home circumstance, Walt developed invisible friends and a rich imagination which would later serve to help him build his Creative Platform company. Eventually, he began to sketch these figures, and became an accomplished amateur cartoonist. However, when he applied for a cartoonist job at the Kansas City Star he was rejected.

TWO PAINFUL LESSONS

In those days, the entertainment field was still a fragmented industry and it was not hard to find a venue for one's work. So, in 1922 Walt and a friend began a small enterprise to make short animated films, called Laugh-O-Gram. They did good work, but their creative products were never released because soon thereafter their distributor declared bankruptcy.

The distributor's bankruptcy was the first of two painful lessons that offered young Walt some wisdom about the business strategies required to support resilience in the Creative Platform. Quickly, this cash-strapped young man got onto a train with $40.00 in his pocket and headed to

Hollywood with the ambitious intention of becoming a movie director. Of course, his arrival in Hollywood went unnoticed by the movie moguls, and he began to run out of money. Fortunately, he had two relatives in the Los Angeles area, his brother Roy and an uncle who allowed him to live in his home.

He found a new distributor for his creative work, not in Hollywood, but in New York. This was Margaret Winkler who loved his creative ability to insert a human child into a cartoon movie. In 1923 she offered Walt and Roy Disney $1,500 for each copy of their new film, *Alice's Adventures.* Upon signing the contract with Winkler Pictures, Disney Brothers animation studio was launched. However, his second painful lesson was about to follow. Over the next five years, they produced several short animated movies featuring Oswald the Lucky Rabbit, an adorable little creature who developed some popularity. During these years, Margaret turned this work over to her new husband, Charles Mintz, and when Walt went to New York in 1928 to review their contract, he discovered that the original agreement allowed the distributor to own the Oswald character. Mintz planned to continue production, had already hired away most of Walt's animators, and informed Walt he simply didn't need Disney Brothers any more. The business side of the Creative Platform is treacherous, and resilience eluded these young entrepreneurs.

Young Walt went back to Los Angeles depressed and bitter. A superficial interpretation of these events might suggest that this entire experience was a loss for him, but there was more going on here. This was a valuable lesson regarding how to build resilience using the Creative Platform and the wisdom gained here influenced the course of his career from then on. He learned that simply creating or inventing something valuable would not be sufficient to achieve either success or resilience. One must look at whether the overall strategy supports resilience. One must ask who will own which part of the value (profits) as the creative product moves along the value chain from inception to consumption. As we will soon see, Walt Disney learned this lesson well, thanks to a bankrupt distributor, and then a selfish one. Also, Walt was participating in a competitive field that was moving from a cottage industry to a less fragmented mature industry and he would have to do some developmental adaptation if he wished to enter a state of resilience.

His first move was to make a vow to remain independent of film distributors forever, and distribute his creative products himself. This plan worked for a while and he produced a new character, a mouse named

Mickey with big ears and an affable personality. (In early productions Mickey's voice was actually that of Walt, and it is rumored that Mickey's personality was a copy of Walt's as well.) In Mickey's Hollywood debut, *Plane Crazy*, Walt saw how enchanted and delighted audiences were with this new character. They were equally thrilled with the next film, *The Gallopin' Gaucho*. But Mickey's place in history became solidified in *Steamboat Willie*, a talkie in which Disney used new technology so the sound was perfectly synchronized with the changes in animation.

THE FIRST DOMINANT STRATEGIC MODEL

The dominant strategic model in early Hollywood was to compete straightforward on creativity. Despite the fact that the Disney enterprise was so young, we see the defining characteristics of the Creative Platform emerge and begin to dominate the small firm. As early as the release of *Steamboat Willie*, Walt had gathered some remarkably talented animators. He was good at leveraging their skills in order to invent something new and exciting, and he quickly adopted new technologies. His creativity brought about a good deal of ambiguity, because no other animator could quite copy his work. The Disney workplace was one of the first to allow a culture of casual attire and unusual work hours for the artistic staff, now so commonly found in Creative Platform companies.

However, his efforts to distribute his film independently meant he was resisting the large Hollywood distribution networks wherein the movie studios owned chains of theatres. By remaining so small he was limiting his ability to establish market presence for Mickey because Disney had to distribute only to independent theatres. This was a self-limiting and exhausting strategy. So in 1930 he signed an agreement to have Columbia Pictures distribute his work, but this time he kept the rights to the characters. Disney was in Quad 1 Growth, was solidly built on the Creative Platform, had established a culture congruent with this platform, and was in compliance with the industry's dominant strategic model. This firm had entered a state of resilience, but the requirements of resilience were about to change.

THE SECOND DOMINANT STRATEGIC MODEL

A second dominant strategic model was emerging. As production and distribution of films became more expensive, some major Hollywood studios were becoming better managed and had begun to master the skills associated with the Marketing Platform.

Up to this point, movie studios owned large chains of theatres, for example MGM owned Lowe's, Inc. In the 1930's they began to discard various aspects of their integrated value chain including some studio production tasks and ownership of the theatres. This was the beginning of vertical specialization as the industry developed. Then the industry went through a shakeout and several players were hurt. Universal Studios was taken over by its creditors in 1936, who then ran the studio. Fox (later named Twentieth Century Fox) went bankrupt in 1936. Across town, things were different at MGM. It soared through the Great Depression, remained financially solvent, and grew into the largest film powerhouse in the world. How could MGM have had such a meteoric rise while its peers were failing?

Instead of promoting and advertising only the movie and the studio, MGM heavily marketed the actors as stars. During the Great Depression the public had a need to believe that life was easy for someone, and that some people were just graceful, glamorous, rich, and blessed. The public could identify with and share this glamour for only the cost of a movie ticket. So the second dominant strategic model involved a new platform, the Marketing Platform. The impact of this platform was profound. While other studios had a few A-list actors mixed in with long registers of B-list actors, MGM created brand images around Greta Garbo, Clark Gable, Joan Crawford, Jean Harlow, and more.

BUILDING RESILIENCE

Resilience Builder Walt Disney's good wisdom as this environment changed came as a result of his early education at the hands of the two unkindly distributors as well as his early experimentation with his own artistic talents. This was the point at which he really moved out of being a short-term creative success and into becoming a world class Resilience Builder. He did two things. First, he marketed star-level characters with whom the public could identify and idealize. Having done so, he decided he could compound his creativity. If the world loved Mickey, wouldn't it love another innocent and wonderful character? He introduced an easily flustered but endearing and naive guy named Donald Duck in 1934. Not only could the audience identify with him, it loved him. In the safety of a movie theatre, people could share Donald's awkward frustrations and enjoy how easily life's problems could be resolved. Soon Disney created Pluto and Goofy, and as it added new characters it added more cartoonists, writers and musical composers.

This adaptation to the new dominant strategic model reached his audience with a Marketing Platform brand image for each character that touched one piece of the human experience. It allowed the audience to identify with the character. All of this fit nicely with what the successful studios were doing with live actors; marketing their brand image.

The second step Disney took to plunge further into the Marketing Platform was to sell promotional paraphernalia, toys, books, comic books, and apparel featuring each of its characters. Disney licensed Mickey's image in newspaper comic strips, as well as on ice cream containers, cereal boxes and bread wrappers. In 1933 it produced the first Mickey Mouse watch and sold over 2 million watches in the first two years. During that same time, Disney's income from promotional materials and licensing accounted for about one third of its revenues. Mickey Mouse was as famous as Santa Claus and Coca Cola.

Not only had this firm maintained its Creative Platform, but it dialed up a second platform, the Marketing Platform, and from that point to the present day, the success of Disney has been built on a unique and ambiguous combination of the large number of core competencies that support these two platforms. Even now, every Disney movie and Broadway show is accompanied by musical hits, clothing, book bags, and toys, all sold separately, and all serving to further promote the biggest product, the Disney image. Disney's greatest resilience-building skill is its ability to combine its unique collection of artistic and organizational competencies so carefully that competitors are unable to imitate it. This has given Disney the benefit of ambiguity. This has given Disney not simply a competitive advantage, but truly a sustainable competitive advantage. And, this has placed Disney in a state of resilience for a very long time.

Two Examples of Late-Stage Adaptation

The discussion thus far has focused on early and mid-stage issues, such as how to establish resilience by building a company around a platform, working within the developmental frame, establishing a resilience-supporting culture, and creating a strategy that is congruent with all of this. Sun's story is instructive, but despite its stunning advances in recent years, the field of technology is not a late stage industry. Notice also that the discussion about Disney stopped in the 1930's. What wisdom do Resilience Builders have about strategy in the late stages of an industry's life cycle?

There are some late-stage patterns that occur in almost all industries. As an industry enters its last stages, we see it become progressively more crowded. Then firms begin to compete on price. This causes the Resilience Builder to choose whether to use the firm's current assets to move to another competitive field or to stay with the industry and therefore become the producer with the lowest cost structure. Resilience can be had either direction, but is rarely achieved unless the firm excels at one or the other of these strategies (new field vs. low cost structure).

Many late stage firms have attempted to leave their industries and start over in more promising fields, but few have succeeded. Those who have succeeded have most often done so by applying their pre-existing competencies in the new industry rather than trying to establish new competencies.

Typically those who decide to remain in the field see prices and profits continue to decline even if revenues increase, causing the industry to operate on very thin margins. Despite this, each firm's products and services are required to become more complex. So as rationalization begins, healthy firms thrive and all of the weak competition fails. Friendly and unfriendly acquisitions allow large firms to continue to grow, and eventually the field is more comfortably shared by fewer competitors.

The Thomson Corporation Leaves Its Industry To Become Thomson Reuters

In 2008, the 78 year old Thomson Corporation bought 158 year old Reuters Group, PLC to form a worldwide giant of business and professional information, Thomson Reuters. This is a narrative about how Thomson Corporation has adapted to its industry's late stage development by leaving its industry.

Thomson Corporation started in the newspaper industry, left that industry, but took with it all of its skills and competencies to enter the information industry. It retained its competitive platform throughout this process, and has made the transition beautifully. It has remained respected, admired, and resilient.

This company has been called the quiet giant. Professionals in finance, law, science, healthcare, and publishing use its tools, sometimes unaware which firm provides the products. Brokers, investment bankers, and analysts use its endless supply of financial data on a minute by minute basis. It has a market capitalization of $25 billion and revenues of $13 billion, with 53,000 employees and a remarkable history of steady growth. Even though 2008 was a terrible year for the finance industry, Thomson Reuters' revenues increased 8%. This is a Canadian company headquartered in Stamford Connecticut. It manages worldwide operations, and has a stunning record of maintaining a state of resilience and returning to Quad 1 Growth after each of its challenges. There is much to learn from the journey of Thomson Reuters, especially for leaders whose enterprises are challenged by late-stage industry development. But first, let's begin at the beginning.

A DIFFICULT START

Roy Thomson was born in Toronto in 1894, the son of a poor barber and a mother who took boarders into the home to help pay the bills. The family circumstance was austere, and helped to motivate Roy toward success. When he quit school at 14 to work in a coal yard, he also worked for a kindly aunt who ran a mortgage company and tutored him about the world of business. As a young man he openly boasted that he would become a millionaire by the age of 40. In the end he became a millionaire many times over, but first he had some wisdom to gain. He failed at farming and failed again at selling auto parts, but he never lost his drive, optimism, and powerful ambition. He then began selling radios in the Ontario town of North Bay. While he was considered a charming and irresistible young salesman, he failed to ask whether this town was fertile ground for radio sales. It turned out that the area had poor radio reception and too few stations, so once again he struggled. 9

In order to influence demand for his radios he decided to open a radio station of his own, even though he had no knowledge of radio technology and no money to support the operation. The Canadian government was not issuing new licenses, so in 1931 he rented an existing license for $1.00 for a year, obtained a transmitter on credit, and set up a station in North Bay. All went well briefly until the local newspaper began to lose advertising revenue to this young man, and the owner retaliated. Roy believed he could win the competitive war if he could get another license for a station in nearby Timmons. With some persuasion, the authorities consented, and he expanded his little company.

The Timmons station was housed upstairs in a rundown building and the first floor was occupied by old printing presses and equipment, all in poor shape. Eventually the landlord started a small newspaper using the equipment and called the newspaper "The Press". When Roy sold radio advertising to a competing newspaper, the landlord protested and threatened to kick him out of the building. So, in 1934 Roy offered to buy the man's paper. He had no idea the impact of what he had done, because this was the start of one of the world's greatest newspaper empires, and it would last for the remainder of the 20th century.

USING AN EFFICIENT STRATEGY IN AN EARLY-STAGE INDUSTRY

Quickly Roy began a program of rapid expansion. Within a year he owned four small radio stations and the newspaper. He expanded completely on credit, and often had to forestall one creditor to pay another. Sometimes in order to gain time for cash flow to catch up he had an associate tell creditors that he was traveling abroad for the following six weeks. As we might expect in Quad 1 Growth, he used income to offset debt, and even used one debt to service another. The small-town newspaper industry was fragmented and he knew this was an opportunity to grow, so he began buying every newspaper he could find. He observed that these family owned papers were loosely run, so he began a policy of tight financial controls and required constant growth of advertising revenues. He pushed again and again to establish his business on the Efficient Platform. However, he did not interfere with editorial policies or the content of the reporting. His intent was simply to grow a business and to make money, not to be a reporter. This remained his approach throughout his lifetime.

Years later Roy began to suffer the price of incumbency and he began to be seen in negative terms by the press and public, simply because of his huge success. In addition, his firm owned so many newspapers in Canada that there were few remaining prospects to buy. So, in 1953 he traveled to the United Kingdom and bought the Scotsman, a distressed Scottish newspaper. Thomson Corporation retained the Canadian operations, and in 1954, at the age of 60, he moved to Scotland and proceeded to make history repeat itself. In Europe, Thomson Corporation bought magazine publishers, entire newspaper chains, and book publishers. In 1957 it bought a Scottish television station and Roy commented that being in television broadcasting was like having a license to print money. His crowning achievement was the purchase of the prestigious London Times and the Sunday Times in 1967.

Examination of the firm at each point along this journey reveals a resilient organization firmly built on an Efficient Platform, with a congruent culture focused on keeping this company in Quad 1 Growth. Strategically, Thomson Corporation had discovered an entire cottage industry of sloppily run family owned newspapers, managed by their own editors and reporters. His well-disciplined business managers knew how to make the balance sheet as well as the profit and loss statement the central focus of the enterprise. This was unique in the newspaper industry and made it difficult for others to imitate, gave the firm ambiguity, and offered it a sustainable competitive advantage. This industry was ready for the second dominant strategic model, and by applying strict business methods including the skilled use of debt to foster growth, Thomson Corporation had delivered it.

DIVERSIFICATION

During the 1960's and 1970's regulators in Europe and America were preoccupied with antitrust, so most big businesses diversified into unrelated fields. This was all right with the elderly Roy Thomson, since he had bought and sold many divergent businesses along the way. But now Thomson Corporation did so in earnest, and two of these sidelines struck gold. The first important diversification came in 1965 when Thomson established Thomson Travel, a travel agency that sold tour packages. It also bought Britania Airways. In those days, as today, people in the UK were very enthusiastic about vacation and travel, and the most common way to obtain tickets was by using a travel agent. Both the travel service and the airline were successful.

The second diversification was in 1971 when Thomson joined a consortium to look for oil in the North Sea. Critics rendered scathing judgments of this newspaper oilman, but the firm persisted. Eventually this investment produced a flood of oil and money that lifted the company to new heights.

These divergences into other industries may now seem like nothing more than distractions, but in fact they served to create a learning-set inside the organization that Thompson could apply its sophisticated core competencies anywhere. It could even move out of its own industry if it needed to.

LATE-STAGE ADAPTATION

In 1978 Roy Thomson died and was followed as CEO by his son, Kenneth, but this story of resilience did not end there. Roy had tutored Kenneth for a lifetime and Kenneth knew how to continue the magic of the Thomson ambiguity and sustainable competitive advantage. He had learned that the ownership of a company or business unit is only in the service of success, and that at some time the larger firm must exit any business so it can rejuvenate another. He was about to put these skills to work.

Kenneth saw that the newspaper industry was in late-stage, and the handsome profits that had supported the firm in his father's day were gone forever. Advertising revenue was declining and so was subscribership. Costs of labor, paper, and distribution had inched up steadily over the years, and it seemed everyone benefited from the industry but the owners. His options were to become the low cost producer in a difficult industry, or modify his offerings.

Kenneth quickly lunged forward with the intent of owning publishers which had healthy margins, steady cash flow, and avoided the hectic and cyclical requirement of selling weekly or daily advertisements. So, Thomson purchased Wadsworth, a publisher of college texts and sophisticated professional books in America in 1978. In 1985 Kenneth installed a young and fresh Michael Brown as president, moved the headquarters to the United States, and together they purchased law book publishers on three continents, Sweet & Maxwell (UK), Carswell (Canada) and The Law Book Company (Australia). During the 1980's the Thomson organization worked hard to become the "go to" source for legal facts, regulatory compliance, and written opinions. In 1989 it grew this strategy further by purchasing Lawyers Cooperative Publishing Company and Research Institute of America. Thompson was still in the publishing business, but now it had become a respected name in law publishing.

The one purchase that would guarantee a healthy future came in 1996 when the firm acquired West Publishing in Minnesota for $3.4 billion. West is best known for its Westlaw service which supplies legal case law, precedents, statutes, and law reviews. It also provides commentary and organizes this material in understandable and useful manner.

ADAPTING BY EXITING THE INDUSTRY

These second generation Resilience Builders, Kenneth Thomson and Michael Brown, knew how to answer the question, "Is this business planted in fertile ground?" As a result, Thomson sold the Times Newspapers in London (after bitter strikes) and the North Sea oil operations (as revenues began to drop about 20% per year and after a tragic fire on an offshore rig). Along the way, as it became clear that various segments of the newspaper industry were not planted in fertile ground, it began selling newspaper subsidiaries, and in 2000 it sold its last newspaper. It was now out of the newspaper industry that had started it all and had brought about such resilient prosperity. But it wasn't out of the information business.

It is worth noting that as this firm moved into new and different industries, it did not undergo a Quad 4 Conversion. That's because it never entered Quad 3 Degeneration. These Resilience Builders were insightful enough to know when their competitive fields were declining and when to get out. Thomson remained squarely built on the Efficient Platform and the rapid transmission of information. Because of its long history of building efficiencies into every endeavor, this firm had positioned itself perfectly to respond well to yet another new dominant strategy that was emerging in this competitive field. This new model would be the digital transmission of information including the use of the Internet. Thomson was far ahead of its peers in using these media to publish Westlaw and other materials. It had moved from its newspaper days when it was a company that sold ink and paper to a company that now efficiently compiles, organizes, simplifies, and digitally transmits highly complex information. Westlaw is an essential tool found in nearly every major North American law firm. It gathers data from over 28,000 databases and employs over 1,200 attorneys who ensure that the discussions of case law are thoughtful, accurate, and valuable to practitioners. As with all digital media, Westlaw's updates are transmitted instantly – a sharp contrast to the cumbersome days of printing information on paper and delivering it to customers' homes on trucks and bicycles!

Westlaw now accounts for about 60% of the revenue in this firm's professional division. It has done such a good job of integrating this massive legal and regulatory material that Westlaw can be said to give the whole company a sustainable competitive advantage. Any competitor who attempts to imitate it will likely find the task too ambiguous and expensive.

THE REUTERS MERGER

In April 2008 Thomson Corporation purchased UK based Reuters Group PLC for $15.6 billion. Reuters was a famous newswire firm started in 1850 by Paul Julius Reuter in Germany. When telegraph lines were built between Aachen and Berlin, Reuters sent news stories to Berlin by telegraph. However, there was a 75 mile gap where the line had not been built, so rather than wait for trains to arrive, he used homing pigeons for that leg of the trip. Speed and efficiency were always important to him, and in the 1860's when telegraph lines were built in Ireland, he sent small boats out to greet ships coming in from America. The ships would drop canisters containing news into the water and the small boats would get the news into port and on the wire long before the ships actually landed. Early on he focused on general news as well as financials which he provided for the stock exchanges in London, Paris, and Berlin.

The new chief executive of Thomson Reuters is Tom Glocer, former head of Reuters. The firm has six business units; financial, tax & accounting, healthcare, legal, science, and media. In its healthcare segment it provides, for example, the famous *Physician's Desk Reference* or PDR, and software to manage drugs, interactions and dosing. Its media information goes to over 1 billion people each day, moving either to the web or directly to newsrooms, including world news, sports, health, and local reports.

RESILIENT STRATEGIES

Roy Thomson's enterprise has been in a state of resilience for almost 80 years. Its relentless drive for efficiencies, platform-supportive culture, ability to work within the developmental frame of each of its business units have all created the durability and resilience that others seek to achieve. Its choices of resilient strategies have been impressive. From the very beginning, this firm has had the ability to objectively see the opportunities inherent in a fragmented field, the efficiencies built by tight financial controls, the value of combining its core competencies in an ambiguous way, and the ability to anticipate the adaptive steps required as each industry changed its dominant strategic model and matured. In 2008 this firm merged with another competent firm, built on the same competitive platform, which had been in the business of efficiently transmitting intelligent information for 158 years. This merger has a remarkably high likelihood of success because of the similarities of platform, frame, culture and strategy in both firms.

It is too bad that Roy Thomson and Julius Reuter never met each other. These men shared the same love of their enterprise and they set in motion internal cultures that prepared their enterprises to adapt strategies as their industries and the world changed. And, both men had the wisdom of Resilience Builders.

CON-WAY, INC. BUILDS RESILIENCE WHILE STAYING IN ITS INDUSTRY

It may seem simpler or even easier to remain in your industry rather than exit it as the industry enters late stage development, but this is not necessarily so. Consider these possibilities: Not only do your competitors know you, but it is likely that their senior managers or even their CEO worked for your firm at one time. All firms have equivalent if not equal strategies, and the limited number of customers know all participants well. Often there are too many competitors, and this leads to bloody price battles, as well as "dirty" sales tactics. As you plan to change the way you compete in your matured industry you will find that there are some powerful forces in place, like unions and regulators, which seem to thwart you at every turn. You may need to make and remake your firm several times just to stay alive. So, the decision to stay in your aging industry should not be made by default. Staying in your industry will require aggressive action and persistence.

As I write this, we are in the darkest days the trucking industry has seen in 70 years. YRC Worldwide, Inc., the nation's biggest carrier fell from a position of robust health in 2007 to a state of despair in 2009. It has sold its headquarters to raise cash, received major wage concessions from its unions, delayed pension contributions for 18 months, closed facilities, and laid off employees. It is not alone, nearly every trucking company is suffering. [9]

So, how has Con-way Inc. managed to remain financially stable despite reducing its prices? How did it get to be on Fortune's list of Most Admired Companies? How has it maintained a positive internal climate, despite the fact that its nonunion workforce is expected to do more? And why was Con-way featured on a 60 Minutes spot for how well it treats its employees that are called to military service?

This firm was started in 1929 in Portland Oregon by Leland James. As the American economy formed and grew, so did the company. In its early days it bought several other trucking firms and took the name Consolidated Freightways. Then it changed its name to CNF, and ultimately Con-way. Today Con-way delivers over 50,000 shipments each day, has 26,000 employees, and is making smart strategic acquisitions. It has $935 million in debt, which is nicely serviced by $4.5 billion in annual revenues and $397 million in cash; enough to safely weather the present-day economic storm.

This company is a good example of an enterprise that is thriving despite the fact that its industry is in late stage development. Unlike Thomson Reuters, Con-way has maintained its resilience by remaining in its industry.

EVOLUTION OF THE TRUCKING INDUSTRY

Before looking at Con-way, it is important to understand the industry life-cycle of the trucking industry. In the last 30 years, it has moved from a simple, fragmented industry to a sophisticated, high tech, late stage industry.

Comfortable Beginnings. For most of the twentieth century the trucking industry was a complacent gold mine in the United States. That was because the American congress had viewed it as essential for the functioning of the nation, so it regulated trucking along with rail and airlines. This regulation created a competition-proof protective shield around every trucking firm and resulted in high fees, excessive wages, and an attitude of entitlement. The entire industry was inefficient and costly for the consumer. Trucks were only allowed to travel certain routes and times. So, in order to send a shipment from Portland to nearby Seattle at an off time, the trucking firm might have to route the first truck to Yakima (185 miles east) and then a second truck would go from Yakima to Seattle. Up to this point, none of this could have been called the dominant strategic model, because firms really didn't have to establish a sustainable competitive advantage. Prosperity came to these firms simply because they existed.

During the time of regulation a familiar pattern happened again and again. All trucking firms charged the same rates due to price regulation. Although the drivers were well paid, the Teamsters demanded wage increases every time the contract renewed. If negotiations came to an impasse, the drivers would go out on strike. Eventually the parties would agree to a wage hike, but then the trucking firms would seek permission to raise rates to cover the wage hikes and the Interstate Commerce Commission would give its approval.

It is widely believed that when the Teamsters got a 30% wage increase in the crippled economy of 1979 and then the ICC approved commensurate price increases, the public outrage caused the industry's deregulation to sweep through congress, nearly unopposed.

First Dominant Strategic Model: Basic Efficiency Equals Direct Routes. Everything changed when the Motor Carrier Act of 1980 deregulated trucking. The result was a multilevel competitive skirmish throughout the industry in the United States. The most notable feature of this fight was the fact that shippers were no longer limited to geographic regions, so there was a rush to get into the long distance hauling market. Very few of the pre-existing firms ever developed the skills needed to compete in this new free enterprise environment, and most vanished. Eventually a small number of competent market leaders emerged who were efficient, used carefully drawn routes, and abhorred returning with an empty trailer. They bargained for cheaper fuel and parts. Despite the outcries of unions, they paid only reasonable wages. Direct routing became the industry's dominant strategic model, squarely built on the Efficient Platform.

However, even though all participants in the industry attempted to operate more efficiently, the nature of this Efficient Platform was simple: Direct routes and efficient daily operations.

Second Dominant Strategic Model: Extreme Efficiency. A second strategic model became dominant in the early 1990's when manufacturing firms started using "Just-In-Time" manufacturing systems. Prior to the Just-In-Time systems, most manufacturers had poor control of their warehouse inventories. So, large quantities of some materials would build up while others ran out. This resulted in patchy work schedules for manufacturing employees. Also, under the old systems, sometimes manufacturers incorrectly misjudged the consumer's level of demand, and large amounts of supplies simply sat on the shelf as demand ebbed, never to be used.

Just-In-Time inventory management requires that suppliers gather information from inside their customer's operations. So, parts suppliers retrieve signals that more supplies will soon be needed on an assembly line. This can produce synchronized flows of parts, not just of one supplier, but of several. Whereas under the old system most suppliers were unaware of each other, this new arrangement is a smart supply system and requires complex data and coordination of suppliers with each other.

Once a product is made, it might be sent to a retailer under another new system, Vendor Managed Inventory (VMI). This requires the manufacturer to gather real-time data at the point of sale, maintain inventories, and replenish the stores or outlets automatically. Software for this gathers data and allows a smooth flow of product to its final destination.

All of this saves time, money and labor. It requires sophisticated, timely and trustworthy IT systems and it all needs the support of trucking companies. As a result, the trucking industry was changed from simply transporting goods to managing inventory. During the late 1990's and early 2000's trucking companies began taking responsibility for their role in these smart supply chain systems.

These changes demanded that trucking firms severely raise the bar on their own efficiencies and abilities to deliver large and small shipments with little notice. As a result, Less Than Truckload (LTL) trucking firms became smarter. One way to think of the LTL system is to draw a horizontal line across a page. At each end of the line, draw some fingers. The fingers on the left side of the line represent inputs that are picked up by the trucking company from many suppliers. The point at which the fingers meet is either a warehouse, truck terminal, or a "breakbulk". Here the items are taken off the trucks, re-sorted, re-combined per customer, and placed on new trailers. They might be sent locally by LTL carriers or over long distance by Full Truckload (TL) carriers. At delivery (the fingers on the right side of the diagram) the items are re-sorted, put in new trailers and delivered. Of course, saving steps here is very valuable.

Con-way's Strategy

Con-way has worked hard to meet the requirements of survival as its industry has moved into late stage. Con-way went non-union, failed and later succeeded at ocean transport, failed and then succeeded at rail multimodal, and had more than one failure at air transport shipping. It established a highly technical third party logistics subsidy, has partners and business units all over the world, and now can get packages anywhere in the world "day definite" 99% of the time. Con-way's story is both complicated and refreshing in its message of survival by renewal in a late stage industry.

Building a New Company. Creating the modern Con-way was not easy. After deregulation this company moved from an old-school union company to a nimble, adaptive non-union shop. Its desire to go non-union was born out of its long struggle with unions. It also came from some personal tragedies. For example, during a strike about 10 years before deregulation, Gary Kistler, a Consolidated employee and 30 year old father of four was shot and killed by a sniper as he drove in a convoy in St. Louis.

So, when deregulation arrived these leaders were eager to exit their union structure. They wanted to begin competing on low price and they wanted their drivers to help their customers unload the trucks and sort the shipments at the final destination. None of this was allowed under their biggest union contracts. They also sought to build a firm in which employees would have loyalty to the company rather than to the union.

In 1983 CEO Raymond F. O'Brien created three regional companies, Con-way Western Express, Con-way Central Express, and Con-way Eastern Express. 10 O'Brien intended for all three regional companies to be non-union, but he believed that a non-union shop in New York would be a lightning rod for conflict, so Con-way Eastern was a union shop. At this point the firm also owned Consolidated Freightways, a long-haul carrier. 11 Eventually regional carriers were also established in the Southeast and Southwest, thus covering the entire country.

In 1990 when negotiations failed with the Con-way Eastern Teamsters the Eastern drivers went out on strike. One week later the company announced that Con-way Eastern was permanently closed. Within hours, employees from other parts of the company removed equipment and trucks from the Eastern terminals, before the union could react. One year later the company expanded Con-way Central as a non-union competitor in New York, and Central began expanding rapidly.

The fight that followed included the National Labor Relations Board, local courts and a federal district court, all of whom sided with the company.

By 1993 it became clear that the regional Con-way companies were taking business and union jobs away from the firm's long-haul company, so the Teamsters protested to the NLRB. Their protest was in vain and the regional carriers continued to gain strength. In 1996 the parent corporation spun off Consolidated Freightways, the long-haul carrier. This was the last major piece of the firm that was unionized.

Ocean and Skies. In the 1980's CEO Larry Scott took several bold steps to enter the worldwide shipping market. The firm attempted to establish Ocean Service intermodal freight, but there were too many tariffs and layers of profit-takers for it to be feasible. It also tried transporting large containers on flatbed trucks that could be transferred to rail, but this also effort was ahead of its time and it failed. Larry Scott's biggest mistake, however, was when he approved the purchase of freight airline, Emery Worldwide, without completing adequate due diligence before the purchase. It turned out that Emery had been losing as much as $1 million per week at the time. 12

Within a year Emery caused the entire firm's debt to increase from less than $50 million to more than $480 million, and Emery was losing $4.2 million per week. In February 2000 an Emery flight departed from Sacramento's airport, flew only a few minutes and then crashed, killing all three crew members. In December 2001 the firm closed Emery and sold all of its aircraft.

Meanwhile, the firm had started Con-way Air Express which did not own any aircraft, but shipped on third party air carriers. This service was shut down in 2006 and its operations were converted to a new shipping brokerage business.

Meeting Global Demands. All of the emerging nations of the world became manufacturing powerhouses at about the same time, during the mid 1990's. Suddenly manufacturing plants in America and Western Europe were closing and capacity was opening in Brazil, Guatemala, Mexico, India, Viet Nam and Eastern Europe. Undisputedly, the overwhelming power here was China.

Going global is not easy for a trucking company. In China, for example, there are magnificent roads, ports, and highways all along the coast. But once you venture inland, these things begin to disappear. Shipping from province to province in China might require the truck to clear customs multiple times. Most of China's own trucking companies consist of only one truck or a few trucks. There are many stories of rural Chinese trucks that pick up a load of goods, then the driver takes the loaded truck home, unloads the items, uses the truck to take his farm products to market, reloads the truck and goes on with his journey. Sometimes manufacturers load trucks and track them only to the first Chinese depot, and then the items disappear until they reappear in Long Beach, hopefully intact and ready to be put on US trucks. All of this represents a great strategic opportunity for a competent large trucking company to enter this market.

Meeting the Late Stage Requirements. The new complex supply requirements imposed by Just-In-Time and other efficient systems apply to operations in the developed nations as well as those in emerging markets. So Con-way launched Menlo Worldwide Logistics in 1991 as a 3PL (Third Party Logistics) firm to provide advanced services such as managing warehouses and depots, tracking inventory through its entire route, and cross-docking services. All of this has given it an ever-more powerful Efficient Platform. In 2007 Con-way's Menlo Worldwide Logistics purchased Chic Holdings, Ltd, and Cougar Holdings Pte Ltd. Chic is based in Shanghai and Cougar is in Singapore. Both are logistics, distribution management, freight forwarding, and warehousing firms. These acquisitions created 155 operating locations, 2,000 employees, and 3.5 million square feet of warehouse space in Asia for Con-way. The Resilience Builder behind all of this strategy is Douglas Stotlar, CEO since 2005.

Con-way established Con-way Truckload (TL) in 2005 which offers seamless transport to and from Mexico and Canada. In 2007 Stotlar bought another TL provider, now named CFI for $750 million.

Con-way offers guaranteed day-definite delivery of goods anywhere in the world, uninterrupted transitions through customs, tracking of shipments the entire route, and coordination with Multimodal systems through rail carriers and its new OceanGuaranteed® service.

CONGRUENCE

This book has proposed that the four essential elements of resilience should match each other in order to establish resilience. Con-way has done just that. It is nicely built on the Efficient Platform. It knows its place on its developmental frame, and after deregulation it performed a Return to Growth. Its culture is clearly the product of its platform and frame; everyone builds efficiency. Its culture also has a significantly positive Interpersonal Component. And Con-way has altered its strategy several times to maintain a good fit to its platform and its location on its frame.

THREE STRATEGIC QUESTIONS

This chapter has suggested that Resilience Builders answer three questions better than other business leaders. The first question has to do with strategic viability: Is this business planted in fertile ground? For Con-way, the answer is yes, but the ground has become progressively more difficult to till over the years.

The second question has to do with ambiguity: Is our collection of strengths hard for others to imitate? Again, the answer is yes. Con-way has dialed up the Efficient Platform so high that others will have difficulty imitating it. Menlo Worldwide Logistics' competent use of advanced technology has further added to this firm's strategic ambiguity.

The third question pertains to developmental adaptation: How mature is the overall industry? As the trucking industry entered late stage it became clear that only the low-cost providers would thrive. The difficult task was that the firm needed to be low cost but offer progressively more complex services. As the industry aged, Con-way established a lower cost structure and adapted well to the late stage development of the trucking industry.

RELENTLESS PURSUIT OF THE EFFICIENT PLATFORM

The Con-way story points to the tremendous amount of work it takes to retain resilience in a late-stage industry. Anyone who might think that his or her firm should remain in the same industry at this stage because it might be easier than stitching industries must look at the tremendous effort Con-way has generated again and again.

If past Resilience Builder Leland James could see Con-way today he might not recognize it. This firm was a strong TL carrier, then it discontinued the TL service and later re-entered it again. It was a Teamster stronghold, but after great struggle those days are gone. Even Raymond O'Brien who gets credit for redesigning the company after deregulation must look at this company with some awe. All of this required the hard work of entering new fields, like intermodal transport, exiting them, and then re-entering to succeed. It is high tech, and seamlessly moves products anywhere in the world.

Con-way has been relentless in its pursuit of efficiency for itself and then it has handed the benefits of that efficiency to others. In 2009 it won the "Green 15 Award" from IDG's Infoworld for its use of its new line-haul simulator software. This allows it to model several freight distribution route scenarios in order to save fuel. It won the award for its beneficial impact on the environment, but it also saves Con-way 4.9 million gallons of fuel per year. In 2008 it was named LTL Carrier of the Year by Wal-Mart for the third time as a result of its efficiency, on time performance, and mastery of complex order management. The journey of Con-way has given its leaders the wisdom of Resilience Builders, and everyone at Con-way benefits from that wisdom today.

Chapter 11

The Wisdom of Resilience Builders

Some scholars and advisors would suggest that to build a resilient company you should first decide how to make a great product. Others would say you should start by putting together a great team. This book suggests that you begin by building your enterprise on one competitive platform. Choose your platform carefully by figuring out what makes you great and then doing it on purpose. As you invest your time, your energy, and your very self into your company, strive to ensure that all of the appropriate parts of your enterprise match this platform. Carefully study where your firm is in its development and manage according to its location. Then build a "cult-like" culture that matches all of this. Doing these things builds a competent organization. This is the work of Resilience Builders. 1

Understand that the strategies you have used to create past successes may not bring prosperity in the future. So, look carefully at how the industry in which you reside is changing. Ask whether there has been a platform shift or a new dominant strategic model in your industry and ask how well your firm has adapted to them.

In this volume we have heard the stories of many Resilience Builders. All had triumphs. All struggled with painful issues that threatened the existence of their firms. All gained the wisdom to avoid those struggles subsequently.

My favorite quote from these great Resilience Builders is Chester Cadieux saying, "We were dumber than dumb." He also said, "We made every possible mistake." We all know that neither he nor any of these great leaders is "dumb". He, for example, was a very bright college student and then turned a small store-front grocery into a highly admired $9 billion company. What Chester meant was that he had wished that he could have seen his struggles ahead of time, and known how to avoid them.

As I have interviewed and known Resilience Builders I have heard each one of them say that he or she was unable to anticipate so many avoidable struggles when the journey began. All of these leaders would want you to gain the wisdom they gained, without having to suffer in order to get it. Also, I have observed that every one of them was still hopeful and optimistic about the future, still cared deeply about their people, and still cared passionately about their enterprise despite the struggles and despite the long journey. They all believed their work was valuable because it brought prosperity to others.

I wish for you the same hope and optimism. I want you to have a good journey and in the end to say that you cared deeply about your people and your enterprise as you generated prosperity. I hope that this book has helped you learn from the triumphs and trials of others and that perhaps in some way, having read this book you have grown in the wisdom of Resilience Builders.

Notes and References

CHAPTER 1

1. The responsible people at Steinway & Sons have informed me that the other 99½% of the harvested wood is put to good use.

2. Anderson, Terry. *Den of Lions,* Ballantine Books, New York, 1993.

3. Firestone was once one of the most resilient companies in the world. It responded too slowly to the onset of radial tire technology and lost its resilience. It was bought by Bridgestone in 1988 and the combined firm is resilient again. This firm is used as an example of the power of strong brands.

4. Collins, James C. & Porras, Jerry I. *Built to Last,* Harper Business, New York, 1994.

5. Stadler, Christian. The Four Principles of Enduring Success, *Harvard Business Review,* July 2007, 85, p. 62.

CHAPTER 2

1. In *The Discipline of Market Leaders* (Perseus Books, New York, 1997), Michael Treacy & Fred Wiersema describe three "disciplines" that they say are the way companies become "market leaders". They are: operational excellence, product leaders, and customer intimacy. This book obviously influenced my current work. However, I suggest that Efficient Platform goes beyond operations. I suggest herein that customer intimacy also goes further than they had suggested, to Relationship Platform. I suggest that product leaders are really Creative Platform firms. And, they did not propose a Marketing Platform, as I do.

2. Squawk Box, CNBC, May 15, 2006.
3. Hindo, Brian. At 3M, A Struggle Between Efficiency and Creativity, *BusinessWeek*, June 11, 2007, p. 8.
4. Packard, David *The HP Way: How Bill Hewlett and I Built Our Company*, Harper Business, New York, 1995.
5. Deal, Terrence & Kennedy, Allan A., *Corporate Cultures*, Addison-Wesley Publishing Co, Reading, MA, 1982.

CHAPTER 3
1. Personal conversation with Chester Cadieux, former CEO, QuikTrip Inc., March 20, 2008.
2. Deal, Terrence & Kennedy, Allan A., *Corporate Cultures*, Addison-Wesley Publishing Co, Reading, MA, 1982.
3. Cadieux, Chester. *From Lucky to Smart,* Mullerhaus Publishing Group, Tulsa, OK, 2008.
4. Personal conversation with Alvin Howerton, former Vice President, QuikTrip, Inc.
5. From Hoover's, a division of Dunn & Bradstreet.
6. Bye-bye Number 56, *Fortune* Jan 25, 1999, v 163, 2, 66-69.

CHAPTER 4
1. Post, Tom. 85Years & Ideas, *Forbes.* December 23, 2002, pp. 123.
2. Note, Campbell's subsequently improved marketing by offering a broader product line with its Select line and other offerings.
3. Bandler, J. & Drucker, J. Kodak, Cingular form Pact on Photos, *The Wall Street Journal*, November 12, 2003, p B6.
4. Love, John F. *McDonald's: Behind the Arches,* Bantam Books, New York, 1995.
5. Brooker, Katrina. The Un-CEO. *Fortune*, Sep 16, 2002, pp. 88.
6. Note, In *The Discipline of Market Leaders* (Perseus Books, New York, 1997), Michael Treacy & Fred Wiersema argue strongly that trying to pursue multiple "disciplines" can have detrimental effects on an enterprise.
7. See, Brooker, Katrina, p. 92.

CHAPTER 5
1. The 100 year old companies, excluding schools, hospitals, and institutions are: Great Western Manufacturing, First National

Bank of Leavenworth, Mid-America Bank, Citizen's Savings and Loan, McAffree-Short Title Company, Biringer's, Mount Muncie Cemetery, The Corner Pharmacy, The Chronicle Shopper, Davis Funeral Chapel, Belden-Sexton-Sumpter Funeral Chapels, and Geiger Ready Mix.

2. In order to avoid confusing the reader, I call the current CEO Bill Geiger, which is what he is called by all who know him. His actual name is Edward William Geiger III.

3. Collins, James C. & Porras, Jerry I. *Built to Last*, Harper Business, New York, 1994.

CHAPTER 6

1. This concept is taken from Churchill, Neil C., Breaking Down the Wall, Scaling the Ladder, *FT Mastering Enterprise*, January, 1997.

2. The 100 Fastest Growing Companies, *Fortune*, September 18, 2006, p. 138.

3. Hot Growth Companies, *BusinessWeek*, June 4, 2007, p. 70.

4. The Inc 500, *Inc.* September, 2009, p. 93.

5. Rubin, James Peter, Business Acceleration, *The Wall Street Journal*, June 12, 2000, Breakaway, p. 6.

6. Porter, Michael E. *Competitive Strategy*, The Free Press, New York, 1980.

7. Sloan, Alfred P., *My Years with General Motors*, Currency Doubleday, New York, 1963. p. xx.

8. Esterl, Mike. Labor Demands Cloud AMR Outlook, *The Wall Street Journal*, April 4, 2009, p. B1.

9. Ellison, Sarah, Inside Campbell's Big Bet: Heating up Condensed Soup. *The Wall Street Journal*, July 31, 2003, p. 1.

10. Slywotsky, Adrian & Wise, Richard. *How to Grow When Markets Don't*, New York, Warner Books, 2003.

11. Financial Information, *Nissan Corporation Report*, March 31, 2008.

12. Muller, Joann. The Impatient Mr. Ghosn, *Forbes*, May 22, 2006, p 107.

13. Churchill, Neil C. & Mullins, John W., How Fast Can Your Company Afford to Grow? *Harvard Business Review*, May 2001, p. 135.

CHAPTER 7
1. Information about Altitude was gathered through several telephone interviews with Altitude and its customers, as well as on-site interviews with Brian Matt, designers, engineers, artists, marketing experts and other staff at Altitude Inc.

CHAPTER 8
1. For example, Thompson, Arthur and Strickland, A. J. *Strategic Management,* Thirteenth Edition, New York, McGraw-Hill, 2003, p. 423.
2. Collins, James and Porras, Jerry, *Built to Last,* Harper Business, New York, 1994.
3. Examples would be Geoffee, R. & Jones, G. What Holds the Modern Company Together? *Harvard Business Review,* Nov 1996, p. 133. And Kanter, Rosabeth Moss, *You are here.* INC, February 2001, p 85.
4. The Wal-Mart of Meat, *BusinessWeek,* September 20, 2004, p. 90.
5. For a more comprehensive discussion of artifacts, rituals, ceremonies and heroes in corporate culture, see Deal, Terrence & Kennedy, Allan A., *Corporate Cultures,* Addison-Wesley Publishing Co, Reading, MA, 1982.
6. Nocera, Joseph, I Remember Microsoft, *Fortune,* July 10, 2000, p. 114.
7. Bardwick, Judith. *Danger in the Comfort Zone.* AMACOM, New York, 1991.
8. Regarding Kodak, see: Norris, Kim, Companies Learn the Pitfalls of Overexpansion, *St. Petersburg Times,* Knight-Ridder, Sep 30, 1996. p. 9B. Also, please note that Polaroid still exists. See The Rush to Grab Orphan Brands, *BusinessWeek,* Aug 3, 2009, pp. 047.
9. FCC Report: *Review of the Radio Industry,* 2001, Executive Summary.
10. Facts from Frank, Robert & Craig, Susanne, Banker to the Rich, U.S. Trust Stumbles After Sale to Schwab, *The Wall Street Journal,* September 15, 2004 p. A1. And, Frank, Robert, & Bauerlein, Valerie, Bank of America Hit a Snag in Bid To Woo the Rich, *The Wall Street Journal,* April 4, 2007, p. A1.

11. Bower, Joseph, Not all Mergers are Alike – and that Matters, *Harvard Business Review*, March 2001, p. 94.

12. Please note, this discussion intentionally ignores the Chrysler bankruptcy in April 2009, which occurred for different reasons.

CHAPTER 9

1. Machine of the Year, and The Updated Book of Jobs, *Time Magazine,* January 3, 1983.

2. Rose, Frank. *West of Eden: The End of Innocence at Apple Computer.* Penguin Books, New York, 1989.

3. Young, Jeffrey S. and Simon, William L. *iCon.* John Wiley & Sons, Hoboken, New Jersey, 2005.

4. Hertzfeld, Andy. *Revolution in the Valley: The Insanely Great Story of How the Mac was Made.* O'Reilly Media, Inc, Sebastopol, CA, 2005.

5. As reported by Young & Simon.

6. See, Hertzfeld, Andy. 2005., p. xv.

7. Kendall. Martha E. *Steve Wozniak: Inventor of the Apple Computer.* Walker Publishing Company, Inc., New York, 1994, p. 51.

8. See, Young, Jeffrey S. and Simon, William L. 2005, p. 73.

9. See, Rose, Frank. 1989, p. 54.

10. See, Rose, Frank. 1989, p. 65.

11. See, Rose, Frank. 1989, p. 128.

12. See, Young, Jeffrey S. and Simon, William L. 2005, p. 99.

13. See, Rose, Frank. 1989, p. 176.

14. Bellew, Patricia. Apple Computer Co-Founder Wozniak Will Leave Firm, Citing Disagreements. *The Wall Street Journal*, February 7, 1985, p. 1.

15. Wozniak, Steve with Smith, Gena. *iWoz.* W. W. Norton & Company, New York, 2006. (See pages 259 -267 for his explanation of why he left Apple.)

16. Price, David A. *The Pixar Touch: The Making of a Company.* Alfred A Knopf, New York, 2008.

17. Burrows, Peter. Apple: Yes, Steve, You Fixed It. Congrats! Now, What's Act Two? *BusinessWeek*, July 31, 2000.

18. Wingfield, Nick. iPod Sales Shine Up Apple's Profit. *The Wall Street Journal*, January 13, 2005, p. A3.

19. Burrows, Peter. An iPOD a Day. *BusinessWeek*, March 7, 2005.

20. Wildstrom, Stephen H. The Unstoppable iPhone. *BusinessWeek*, June 29, 2009.

CHAPTER 10

1. Smith, Adam. *The Wealth of Nations*. Alfred A. Knopf, New York, 1776.
2. Schumpeter, Joseph A. *Business Cycles: A Theoretical, Historical and Statistical Analysis of the Capitalist Process*. Two Volumes. McGraw-Hill, New York, 1939.
3. Porter, Michael E. *Competitive Strategy*. The Free Press, New York, 1980. And Porter, Michael E. *Competitive Advantage*. The Free Press, New York, 1985.
4. For a more complete discussion of what strategy is and isn't, see Porter, Michael E. What is Strategy? *Harvard Business Review*, Nov. 1996, p. 61.
5. The Doctor Won't See You Now. *BusinessWeek*, Feb 5, 2007, p. 30.
6. Hamilton, David P. Sun Microsystems Basks in the Glow of Internet Aura, *The Wall Street Journal*, Jan. 21, 2000, p. B4.
7. Kerstetter, James & Burrows, Peter. Sun: A CEO's Last Stand. *BusinessWeek*, July 26, 2004, p. 64.
8. Historical information about Roy Thomson taken from *Thomson Corporation Home Page*, 2007.
9. Roth, Alex & Sidel, Robin, YRC to Apply for Bailout Funds, *The Wall Street Journal*, May 15, 2009, p. B3.
10. Note: Con-way Eastern Express was actually named Pen-Yan Express when Con-way first purchased it.
11. Note: Consolidated Freightways was also called CF MotorFreight.
12. Note: The best historical review I have found of Con-way is: Rodengen, Jeffrey. *The Legend of Con-way*. Write Stuff Enterprises, Inc. Ft. Lauderdale, FL, 2008.

CHAPTER 11

1. The term "cult-like cultures" is taken from: Collins, James and Porras, Jerry, *Built to Last*, Harper Business, New York, 1994.

CPSIA information can be obtained at www.ICGtesting.com
Printed in the USA
LVOW13*1424150414

381821LV00002B/42/P